Women on Corporate Boards

T0293136

Female presence and involvement on boards improves firm performance, transforms corporate governance and leads to the transition towards more responsible business.

Corporate boards are essential bodies for governance and management and their efficiency determines a company's performance. The board is a crucial element of the corporate governance structure and its efficiency and performance determines the success of the operation and monitoring of the company. The board is viewed as the liaison between providers of capital (shareholders) and managers who use this capital to create value. The board role is to represent, formulate and fulfill the interests and expectations of shareholders as the owners of the companies. The discussion surrounding female participation in business inevitably needs to refer to their presence on corporate boards. It is also a reliable indicator of a gender equality policy and advancement, adopted by countries and companies.

The book traces the logic behind the decision patterns of female involvement in governance and management. In particular, it identifies the patterns of women's presence on corporate boards, with respect to theoretical and conceptual argumentation, policy and regulatory implication, as well as practical adaptation. The phenomenon of women on corporate boards is analyzed in the context of different political, cultural and institutional environments addressing challenges in both developed and emerging economies. The role of female directors is viewed as one of the crucial aspects in corporate governance, adding to the quality of control and management.

Maria Aluchna is an associate professor at the Department of Management Theory, Warsaw School of Economics, Poland.

Güler Aras is a professor of Finance and Accounting at Yildiz Technical University, Istanbul, Turkey, and a visiting professor at Georgetown University McDonough School of Business, USA.

Finance, Governance and Sustainability: Challenges to Theory and Practice Series
Series Editor: Professor Güler Aras
Yildiz Technical University, Turkey;
Georgetown University, Washington DC, USA

Focusing on the studies of academicians, researchers, entrepreneurs, policy makers and government officers, this international series aims to contribute to the progress in matters of finance, good governance and sustainability. These multidisciplinary books combine strong conceptual analysis with a wide range of empirical data and a wealth of case materials. They will be of interest to those working in a multitude of fields, across finance, governance, corporate behaviour, regulations, ethics and sustainability.

Transforming Governance
New Values, New Systems in the New Business Environment
Edited by Maria Aluchna and Güler Aras

Strategy, Structure and Corporate Governance
Nabyla Daidj

Corporate Behavior and Sustainability
Doing Well by Being Good
Edited by Güler Aras and Coral Ingley

Corporate Social Responsibility and Sustainable Development
Social Capital and Corporate Development in Developing Economies
Risa Bhinekawati

Cosmopolitan Business Ethics
Towards a Global Ethos of Management
Jacob Dahl Rendtorff

Sustainability Accounting and Integrated Reporting
Edited by Charl de Villiers and Warren Maroun

Women on Corporate Boards
An International Perspective
Edited by Maria Aluchna and Güler Aras

For a full list of titles in this series, please visit www.routledge.com/Finance-Governance-and-Sustainability/book-series/FINGOVSUST

Women on Corporate Boards

An International Perspective

**Edited by Maria Aluchna and
Güler Aras**

Routledge
Taylor & Francis Group

LONDON AND NEW YORK

First published 2018 by Routledge

2 Park Square, Milton Park, Abingdon, Oxfordshire OX14 4RN

52 Vanderbilt Avenue, New York, NY 10017

Routledge is an imprint of the Taylor & Francis Group, an informa business

First issued in paperback 2020

British Library Cataloguing-in-Publication Data
A catalogue record for this book is available from the British Library

Library of Congress Cataloging-in-Publication Data
Names: Aluchna, Maria, editor. | Aras, Gèuler, editor.
Title: Women on corporate boards : an international perspective / Maria Aluchna and Gèuler Aras.
Description: Abingdon, Oxon ; New York, NY : Routledge, 2018. | Includes bibliographical references and index.
Identifiers: LCCN 2017059068 (print) | LCCN 2018000324 (ebook) | ISBN 9781315183701 (eBook) | ISBN 9781138740181 (hardback : alk. paper)
Subjects: LCSH: Boards of directors. | Women executives. | Corporate governance.
Classification: LCC HD2745 (ebook) | LCC HD2745 .W645 2018 (print) | DDC 658.4/22082—dc23
LC record available at https://lccn.loc.gov/2017059068

ISBN: 978-1-138-74018-1 (hbk)
ISBN: 978-0-367-59136-6 (pbk)

Typeset in Times New Roman
by Apex CoVantage, LLC

Contents

Figures

Tables

Contributors

Maria Aluchna, PhD
Associate Professor, Warsaw School of Economics
Director, Center for Research on Responsible Management

Maria Aluchna, PhD is Associate Professor, Department of Management Theory, Warsaw School of Economics; Director of Responsible Business Center and Post-graduate Studies on Products and Services Management at Department of Management Theory Warsaw School of Economics; counsel at the law firm Głuchowski, Siemiątkowski i Zwara; and the expert of Ministry of Economic Development in the EU Operational Program Intelligent Economy. She specializes in corporate governance, strategic management and corporate social responsibility. She is also Fellow of Deutscher Akademischer Austauschdienst (research stay at Universität Passau), US-Polish-Fulbright Commission (research stay at Columbia University), Soros Foundation, Volkswagen Foundation and Foundation for Polish Science Development. Further, she is Visiting Scholar at London Metropolitan Business School and Sydney University School of Business. She teaches corporate governance, responsible management (within the cooperation of University of Illinois, Springfield, US) and strategic management for MBA, postgraduate, PhD, MA and BA studies. She has given guest lectures at Cambridge University, Nottingham Business School, BPP University College, ZHAW School of Management and Law (Winterthur) and Universidad Internacional de Cataluña. She is a member of European Corporate Governance Institute, International Corporate Governance Society, Finance Watch, European Academy of Management, Academy of International Business, Council of Management and Finance Collegium, as well as of the editorial committees of *International Journal of Corporate Social Responsibility, European Journal of Economics and Management, Journal of Knowledge Globalization*, Przegląd Organizacji and e-Mentor. She publishes in Poland and abroad (four monographs, including one in English published by LAM Academic Publishing; three edited books, including one in English, published by Gower; over 70 articles and conference papers [EURAM, AIB, ISBEE]), and she takes active part in international conferences.

Güler Aras, PhD, CPA
Professor of Finance and Accounting, Yildiz Technical University
Founding Director of Center for Finance, Governance and
  Sustainability (CFGS)
Founding Chair, Integrated Reporting Network Turkey

Güler Aras is Professor of Finance and Accounting at Yildiz Technical University, and the founding director of Center for Finance, Governance and Sustainability (CFGS). Professor Aras is the founding chair of the Integrated Reporting Network Turkey. She was a visiting professor at Georgetown University McDonough School of Business and is the former Dean of Faculty of Administrative and Economic Sciences and the former Dean of the Graduate School. Her research focus is on financial economy and financial markets with particular emphasis on the relationship between sustainability, corporate governance, corporate social responsibility and corporate financial performance. She has published more than 25 books and has contributed over 250 articles in academic, business and professional journals including *Journal of Business Ethics, Management Decision, Emerging Market Finance and Trade*, and *Journal of Applied Accounting Research*. She has also edited several book collections and conference proceedings. Her latest book, *Sustainable Markets for Sustainable Business: A Global Perspective for Business and Financial Markets*, and co-authored book, *Transforming Governance* and *Corporate Behavior and Sustainability: Doing Well by Being Good*, were published by Routledge. She is Editor in Chief of *Journal of Capital Market Studies*, the editor of the Routledge book series "Finance, Governance and Sustainability: Challenges to Theory and Practice",and the editor of the Routledge book series "Corporate Social Responsibility"; she has also served as an editor of *Social Responsibility Journal* and "Emerald Development of Governance and Responsibility" book series. Professor Aras has spoken extensively at professional and academic conferences and has served as a consultant to a number of governmental and commercial organizations such as Minister of Development, Undersecretary of Treasury and Minister of Labour and Social Security Employment in Turkey. Professor Aras works with business closely and acts as an independent board member of Allianz Turkey and Turkish Capital Market Association (TCMA). She is the founding president of the International Financial Management Institute in Turkey (IMA, Turkish Chapter), and founder of the Turkish Chapter of Transparency International. She has served as a board or a committee member of many national and international associations and research centres.

***

Leszek Bohdanowicz is Associate Professor at the Department of Finance and Strategic Management, University of Lodz, Poland. He has MA and PhD degrees from the University of Lodz. His research interests are in the areas of corporate governance and strategic management. He has published his research in various Polish and international journals. He has carried out numerous research projects financed by the Polish Ministry of Science and Higher Education and conducted training and consulting activities for many Polish companies. Leszek is a member of the European Academy of Management and the Scientific Society of Organization and Management.

Kevin Campbell is Director of the MSc in Investment Analysis Programme at the University of Stirling, a University Affiliation Program partner of CFA Institute. He is a senior lecturer in Finance within the Accounting and Finance Division of Stirling Management School. He has MA and PhD degrees from the University of Glasgow. He researches primarily in the fields of corporate finance and corporate governance and has published in journals such as *Review of Finance, Energy Economics, Journal of International Financial Markets, Institutions & Money, International Journal of Accounting, Baltic Journal of Management, Managerial Finance, Journal of Business Finance and Accounting, Journal of Business Ethics, Journal of Management and Governance, Corporate Governance* and *Journal of Law and Society*. He has held visiting positions at the University of New South Wales, the University of Western Australia and the Graduate Business School at the University of Cape Town. He is currently an Honorary Visiting Professor at the University of Gdansk.

JF Corkery has been the founder and head of law programs, research centres and law journals over his career as Professor of Law at Bond University and, before that, at the Universities of Adelaide and Otago. He writes and teaches in corporate law, taxation law and sports law. His most recent book is *Corporate Social Responsibility: The Good Corporation and Companies Law*.

Nabyla Daidj is Associate Professor of Strategy at Telecom Ecole de Management (Institut Mines Telecom). Her teaching and research interests are corporate strategy, inter-organizational relationships (strategic alliances, clusters, business ecosystems and cooperative practices), corporate governance and CSR. She has published in international journals and conference proceedings and, in 2008, she published a book about cooperation, game theory and strategic management.Her current research investigates sources of value creation in international firms operating in the ICT sector within the context of convergence. Her work has also been published in *Journal of Media Business Studies* and *Journal of Media Economics, Communications & Strategies*.

Helena Desivilya Syna is Professor of Social and Organizational Psychology and a faculty member in the MA Studies Department in Organizational Development and Consulting at the Max Stern Yezreel Valley College. She conducts research on social conflict, organizational behaviour and diversity management. She has published about 40 articles in peer-reviewed journals and 20 book chapters, as well as edited two books: *A Paradox in Partnerships: The Role of Conflict in Partnership Building* and recently *Women's Voices in Management: Identifying Innovative and Responsible Solutions* published by Palgrave Macmillan. She is on editorial boards of *Conflict Resolution Quarterly*, *International Journal of Conflict Management* and *Negotiation and Conflict Management Research*.

Diana Eerma holds a PhD in Economics from University of Tartu, Estonia and Master's of International Affairs in Economic Policy Management from Columbia University, New York City, USA. She is Associate Professor on Economic Policy at the School of Economics and Business Administration, University of Tartu, Estonia. She has been a guest lecturer at the University of Joensuu, Finland, University of Deusto, Spain and University of Economics in Bratislava, Slovakia. She is author/co-author of more than 60 scientific articles and three books. She was a short-term consultant at the World Bank Rural Development and Natural Resources Unit of East Asia and Pacific Region, Washington DC, USA, in 2000. She has been expert for Regional Program Projects in the Enterprise Estonia since 2002, evaluation expert of educational intensive programs of the Estonian Foundation Archimedes Erasmus (since 2010), expert with the Center for Policy Studies (PRAXIS) in Estonia (2001), expert with the Centre for Applied Social Sciences (CASS) in Eurocollege for 'Intermediate evaluation of structural funds in the period 2007–2013'. She has contributed as Consultant in the international team in "Administrative Capacity Study Phase 2" – Phare Region Project (2002–2003 Nomisma SpA, Italy) and as Project Partner (including management and financial management) for Interreg IIIB Program Project 'Baltic Business Development Network' (2005–2007). Recently (2011–2015) she has been Performer in the Research and Innovation Policy Monitoring Programme in Estonia. She is a member of the Management Committee for the COST Action for European Network for Research Evaluation in the Social Sciences and the Humanities (ENRESSH), starting in November 2015. She leads the Doctoral School in Economics and Innovation in Estonia. She has been a member of Team Europe–Estonia from 1997 to 2009 and is a member of the Estonian Economics Association. Her main research interests are economic policy, including institutional and organizational aspects of state regulation and competition policy, comparative analysis of different economic systems and social accounting.

Rita Goyal is a doctoral researcher at Henley Business School, University of Reading. Her research is on board diversity and its impact on boards' role effectiveness. In her pursuit of research studies she is interviewing chairmen, CEOs and board directors of many listed and closely held companies in the UK. She and her co-authors have written academic papers in the realm of board governance, which she has presented in international conferences. Earlier she worked in the fast-track Indian Civil Services for two decades in various middle and senior management roles. Rita holds an undergraduate degree in Mathematics, Physics and Chemistry and a postgraduate degree in History with silver medal from her university in India.

Melanie Hayden is a corporate lawyer at Allens in Sydney, specializing in public and private M&A. She graduated from Bond University in 2015 with a Bachelor's of Laws (Hons) and Bachelor's of International Relations (Business).

Petra Inwinkl is Associate Professor in Business Administration with emphasis on International Accounting and Corporate Governance at Jönköping International Business School, University of Jönköping in Sweden. She was an undergraduate in Business Administration and pursued doctoral studies in Business Administration at the Vienna University of Economics. She further pursued doctoral studies in Law at the University of Vienna. She is a professional licensed tax advisor in Austria, member of the Research Faculty Board as well as Member of the Centre for Family Enterprise and Ownership at Jönköping International Business School, University of Jönköping. Furthermore, she is author of many articles on issues in international accounting, IFRS, auditing, corporate governance, corporate mergers and takeovers, European company law, European tax law and valuations.

Andrew P. Kakabadse, BSc MA PhD AAPSW FBPS FIAM FBAM, is Professor of Governance and Leadership at Henley Business School and Emeritus Professor at Cranfield School of Management. He is a Board Member on boards of ABIS and Winsor Leadership Trust. He is Visiting Professor at the University of Ulster, Macquarie University, Australia. Andrew's research covers boards, top teams and the governance of governments. He has published over 45 books, 88 book chapters, over 235 articles and 18 monographs. He is Adviser to the UK Parliament and numerous corporations, NGOs and other governments.

Nada Korac Kakabadse is Professor of Policy, Governance and Ethics at Henley Business School. She is the Head of School (Marketing and Reputation) at the University of Reading. She is Visiting Professor at US, Australian, French, Kazakhstani and Chinese universities. She is an elected and active member of European Academy of Science and Arts (EASA) and is the Head of its EU Representation Office at Brussels. She has co-authored 19 books and has published over 190 scholarly articles. Her current interests are leadership, boardroom effectiveness, governance, CSR and ethics, diversity and the policy design of the state.

Maha Karkabi-Sabbah is currently a post-doctor fellow at the Sociology Department, Tel Aviv University, and has recently finished her post-doctoral fellowship at the Center for Gender Studies, SOAS, University of London. She is also an associate researcher at The Van Leer Jerusalem Institute. Her current works concentrate on family, gender, inequality, and Palestinian society in Israel. She is the author of a number of articles on these themes in journals such as *Studies in Family Planning* and *Israeli Sociology* (in Hebrew). She has received several awards and grants for her research, among them the Post-doctoral Scholar Award of The Israel Science Foundation (ISF), The Council for Higher Education in Israel (VTAT), and the Tel Aviv University Post-doctoral Fellow 2016–2017. Recently, she received the Truman Researcher Grant–The Hebrew University of Jerusalem, for her study "Ethno-mixed marriages in a divided society: the case of Palestinian women married to Jewish men in Israel".

Ozlem Kutlu Furtuna is Assistant Professor in the Faculty of Economic and Administrative Sciences at Yildiz Technical University (YTU), Istanbul,

Turkey. She is Vice-President of the Center for Finance, Governance and Sustainability (CFGS) at YTU. Ozlem completed her PhD and Master's degree in the Accounting and Finance Department at Marmara University in Turkey. She teaches Financial Management and Financial Statement Analysis in the undergraduate program and Financial Management: Theory and Application and Research Methods in the graduate program at YTU. She has recently worked on a research project titled "An Alternative Approach for Corporate Sustainability Performance Measurement: An Application on Turkish Banking Sector" supported by the Scientific and Technological Research Council of Turkey (TUBITAK). Her research areas primarily lie in the area of corporate finance topics, specifically agency theory, corporate governance and corporate sustainability.

Anna Lindstrand has been a research assistant at the Jönköping International Business School and now pursues her professional career at the major auditing firms in Sweden.

Anna Masłoń-Oracz (PhD) is a lecturer at Warsaw School of Economics. She is a political scientist, economist and an expert in the area of EU foreign policy, with particular focus on the global trade policy and transatlantic relations (EU, US, Africa). Anna is a member of the International Women's Forum and Vice-President of the Polish European Community Study Association. As a business-oriented researcher, Anna has done analysis on how clusters influence regional development competitiveness from a smart specialization perspective. She is also involved in international projects in many countries in Africa concerning women's empowerment, development of SMEs and regional innovation systems (RIS) to enhance the role and importance of RIS in economic development and growth.

Filipe Morais holds a degree in Human Resource Management and an MBA from Northampton Business School and recently embarked on a full-time PhD at Henley Business School, University of Reading, UK. Since 2004, Filipe has held various positions in HR, both in manufacturing and service companies, as well as a role as Executive Director for Research with two private higher education institutions in Portugal, where he took on the additional role of Editor of the peer-reviewed Portuguese *Journal of Marketing*. While completing his MBA, Filipe developed an interest in corporate governance, boardroom process and effectiveness, and board leadership, which are currently his main areas of research. His research is looking at how boardroom processes lead to balanced decision-making. Filipe is supervised by Professors Nada and Andrew Kakabadse. Filipe also has an interest in the improvement of human resource management practice and is a published author.

Justina Mutale is acclaimed as one of the most influential and inspirational African women. In 2012, she was awarded the prestigious title of African Woman of the Year, sharing a platform with various African presidents and heads of state. Dr Mutale is Founder and President of the Justina Mutale Foundation. She is also Founder of Positive Runway: The Global Catwalk to Stop the Spread of HIV/AIDS. Dr Mutale serves as Global Envoy for Gender Equality and Spokesperson of the International Women's Think Tank. She sits on the Board of the World Leaders Forum and is a Civil Society Delegate and Speaker at the UN Commission on the Status of Women and the African Union High-Level Panel on Gender Equality and Women's Empowerment.

Ida Ohlsson has been a research assistant at the Jönköping International Business School and now pursues her professional career at the major auditing firms in Sweden.

Marta Pachocka holds a PhD in Economics. She is Assistant Professor at the Department of Political Studies of the Collegium of Socio-Economics of the Warsaw School of Economics and at the Centre of Migration Research of the University of Warsaw. She is a coordinator of the project EUMIGRO – Jean Monnet Module on the European Union and the Contemporary International Migration – an Interdisciplinary Approach (2016–2019) and a key staff member in the project CEWSE – Centre of Excellence at Warsaw School of Economics on European Union's Security and Stability in a new Economic, Social & Geopolitical Settlement (2016–2019), both conducted at the Warsaw School of Economics and co-financed by the EU under the Erasmus+ Programme. She has been involved in many national and international projects co-funded by i.a. EU, Polish Ministry of Foreign Affairs, National Bank of Poland and Polish National Science Center. She has been a beneficiary of Young Scientists' Research Grants financed by the Polish Ministry of Science and Higher Education since 2012. She was a visiting research fellow at Centre d'études européennes of Sciences Po Paris (2015) as well as a visiting professor in Bratislava (2015) and Tartu (2016). She is a secretary of the Polish European Community Studies Association (PECSA) and an active member of UACES, IPSA, IMISCOE, IASFM and AIELF. Her main research interests are socio-demographic changes in Europe/EU, Europe/EU and international migration, forced migration and refugee studies, EU policy on migration and asylum, immigration policy and integration policy in France, France's international position, European economy and world economy.

Michal Palgi is Professor of Organizational Sociology and the head of the Institute for Research of the Kibbutz and the Cooperative Idea at the University of Haifa and was the chair and founder of the graduate program in Organizational Development and Consulting at the Emek Yezreel College in Israel. She is among the founders of the Israeli Women's Network and the founder of Gender Studies in her college. She is a former president of the International Sociological Association Research Committee on Participation, Organizational Democracy and Self-Management (RC10), and was the head of the Israeli Sociological Association Committee for Research of Gender Roles. Her areas of research and activity are organizational democracy, organizational change, gender-based inequality, social justice, kibbutz society and community development. Professor Palgi was an adviser to the Austrian–German research project ODEM (Organizational Democracy – Resources of Organizations for Social Behavior Readiness Conducive to Democracy). She has published extensively on kibbutz, organizational democracy, community development and gender.

Irina Pervukhina is Senior Lecturer in the Department of Business Foreign Languages, Ural State University of Economics (Ekaterinburg, Russia). She holds a MA from New Mexico State University (USA). As the department's Head Deputy, she is responsible for curriculum design and quality assurance and is a Member of the USUE Quality Assurance Board. She has both teaching and business experience. She has participated in several international educational projects, such as CHAIN-E: Creation of a Higher Academic International Network for Economists, The European (TEMPUS/TACIS), Bridge, Internationalizing Higher Education, Erasmus Mundus and Erasmus+. Her main research interests are teaching and learning, pedagogy, academic writing, women's studies and corporate governance. She is one of the authors of *English for Academics, Book 1 & 2* (CUP).

Gunnar Rimmel is Full Professor and holds a Chair in Accounting at Henley Business School, University of Reading, UK. He previously worked in Sweden as a professor in Accounting at Jönköping International Business School and Gothenburg Research Institute at the University of Gothenburg. He received his PhD in 2003 for the thesis "Human Resource Disclosures" from the School of Business at the School of Business, Economics and Law at Gothenburg University in Sweden. He has published his articles in international academic journals such as *Accounting, Auditing and Accountability Journal*, *Journal of Accounting and Public Policy* and *Accounting Forum*. Further, he has contributed more than 20 book chapters in international books. His research and teaching interests include accounting communication, human resource accounting, international financial accounting, and social and environmental reporting, specifically integrated reporting. During the past years his research program Accounting for Sustainability – Communication Through Integrated Reporting has been externally funded by the Handelsbanken research foundations. He had also received grants from the NASDAQ OMX Nordic Foundation.

Tomasz Szapiro's degrees include MSc in Physics from Warsaw University, Poland and PhD in Mathematics from Polish Academy of Sciences, habilitation. He is also Full Professor in Economy, Professor in the Institute for Modern Civilization at WSE and Adjunct Professor of International Business Studies at the Carlson School of Business, University of Minneapolis, USA. He is a former president of the SGH Warsaw School of Economics (2012–2016). He is International Partner of the INSID – Instituto Nacional de Sistema de Informação e Decisão (National Institute of Information and Decision System), Universidade Federal de Pernambuco, Brasil. His research interests focus on Operational Research, IT and Economics of Privacy and Economics of Education.

He publishes in Poland and abroad, including two books, a monograph, and over 120 articles and conference papers (in, for example, *Operations Research, IEEE Transactions on System Man and Cybernetics, European Journal of Operations Research*), and actively participates in international conferences. Professor Szapiro is a referee for first-rank international research journals. He worked as Visiting Professor and part-time Lecturer in the School of Business, Carleton University and in the Department of Computer Science, University of Ottawa, Canada. He also worked as an expert for European Commission and Fulbright Commission (project evaluation) for the Ministers of Finance, Economy and National Education. He was Supervisory Board Member of ING-BSK and of Aviva (Commercial Union). He is the recipient of numerous awards for organizational and research achievements and for excellence in teaching.

Aleksandra Szczerba-Zawada is Doctor of EU Law, Head of the Chair of Administrative Science at the Faculty of Administration and National Security of the Jacob of Paradise University in Gorzów Wielkopolski. She specializes in EU law and anti-discrimination law. Aleksandra is a member of scientific associations: PECSA, PSPE, PTSE and scientific committees of *Journal of Administration and Security* and *European Studies Journal* (ECSA-Moldova). Her research interests include the principle of gender equality, EU Internal Market, AFSJ and CFSP. She has didactic experience on EU law, human rights law, EU structural funds and CFSP. She has been an expert in many scientific projects, including EU-funded projects. She is the Jean Monnet Module EUIncSo coordinator (2016–2019). She is an author and co-editor of several books and articles published both in Polish and English. Aleksandra has received several national and foreign scholarships, including prestigious scholarship of the Polish Minister of Science and Higher Education for outstanding young scientists 2016–2019.

Dr Madeline Elizabeth Taylor LLB (Hons.), PhD is an Early Career Development Fellow at the University of Sydney, School of Law. Madeline specializes in corporate governance, energy and natural resource law with her research publications in the corporate law field to date focusing on the governance and regulation of diversity of corporate boards and management. She teaches in the areas of corporations law and real property, and has held research positions within the Centre for Coal Seam Gas at the University of Queensland and the Centre for Land and Food Systems at the University of British Columbia, Canada.

Irina Tkachenko is Professor at Ural State University of Economics, Ekaterinburg, Russia; Director of Institute of Corporate Governance and Entrepreneurship; and Head of the Department of Corporate Economics, Governance and Business and Business Administration. She is a Doctor of Science (Economics). Her doctorate dissertation (2002) 'Institutional and Valuable Basis for Effective Development of Interfirm Corporate Relations' was devoted to the problems of corporate governance. She specializes in topics of corporate governance, corporate social responsibility and public–private partnership. She is one of the co-authors of the book *Transforming Governance: New Values, New Systems in New Business Environment*, edited by Maria Aluchna and Güler Aras (Gower Publishing Limited, England, 2015–240p.). Irina is one of the co-authors of the book *Responsible Corporate Governance*, published by Springer Publishing House (2017) and edited by Maria Aluchna and S.O. Idowu. Irina has won many grants on corporate governance issues, including: the Fundamental Research Fund in the Sphere of Economic Science by the Russian Ministry of Education (1999–2000, 2003–2004); RGNF Grant (2001, 2011–2012); the Russian Foundation for Basic Research (2013–2015); Grant of Bridge Partnership with Ashcroft International Business School of Anglia Ruskin University, UK (2006–2010, 2012); ACTR-RSEP Fellowship, George Washington University, Washington, DC (US, 1995); Canada–Russia Program in Corporate Governance, Schulich School of Business, Toronto, Ontario, Canada, Grant of CIDA, June–July, 2003; Erasmus Mundus Action 3: (SCEE project) – The Warsaw School of Economics (Szkoła Główna Handlowa w Warszawie, SGH) (2013). Irina was a Visiting Lecturer in Karaganda State University, Kazahkstan (2012), in Poland (SGH, 2013), in Italy (Luiss Guido Carli University and Link Campus University, Rome, 2014) and Florence University (2014).

Part I
Overview

Introduction

Maria Aluchna and Güler Aras

Corporate board is the crucial element of the corporate governance structure and its efficiency and performance. The quality of board work, specifically monitoring and oversight over executives determines the company performance. The board functions as the liaison between shareholders, the providers of the capital and managers who use this capital to create firm value. It is also an influential, powerful and prestigious body at the top of organizational hierarchy which bears the ultimate responsibility for company operation. Due to the strategic role of the board the issues of its work, composition and structure are placed among the most dynamically developing research topics in management and corporate governance. Today the board evolved to engage more independent directors, reveal increased transparency and have more diverse composition. This results in the increased representation of women in the boardroom. Board diversity is also a reliable indicator of gender equality advancement and policy adopted by countries and companies.

We address the ongoing debate on corporate governance reforms and company reaction to stakeholder expectations and trace the patterns of women's involvement in governance and management. In this book we intend to outline theoretical and conceptual frameworks and discuss policy and regulatory arguments and the practical implication of women on boards.

Adopting the interdisciplinary approach and international perspective the book traces the logic behind the decision patterns of female representation in governance and management. Specifically, the publication aims at the identification of patterns for women's presence on corporate boards with respect to theoretical and conceptual framework, policy and regulatory implication and the practical adaptation. The phenomenon of women on corporate boards is analyzed in the context of different political, cultural and institutional environments addressing challenges in both developed and emerging economies. The role of female directors is viewed as one of the crucial aspects in corporate governance adding to the quality of control and management.

The book is divided into three main parts, preceded by an overview. The chapters in Part II discuss concepts and policies on female representation on corporate boards. Part III covers institutional and socio-economic perspectives of gender diversity. The chapters in Part IV present studies and analysis on mechanisms which explain female representation on boards in the organizational context. Final remarks are provided in the conclusion.

Part II focuses on concepts and policies of gender diversity in the boardroom. In Chapter 1, "Women on corporate boards: backgrounds, drivers and mechanisms", Maria Aluchna and Tomasz Szapiro provide an overview of the existing literature summarizing key findings. Specifically, they address the background of gender diversity in management and governance, identify main drivers for its development and enumerate five mechanisms referring to the labour market, regulation efficiency, the role of the institutional context and business practice. In the final part they outline directions for further research offer a starting point for the discussion provided in the following chapters.

Chapter 2, "Gender diversity on boards in Norway and the UK: a different approach to governance or a case of path dependency?", is written by a team of Rita Goyal, Nada Kakabadse, Filipe Morais and Andrew Kakabadse. They investigate the cases of Norway and the UK to identify possible reasons for adopting different strategies to achieve gender diversity in boards of these countries. They offer a possible explanation of partial failure of adopted strategies in the UK and Norway in achieving the objective. In their analysis the authors refer to the concept of the path dependency pointing at the prevailing legal systems, corporate philosophies, political orientation and socio-cultural practices which contribute to the adoption of different strategies for boards' gender diversity.

In Chapter 3, "Regulation of the gender composition of company boards in Europe: experience and prospects", Kevin Campbell and Leszek Bohdanowicz offer the review of the enforcement approach proposed by the European Commission pointing at its successes and failures. They discuss the evidence on the mandatory quota system in Norway drawing on factors that contribute to the success of quotas, such as the nature of the sanctions against non-compliant companies, and their enforcement. Kevin Campbell and Leszek Bohdanowicz also evaluate the UK voluntary approach for listed companies included in the FTSE 100 and 250 indices confronting the success of this policy with initiatives in other European countries. Finally, they address the question on the efficiency of hard versus soft law approaches for the increase of the representation of women on boards.

Part III addresses the topic of gender diversity in boardrooms viewed from institutional and socio-economic perspectives. This part starts with the fourth chapter written by JF Corkery, Madeline Elizabeth Taylor and Melanie Hayden titled "Gender balance in Australian boardrooms: the business case for quotas" which explores the importance of improving corporate culture to be more inclusive of women in leadership positions. The authors examine the current Australian policy which follows the soft regulatory intervention supporting the increase of women on boards and assesses the potential benefits of enacting mandatory gender quota legislation. This chapter concludes with arguing that despite the increase of gender diversity in Australia, there is a need for a long-term plan due to the slow progress of the soft policy for female representation on Australian boards.

Chapter 5 was written by Marta Pachocka, Aleksandra Szczerba-Zawada and Diana Eerma and provides the comparison of "Women on corporate boards in

Poland and Estonia in the context of the EU gender equality policy". Aiming to analyze the women's presence in decision-making positions the authors discuss the cases of Estonia and Poland referring to a broader background of the EU gender equality policy. The chapter emphasizes the lack of the EU legislation on women's representation on corporate boards. This results in significant divergence or the absence of such regulation at national level in the EU Member States and hinders the achievement of gender equality in this area. The authors offer the analysis of acts of law and official documents at the EU and national levels, the content analysis, the case study approach and the comparative perspective. This study is supplemented with the analysis of quantitative data.

In Chapter 6, "Socio-economic perspective on women on boards: an African perspective", Justina Mutale and Anna Masłoń-Oracz carry out analyses on female representation on boards on the company and regional levels. They provide the overview of the literature, source materials and program documents as well as deliver a comparative and descriptive study on the policies and business practice of female representation on corporate boards in selected African countries. They document both regional and sectorial differences identifying significant constrains to increase the percentage of female directors.

Helena Desivilya Syna, Michal Palgi and Maha Karkabi-Sabbah focus on the mechanisms underlying women's limited involvement in strategic decision-making in their chapter "Women's experiences in Top Management Teams (TMTs): the case of Israeli national majority and national minority women". They intend to widen the research scope to not only examine the presence of women on boards but also to understand the roles played by women in these forums. For the purpose of the analysis they address the phenomena such as gendered construction of power relations, gender stereotyping in decision-making processes and networking patterns is deemed important. The study aims to diminish the research gaps of what actually happens in top forums shedding light and comparing Jewish and Arab women's experiences at upper echelon forums.

The chapters in Part IV study and identify mechanisms explaining female participation on boards in the organizational context.

In Chapter 8, "Female entrepreneurship and boardroom diversity: the case of Russia", Irina Tkachenko and Irina Pervukhina present the study results on the role of women in corporate governance. Specifically, they examine the presence of women on boards of directors of Russian companies with state involvement in the ownership structure. They analyze the effect of female participation on the board for economic and financial performance. They intend to address the question on whether women on the corporate boards contribute to firm growth and development whether their appointment is viewed just as a tribute to 'breaking the glass ceiling' trend.

In Chapter 9 Gunnar Rimmel, Petra Inwinkl, Anna Lindstrand and Ida Ohlsson present a study of "Female representation on Swedish corporate boards" addressing the role of the women-friendly regulatory and social climate. Using the data from company annual reports they reveal the current state and the dynamics of women's participation on Swedish corporate boards. In their analysis they link the appointment of female board members with a number of factors such as board size, ownership structure and educational level.

The evolution of female participation in the economic sphere and in decision-making positions in France is discussed by Nabyla Daidj in Chapter 10, "Females on corporate boards: French perspectives: towards more diversity?". She provides an analysis of a wide set of documents and data to document the effectiveness of legislative actions for the progress of gender equality policies in France. The author notes that despite undertaken measures the percentage of women's representation on French boards remains still below the objective set by the law.Chapter 11, entitled "The 2017 New Zealand stock exchange directors' network analysis and the effect of 'soft' reporting regimes on board diversity" is written by Rosanne Hawarden. It delivers the first research to assess the effectiveness of the 'soft' initiative of the diversity reporting regime with limited sanctions for non-compliance introduced on the New Zealand Stock Exchange in 2013. The chapter is based on two studies – a census and a network analysis motivated by the methodology of crowd science. The network of the 122 diversity reporting companies was constructed using a 'crowd research' methodology. The analyses document an increase to 14.8% of women directors, with an increase of 1% per annum since the introduction of the reporting regime. This finding remains similar but less marked than the effect noted in Norway of 'hard' legislated quotas.

In the final chapter, Chapter 12, "Women on board: perspectives from BRIC and Turkey", Güler Aras and Ozlem Kutlu Furtuna discuss the gender diversity on boards in the context of Turkish listed companies. The authors deliver statistical data which document the dynamics of percentage of females in top management, female chairperson, percentage of independent female members in board of directors, female CEO-general manager for firms listed on BIST (Borsa Istanbul). While the regression analysis linking the percentage of female members and firm performance emphasize the positive effect of gender diversity, the authors conclude with the observation that the involvement of women on the board remains insufficient in BRIC firms.

Final remarks are presented in the conclusion.

We believe that the international group of authors who contribute to this book add to the understanding of the process, mechanisms and effects of increasing gender diversity in the boardroom. Offering studies about the presence of women on corporate boards across the globe, they examine internal mechanisms and organizational specificities in companies as well as external determinants which impact the presence of women on corporate boards. The authors carry out their analysis in the context of different political, cultural and institutional environments addressing challenges for increasing female representation on boards in both developed and emerging economies. The book elaborates on the consequences of having women on corporate boards indicating the qualitative changes in governing a corporation.

Part II

Concepts and models

1 Women on corporate boards

Backgrounds, drivers and mechanisms

Maria Aluchna and Tomasz Szapiro

Introduction

Research on the presence of women on corporate boards addresses female participation in management and governance. The inclusion of women on boards has over the years evolved to be one of the most intensively investigated and debated issues of – both – academia and corporate practice (Singh et al., 2008; Terjesen et al., 2009; Dalton and Dalton, 2009; Kakabadse et al., 2015; Seierstad et al., 2017). It is confirmed in the growing number of empirical and theoretical studies as well as in the formulation of codes of conduct and the sets of guidelines adopted among companies and public administration. The topic has also turned to be a political issue triggering implementations of regulations and recommendations in various spheres of economic and social lives.

With the growing number of studies, regulations formulated and adopted in the organizational context the topic of women on boards unveils its complexity. The dynamics of organizational reactions and the role of institutional contexts indicate the complexity, multidimensionality and interdependencies of gender diversity in the boardroom leaving questions not addressed. Numerous analyses (Ibrahim and Angelidis, 1994; Sheridan, 2001; McKinsey & Co., 2009, 2010; Davidson and Burke, 2004; Hillman et al., 2007; Dalton and Dalton, 2010) show that active participation of women in enterprises is constrained by structural hindrances which women face while pursuing their careers to reach the board level. This is caused by a number of reasons. First, structural obstacles refer to socio-economic sphere resulting from the unequal dedication to household work and responsibilities (McKinsey & Co., 2016). Second, in the organizational context a corporate career model requires significant geographical mobility and time availability standing in conflict with plans for starting a family and having work–life balance. The "anytime, anywhere" career model appears to be more problematic for women who statistically devote more time to raise children than for men. Third, in the socio-cultural framework females may jeopardize their career once they underestimate their skills, neglect networking, and do not build connections, professional alliances or coalitions (Haigh, 2008). In addition, the socially viewed gender role may hinder females' promotion up the organizational ladder. Women as compared to men may reveal a less confrontational leadership style which may be perceived as low ambitions determination (Wood and Eagly, 2012). On the other hand, in the case of dedication shown at work, women may be criticized as extremely aggressive and excessively determined.

In this chapter, we intend to draw upon the theme of female participation on corporate boards. Our aim is to provide an overview of the literature and research reports to recognize the main contributions to this field and synthetize key findings. This chapter intends to open the discussion on women's presence on corporate boards, which is elaborated in the following chapters. Specifically, we address the background of gender diversity in management and governance, tracing the main drivers for its development and identifying mechanism which determined the current state of art and shape future prospects.

The remainder of the chapter is the following. Backgrounds and statistics on gender diversity in boardroom are outlined in the first section. In the second section, we discuss motivations and drivers for increasing women's participation on boards offered by different conceptual and theoretical frameworks. The third section reviews existing studies and research and addresses the main empirical developments which document the mechanisms which explain the role and contribution of women on corporate boards. The discussion of directions for future research is revealed in the fourth section. The argument is concluded with final remarks.

Women on boards: backgrounds

The board constitutes the essential organizational body in a company and is a crucial element of the corporate governance structure (Carter and Lorsch, 2004; Larcker and Tayan, 2011). Boards may operate as unitary boards of directors (one-tier model) or dual supervisory and management boards in the two-tier model (Mallin, 2004). In both models the quality of board work, monitoring and counselling determines the efficiency of governance and the board directors bear the ultimate responsibility for the company performance. Monks and Minow (2004: 195) notice that boards "are the link between that people who provide capital (the shareholders) and the people who use that capital to create value (the managers)". Boards constitute the connection between concentrated or dispersed shareholders of different identities (individuals, funds, companies, banks etc.) who exert the residual rights and executives who run the company (Roe, 1994; Fisch, 2004). The task of board directors is to align the goals of managers with the interest of shareholders (Hambrick and Jackson, 2000). The main board responsibilities include (Monks and Minow, 1996; Carter and Lorsch, 2004) the review of strategy, providing accountability, monitoring and counsel to top managers as well as the selection, evaluation, replacement of CEO.

Corporate boards are powerful groups of strategic importance packed with high-profile directors tied with a network of relations and behavioral patterns (Hambrick et al., 2008) whose work determines the company performance and shareholder value. With the understanding of the strategic role of the board, its structure, composition and work standards have evolved to be a leading topic in corporate governance. Numerous studies (van Knippenberg et al., 2007; Terjesen and Singh, 2008; Terjesen et al., 2009; Nielsen and Huse, 2010; Bear et al., 2010; Hafsi and Turgut, 2013; McGuinness et al., 2015) aim at the understanding of the role and importance of selected board attributes (size, structure, demographics, turnover, independent/affiliated directors, specialized committees) for specified company performance (strategy, financial results, value, CSR/environmental performance). With the consequences of globalization and growing stakeholder pressure companies need to adjust their strategies and operation (Idemudia, 2011; Verdeyen et al., 2004; Donaldson and Preston, 2008). These reforms are also expected at the board level – directors should acquire new skills, and show understanding of information technologies as well as social and environmental challenges and respond to new stakeholders' expectations (Moon and Matten, 2008; Moon et al., 2010; Riyanto and Toolsema, 2007; Jamali et al., 2008). The business cannot be done as usual, so boards cannot operate according to prior agendas.

At the company level appointing women to corporate boards is viewed as an upright business decision, a move to enhance corporate governance standards, an element to understand and represent wide stakeholder groups and a contribution to improving company performance (Simpson et al., 2010; Colaco et al., 2011). Studies indicate that "women are not substitutes for men director of equal ability and qualifications, but women instead may have unique attributes that increase the performance of the board, and ultimately the performance of the firm" (Simpson et al., 2010: 27). These attributes help develop communication skills, preference for dialog and compromise versus confrontation, risk-aversion, long-term orientation and social/environmental empathy. Women help mitigate group-thinking syndrome increasing diversity on boards.

Studies reveal continuous increase in the number and percentage of board seats held by women and the decrease in the number of companies with no female on the board (PWC, 2016). Data reveal however significant differences globally. Figure 1.1 presents the percentage of board seats held by women in selected countries.

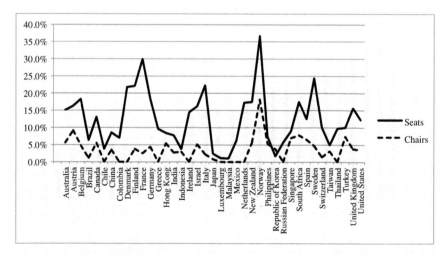

Figure 1.1 Board seats held by women

Source: based on Deloitte (2015: 68)

Data in Figure 1.1 indicate that the percentage of board seats held by women differs significantly for the analyzed countries ranging between 36.7% for Norway and 3.7% for Indonesia. Overall, the strongest women's presence in the boardroom is noted in Europe. Interestingly, increase in the participation of women on boards does not necessarily lead to the increase in female chairpersons of the board. Data for the EU are presented in Figure 1.2 with the breakdown for Member States.

In order to capture the dynamics of women's engagement on boards, the overview by Catalyst (2016) documents a moderate change reporting the following:

• Credit Suisse on the sample of more than 3,000 global companies found that women held 14.7% of board seats in 2015, which represents an increase of 54% since 2010.
• In MSCI's study out of the 4,218 companies, women held 15% of board seats in 2015, which is up from 12.4% the previous year;
    • of those companies, 73.5% had at least one woman director, while 20.1% had boards with at least three women.
• In Deloitte's analysis of nearly 6,000 companies in 49 countries, women held 12% of board seats;
    • of which 4% of board chair positions were held by women.

Figure 1.3 presents the data from the 2016 Global Board Diversity Analysis documenting "slow but positive Gender diversity progress globally" (EgonZehnder, 2017).

Interestingly, as shown in Figure 1.3, despite the debate on the benefit of female participation in corporate boards and a series of regulations introduced, the dynamics in the boardroom differ across the world. While over the analyzed

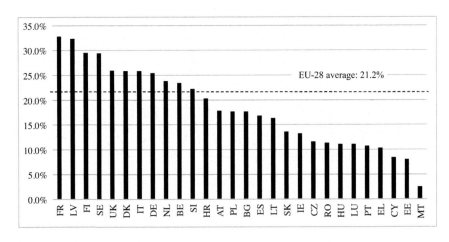

Figure 1.2 Representation of women on the boards of large listed companies in the EU
Source: European Commission (2016)

period 2012–2016 the majority of countries note the growth of percentage of board positions held by women, according to data by EgonZehnder (2017) the change is marginal for Brazil, the US, Argentina and Russia and slightly negative for China, Mexico, the Czech Republic and Turkey.

Finally, Figure 1.4 shows the data for 2011–2016 according to Gender Diversity Index (2017) for US companies revealing improvement for female participation on boards.

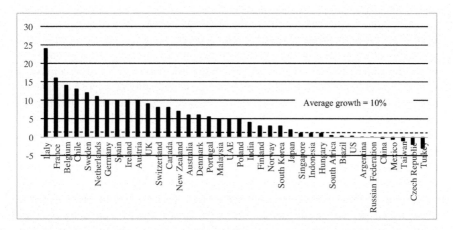

Figure 1.3 Four-year growth, percentage of board positions held by women (2016 versus 2012)

Source: EgonZehnder (2017: 5).

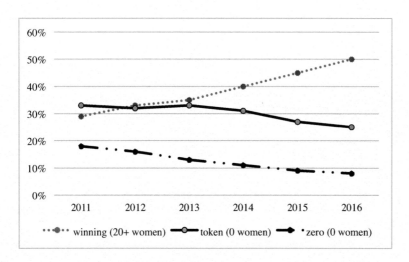

Figure 1.4 Gender Diversity Index (2011–2016)

Source: based on Gender Diversity Index (2017: 3)

As shown in Figure 1.4 women on boards made a steady progress as measured by four indicators called "winning" (20%+ women on board), "very close" (11–19% women on boards), "token" (1 woman on board) and "zero" (0 women on board). In 2016 half of the companies in the Gender Diversity Index belong to the winning category, while the percentage of "zero" companies fell to an all-time low of 8% (Gender Diversity Index, 2017)

At the institutional level, corporate practice is backed with regulatory efforts. Increasing the number of women on boards is often perceived as an exemplification of the change supported with actions in the regulatory environment with many actors affecting the adoption of new guidelines and policies (Seierstad et al., 2017). Both situations – unbalanced board and the gender gap at the labor market – may negatively affect the company performance and may hinder country social and economic development. Actions to increase female participation on boards recommend voluntary adoption of best practice, promote gender equality or impose regulatory quotas. Using Norway, the first country to introduce binding quotas of 40% female representation on boards, as a benchmark, a number of the following initiatives were adopted. Documents of the European Parliament exemplify tools for assuring larger female involvement calling for bridging the gender gap, eliminating discrimination and suggesting quotas for the female presence on boards. This pragmatic attitude enriches earlier purely gender equality-oriented debate as documented in Figure 1.5.

EU strategy for gender equality was presented in a series of documents (Aluchna, 2017) which address the equality between women and men; a roadmap for equality between women and men; and the context of discrimination, practices, policies and laws. As shown in Figure 1.5 the average increase in women on boards is estimated for 0.5 percentage points between 2005 and 2010 and for 2.1 percentage points between 2010 and 2015 when legislative actions were introduced.

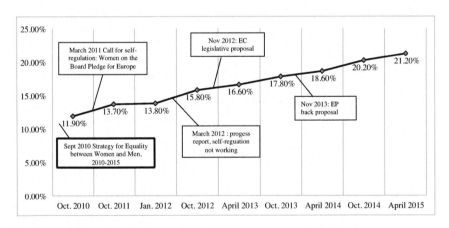

Figure 1.5 Gender equality in EU legislations and female representation on boards (2010–2015)

Source: European Commission (2016)

Another stream of conclusions refers to economic matters – gender pay gap, gender budgeting in the EU budgetary process, promotion of women innovators and entrepreneurship, and attracting women to research and science and technology. A set of gender equality rules was identified including, among others, equal economic independence for women and men, better reconciliation of work and private family life, promoting equal participation of women and men in decision-making, eradicating gender-based violence and promoting gender equality outside the EU.

Women on boards: motivations and drivers

Empirical studies, particularly in recent years, have been dominated by the seminal question on the impact of female presence on boards on performance, yet numerous approaches and theories mirror different motivations and rationales. These perspectives, briefly presented in the following subsections, intend to formulate arguments supporting women's presence on boards. While the socio-political approach places the inclusion of women in boards in the affirmative action and justice rationales (Seierstad, 2016), the institutional approach reveals hindrances and obstacles which deteriorate women's promotion to the top position in organizations, the managerial theories provide efficiency and performance motivations denoting a business case for women on boards.

Socio-political perspective

This perspective pictures the issue of women on boards within political and social frameworks such as non-discrimination/social justice theory and gender/feminist theory. Let us briefly address these issues.

Social justice/non-discrimination theory

"The social justice viewpoint is based on the key underlying principle of that of an equal society" (Seierstad, 2016: 393) which leads to the claims that half of the society needs to have its representation on corporate boards. The affirmative action streaming from the social justice theory should compensate for injustice and inequality perceived as results of unfair and unbalanced distribution of power and resources. According to the rationales of equal opportunities and non-discrimination, the notion of women's presence on corporate boards is viewed though the perspective of the fundamental civil rights which include the obligation of equal treatment of all the male and female employees irrespective of their sex (EU Directive 2000/43/EC Art 13). The main message of non-discrimination approach is a desire to assure equal rights to every individual. Equal treatment is based on the principle of equal pay, equal work conditions, equality in decision-making processes, and equal access to trainings and promotion. The assumptions of the non-discrimination emphasize the gender equality with the reference of opportunities and chances, antidiscrimination laws and programs to improve living standards of all social groups.

Gender/feminist theory

The feminist theory identifies gender as a source for identification (inclusion) and differentiation (exclusion) (Bourdieu, 1997; Bourdieu and Wacquant, 1992). It recognizes inequalities between two sexes and the abuse of women in society. The basic driver of gender stereotypes is in-group favoritism or in-group preference. Gendered organization's structures result in job segregation, disparities between an organization's hierarchical levels and impact the processes employees use to determine their own gender identities at work (Acker, 1990). Gender stereotypical beliefs (gender roles) can act both as social norms (embedded in others' expectations) and as personal dispositions (embedded in individual gender identities) (Wood and Eagly, 2012). In general, the masculine leadership style based on task-oriented, autocratic, directive, dominant behaviors dominated organizational structures. In effect, women entering the boards of directors may possess the necessary cultural capital in terms of education and professional skills but the social field (boards) has the historically grown social constructions of "masculinity".

With the importance of gender roles in organization Tajfel et al. (1986) offered the social identity theory linked to the social self-categorization theory. This perspective suggests that individuals tend to discriminate against out-group members who display characteristics which differ from their own. This means that women and men are defined by their sex which determines rules of behavior and access to resources. The conflicts between gender groups stimulates the group members to reproduce given characteristics and behavior (Britton, 2000; Kakabadse et al., 2015).

Institutional approach

The institutional perspective has so far not often been adopted to explain the phenomenon of women on boards; however recent comparative analyses have addressed institutional differences among countries. This approach suggests that corporate behavior, strategies and the implementation of best practice are significantly embedded in the institutional context (Meyer and Rowan, 1977; DiMaggio and Powell, 1983; Mizruchi and Fein, 1999). Organizations have theory-specific ways to transform signals from the environment – some of them prove to be highly adaptive and flexible, while others remain laggards (Aguilera and Jackson, 2003; Kang and Moon, 2012). Studies indicate environmental factors characteristics and actors (Seierstad et al., 2017; Terjesen et al., 2015) which either stimulate or inhibit gender diversity in economic and social lives. Specifically, the comparative analyses reveal the importance of cultural and social norms, institutional environment, and legal and political systems (Foster, 2017). Research within this framework shows that the institutional environmental and organizational context in which women operate determine the behavior in companies, shared values, prevalent leadership style and patterns of promotion (Nekhili and Gatfaoui, 2013).

Managerial theories

Managerial theories discuss the presence of women on boards within the organizational framework, culture and leadership, and company performance. These perspectives include principal–agent theory, human capital and resource dependence theory, stakeholder theory and diversity management framework. The inclusion of women at the governance and executive level is explained with the use of efficiency rationale showing that women contribute to the overall company performance delivering unique skills, competences and resources; increasing diversity; and responding to shareholder and stakeholder expectations.

Principal–agent theory

The principal–agent theory remains the most influential approach in corporate governance analysis. It studies the conflicts between principals (shareholders) and agent (managers) which take place in the case of the separation of ownership and control characteristic for large publicly listed firms (Jensen and Meckling, 1976). To mitigate the agency costs arising from the inevitable conflicts and tendency of opportunistic behavior, this theory offers a wide range of governance and incentive mechanisms (Fama and Jensen, 1983; Shleifer and Vishny, 1997). It places boards in the center of monitoring and control suggesting that a given structure and composition assures better monitoring and enhances company performance. According to the principal–agent theory the inclusion of women on boards is the strategy to improve board process, increase the quality of board monitoring and in effect it leads to better financial results. Thus, increasing the participation of women in governance represents the efforts to protect investor rights and create shareholder value. Yet, as noticed by Kakabadse et al. (2015), the empirical evidence cast doubts on the existence of strong and unequivocal relationships between board characteristics and company performance.

Resource dependence and human capital theory

According to the resource dependence theory (Pfeffer and Salancik, 1978; Davis and Cobb, 2010) inner firm resources are sources of competitive advantage (Sirmon and Hitt, 2003). Among different assets human capital represents an important resource which can enhance the development of skills and competences and improve the quality of management and supervision. This perspective suggests "moving away from the concept of the board of directors as a locus of control toward a more multifaceted role determined by a number of environmental factors" (Kakabadse et al., 2015: 267). While boards constitute an essential link between the company and its environment and the external resources on which a company depends, they may provide the organization with useful information, may assure for a communication channel and help obtaining commitments of support from important elements of the environment, and result in improving firm reputation and performance (Hillman et al., 2007).

Stakeholder theory

The stakeholder theory (Freeman and Reed, 1983) addresses the issues of the board securing necessary resources for the company operation. This approach views the role of female directors from the perspective of interests raised by different constituencies and social and environmental performance. The board constitutes the platform for the cooperation of various stakeholder groups (employees, customers, suppliers, NGOs, local communities etc.) in addition to the traditional attention given to investors. The engagement of stakeholder representation is expected to increase the effectiveness of corporate governance. The board is seen as a place where the conflicting interests are mediated, and where the necessary cohesion is created (Luoma and Goodstein, 1999). The board, specifically the one with a number of representatives of various stakeholders, enhances firm legitimacy in the environment the firm operates in. It adds for a deinstitutionalization of a homogeneous old boys' network which changes the behavioral pattern and communication dynamics. Thus, board gender diversity increases real and symbolic representations, women enhance boards' legitimacy and trustworthiness, fostering shareholders' trust in the firm and thus contributing to its market performance (Blair and Stout, 2001).

Diversity management

The concept of diversity management refers to the inclusion of different demographic groups in the workplace in numerous groups and bodies. This approach indicates that "diversity" is a value in itself since heterogeneity stimulates communication, enriches discussion, adds to problem-solving, allows for greater flexibility and provides diverse perspective to strategic choices (Cox and Blake, 1991; Luoma and Goodstein, 1999). The management theory views the concept of diversity as a potential opportunity to create value as team members with different backgrounds and experience increase team performance.

Specifically, according to the concept of diversity management, overcoming the problems of homogeneous perception and group/culture thinking syndrome brings a number of advantages. Greater diversity can lead to a better understanding of local markets and customers, increased ability to attract and retain the best people, greater creativity, better problem-solving and greater flexibility for organizations (Pfeffer and Salancik, 1978). At the board level diversity is also viewed as a necessity for fair and transparent decision-making (Luoma and Goodstein, 1999) and is expected to increase its independence and enhance the quality of monitoring and governance (Jensen and Meckling, 1976; Carter et al., 2010). Studies within the diversity management framework may also be accompanied with the concept of top management team (TMT) and upper echelons theories which explain behaviors at the top level of organizational hierarchies (Dang and Vo, 2014).

Table 1.1 summarizes the overview of theoretical perspective for studies of women's participation on boards.

Table 1.1 Theoretical perspective for studies of women's participation on boards

Theoretical perspective	*Key conceptual assumptions and drivers for women on boards*	*Key findings and contributions*
Socio-political perspective		
Social justice/non-discrimination theory	Women represent 50% of society and should be given rights to have the respective participation on corporate boards	Introducing non-discrimination policies enhances the female participation in management and governance
Gender/feminist theory	Gender shapes social roles, access to power and resources; balancing gender structure may impact behavior and decision-making patterns	Women's presence can help to change stereotypes embedded in others' expectations and embedded in individual gender identities
Managerial theories		
Principal–agent theory	Women may provide effective monitoring and governance	Having women on boards increases shareholder value and company performance
The resource dependency theory	Women have competence and skills complementary to resources provided by men	Women provide experience and competences to improve the board work quality
Stakeholder theory	Women represent a stakeholder group and may show greater response to expectations of firm constituencies	Women reveal stronger understanding for stakeholder expectations and empathy for social and environmental concerns
Diversity management	Diversity with respect to gender is positive for the quality and efficiency of work and decision-making	Women enrich corporate boards contributing to communication, leadership style, different risk attitude and term orientation

Source: own compilation based on Aluchna and Krejner-Nowecka (2017)

Women on boards: mechanisms

The growing interest in the inclusion of women on corporate boards results in numerous studies which address both the institutional/regulatory dimension as well as the corporate practice. The evidence collected from a series of studies allows researchers to identify the characteristic of dynamics of females in the boardroom. Findings help formulate a set of statements and observations which describe mechanisms of women on boards in the organizational context.

Women on boards as a derivative of female position in labor market

The studies on gender equality and effectiveness of gender policies utilize the proportion of women on supervisory boards, executive committees or boards of directors. The intuitive perception of higher presence of female directors supports the belief of respective gender equality and positive evaluation of female role and importance for the efficient management and contribution to performance. The analysis of female presence engagement on boards is a result of change in the labor market towards non-discrimination practice, equal pay and transparent procedures for promotion. While the 2010 study by McKinsey & Co. showed that females made for 30–40% university graduates in the 1970s in the case of France, Spain and Germany, only 7%, 6% and 2% of them, respectively, would complete their career at the top executive level. The data reveal improvement 30 years later – females made for 55–60% of university graduates in 2008, yet the ratio of women on top executive positions rose to 9% for France, 11% for Spain and 4% for Germany. Using the arguments of social justice and human capital theories (Simpson et al., 2010) such evidence suggests the inefficient use of substantial resource and the loss of opportunities for significant social and economic progress. Similar rationales are used to discuss females' position on the labor market indicating lower, as compared to men, employment ratio and pay level with higher part-time employment ratio. The arguments behind the increased female participation on boards show that bridging the gender gap leads to the effective use of educated skilled individuals.

> A best-in-region scenario, in which all countries match the improvement rate of the fastest-improving country in their region, could add as much as USD 12 trillion, or 11% to global 2025 GDP, and USD 2.1 trillion to Western Europe's GDP in 2025.
>
> (McKinsey & Co., 2016: 4)

The estimated GDP growth comes from:

- the increase in hours worked by women
- the higher participation of women in the workforce
- a greater representation of women in high-productivity sectors.

The change on the labor market would also improve the representation of women in leadership positions (McKinsey & Co., 2016).

The inclusion of women on boards can be supported by regulation

Research shows that the highest number of women on boards is found in Norway which introduced quotas obliging listed companies to secure 40% of female participation. Norwegian experience was followed by the European Commission recommendations and the implementation of different variations quotas regulations by several EU Member States such as Italy, France, Spain, Finland, Belgium and Germany. Outside the EU, quotas were introduced also in Quebec (Canada), Israel and Kenya (Seierstad, 2016).

McKinsey & Co. (2009, 2010), European Commission (COM 164, 2011), Bilimoria and Wheeler (2000) provide arguments recommending the introduction of instruments increasing presence of women on boards related to increased board heterogeneity and associated advantages. Critics view quotas as the element of authorities' intervention in business mechanisms contradicting market rules and thus its optimality of market since it deforms the role of corporate boards in company management and autonomy in decision-making. The arguments of the shortage of women with an adequate level of knowledge, experience and skills as well as the prevalence of masculine leadership behaviors by successful women, raised by the opponents of quotas, may also turn to non-optimal outcomes. Finally, quotas may result in instrumental treatment of women to fulfill the recommendation for appropriate gender as opposed to experience and knowledge, as well as result in situations when women are appointed to the board not necessarily as better candidates leading to the phenomenon of "reverse discrimination" (Seierstad, 2016). Figure 1.6 is based on research by EgonZehnder (2017) and shows the percentage of new board hires with multiple board positions.

Figure 1.6 indicates that

> 13% of women versus 10% of men hold multiple board positions globally within the group of 1,491 of the largest traded companies studied. In countries that adopted quotas like France, Germany and Italy, new women on the board were more likely to hold multiple board positions than men; but this gap was not as large in other markets, making the board diversity progress in Canada, Australia and the UK even more commendable.
>
> (EgonZehnder, 2017: 21)

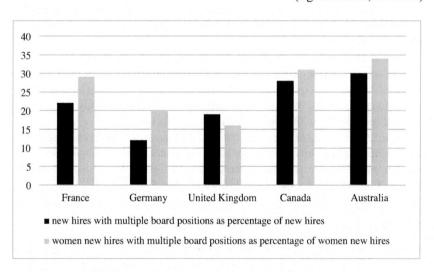

Figure 1.6 Percentage of new board hires with multiple board positions
Source: based on EgonZehnder (2017: 21).

Despite some doubts raised by the concept of quotas, this regulation has so far been the fastest instrument to increase women's participation on corporate boards. A study by MSCI (Lee et al., 2015) provided an estimation of the dynamics of female participation on boards to reach the threshold of 30% following three scenarios – the accelerated conversion, the accelerated turnover and business as usual.

The three projections prepared by MSCI (Lee et al., 2015) reveal that

> the accelerated conversion approach would double the proportion of new board seats taken by women reducing the 30% estimate by five years, while the accelerated turnover approach would keep the current rate of women taking new board seats at the historical rate, but turnover of existing board seats could increase resulting in a less disruptive "refresh" achieving the 30% target by 2020.
>
> (Lee et al., 2015: 2)

Women's participation on boards is significantly embedded in the institutional context

Recent studies show that the inclusion of women on corporate boards is more complex than initially expected. The result in the form of a number and proportion of females on boards derives from mutual relationships of factors, characteristics and actors (Seierstad et al., 2017; Terjesen et al., 2015) which can explain the prevalence of culture of privilege and power (Sayce and Özbilgin, 2014). Culture in a dialectic interaction with other societal norms and beliefs, might explain culturally "dominant aspects of education, career paths, or corporate behaviors" (Kakabadse et al., 2015: 266). The institutional factors include "female labor market and gendered welfare state provisions, left-leaning political government coalitions and path-dependence policy initiatives for gender equality" (Terjesen et al., 2015: 233). In addition, the strategy of political elites and candidate quotas, trade unions activity and the development of civic society are positively associated with the increased female participation on boards (Dahlerup, 2006; Freidenvall et al., 2006; Seierstad et al., 2017). Historical dynamics can be also significantly impacted by regional specificities within one country (Papenfuß et al., 2015).

According to EgonZehnder (2017) the critical mass of women on boards estimated with regard to the country population size is achieved in: France, Germany, Sweden, Italy, Norway, Belgium, Austria, Canada, South Africa, Spain, Denmark, the UK, Finland, Ireland, the Netherlands and Poland.

Increasing gender diversity in companies is a slow process

Reports on introducing measures to increase gender diversity in the top positions reveal two essential findings. First, the vast majority of companies take actions to increase gender diversity.

> The measures mentioned include setting quantitative targets and programs to increase representation of women, launching women development programs

such as training, mentoring and networking, establishing and monitoring gender diversity indicators, as well as HR processes and policies to attract, develop and retain talent.

(McKinsey & Co., 2016: 4)

Yet, the McKinsey report (2016) on the sample of 233 companies and 2,200 employees reveals that companies struggle to achieve significant results:

- Increasing the number of gender diversity initiatives is not sufficient. While reaching the critical mass of diversity measures is important, it does not explain female presence on boards. The report says that 52% of the companies implemented more than 50% of measures, but only 24% have more than 20% of women in top management positions.
- Only 7% of the analyzed companies place diversity among the top three priorities on their strategic agenda.
- Over the last four years the percentage of women of Western Europe's executive committees increased by 6 points and percentage of women on corporate boards of companies listed in the main stock index of their countries increased by 10 points, reaching 17% and 32% in 2016, respectively.
- Of the 2,200 surveyed employees, over 88% declared that they did not believe their company is taking enough effort to improve gender diversity, and 62% of them did not know how to contribute to gender diversity.
- The effectiveness of gender diversity programs raised but still remains insufficient with only 40% of the respondents saying that they were "well implemented" (clear follow-up processes in place, assessed on a regular basis, effectiveness evaluated at various levels of the organization.

Figure 1.7 shows the breakdown by countries by percentage of board with at least one woman.

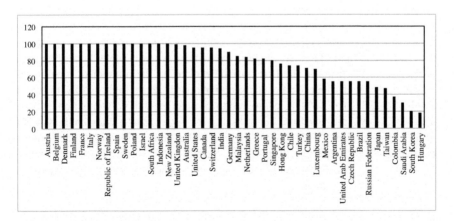

Figure 1.7 Countries ranked by percentage of board with at least one woman

Source: based on EgonZehnder (2017: 8)

As presented in Figure 1.7 based on EgonZehnder's (2017) analysis on the largest listed firms, the countries with 100% of companies having boards with at least one woman are: Austria, Belgium, Denmark, Finland, France, Italy, Norway, Ireland, Spain, Sweden, Poland, Israel, South Africa, Indonesia and New Zealand.

The 2016 special report published in *Harvard Business Review* shows that diversity programs do not work since they "focus on controlling managers' behavior" which "tends to activate bias rather than quash it. People rebel against rules that threaten their autonomy" (Dobbin and Kalev, 2016: 55). Foster (2017) notes that "nearly one-fifth of the world's 200 largest companies have no woman directors at all". In addition, the EY report (2015) reveals that while in 15% of 1,500 analyzed firms the growth of female presence on boards increased in the years 2013–2015, it appears often to be a derivative of the board size rise. The report documents that 54% of firms with seven board members and 98% of firms with 12 board members had at least one woman on board.

Women directors make a difference for financial performance, governance quality, social and environmental performance, board leadership and behavior

Studies aim at the explanation of whether female presence on boards makes a difference and improves company performance with respect to selected criteria such as financial results, risk policy, strategic orientation, ethical behavior and CSR/environmental performance (Terjesen et al., 2009; Kim and Starks, 2016). While the" board process is key to board effectiveness" (Kakabadse et al., 2015: 277) changing the board attributes should have an effect on board work and dynamics. This is possible when the number of women on boards reaches the critical mass of three directors (Konrad et al., 2008). The positive impact is assumed in accordance with the principal–agent and resource dependence theories as well as the diversity management framework.

The research in this stream initially focused on the effect of female presence on boards on financial performance. Studies show in general positive links between the number of women on boards and accounting performance. For instance the McKinsey & Co. analysis (2009) on the sample of 279 companies from six countries (the UK, France, Germany, Spain, Sweden and Norway) notes better financial performance for firms in the first quartile ranked by the number of women on boards. Firms with more females in executive boards reveal higher ROE (by 47%) and higher EBIT (by 56%) as compared to companies with no women on boards. The McKinsey/Amazone Euro Fund (McKinsey & Co., 2009) study on the sample of 89 European firms for 2005–2007 indicates that companies with higher gender board diversity report higher ROE (11.4% versus 10.3% sectorial average), higher EBIT (11.1% versus 5.8% sectorial average) and higher share price increase (64% versus 47% sectorial average).

Research on Finland-related firms with a female CEO to firms with a male CEO showed the positive effect of women leaders – companies with women as CEO noted 10% higher income (Kotiranta et al., 2007). The positive correlation was also found on the sample of 2,500 Danish companies (Smith et al., 2006). On the sample of US companies for the years 1996–2003 Adams and Ferreira (2009) found evidence that women on boards make a difference for corporate governance standards and financial performance. Financial performance measured by shareholder value proved to be positively related to the number of women on boards for S&P500, S&P Midcaps and S&P SmallCap. On the other hand, no statistical effects of higher female presence on boards and performance were noted in the case of the studies on the US banking sector (Richard et al., 2006), firms from Denmark (Rose, 2007) and recently from Norway (Dale-Olsen et al., 2013). For China McGuinness et al. (2015) found a moderate impact of women on boards on dividend policy and no support for risk-aversion.

Recently, MSCI Report (Lee et al., 2015) revealed results of a study of the performance of MSCI World Index with respect to board diversity. The MSCI World Index is a broad global equity benchmark that represents large and mid-cap equity performance across 23 developed markets countries. It covers ca. 85% of the free float-adjusted market capitalization in each country and is not exposed to emerging markets. The results show the following:

- Companies that had strong female leadership generated ROE of 10.1% per year versus 7.4% for those without women on boards.
- Companies lacking board diversity tend to suffer more governance-related controversies than average.
- The analysis did not find strong evidence that having more women in board positions indicate greater risk-aversion.

Studies indicate that female directors have an impact on the board work and the quality of governance. In the study by Adams and Ferreira (2009) women on boards contributed to the higher attendance of members during committee meetings, higher CEO rotation and more frequent structuring of performance-related executive compensation. Nielsen and Huse (2010) using a survey of 201 Norwegian firms found that the ratio of women directors is positively associated with the board strategic control. This effect is mediated through the increased board development activities and through the decreased level of conflict.

In addition, women on boards make a difference for social and environmental performance. Firms having a higher proportion of women serving on their boards do engage in charitable activities (Williams, 2003). Gender board diversity adds to more proactive and comprehensive CSR strategy and improves social (Hafsi and Turgut, 2013) and environmental (Shaukat et al., 2016) factors. It also enhances firms' reputations (Bear et al., 2010).

Agenda for future research

The phenomenon of women on boards remains in the center of management studies. Research relates the participation of females on boards in the context of various concepts and theories addressing issues of institutionalization and diffusion of best practice, dynamics of corporate governance regulation, leadership, board work, ethics, CSR and sustainability, financial performance, investment and organizational efficiency, decision-making and strategic development (BenAmar et al., 2013).

Despite 30 years of analyses studies, there are still many questions on the role of women on the board which are unanswered. They fail to identify the mechanisms of individual and group decision-making as well as to explain how female participation impacts the behavioral patterns. In addition, research on women in the boardroom faces significant methodological shortcomings. Three of those obstacles require comments.

First, management (and board) studies endure misconceptions about mathematical models which may narrow the meaning of abstract concepts to numbers and mathematical definitions. Differently than in mathematics, in management studies abstract concepts are represented by etiquettes (words, terms) which are identical for instances (examples, cases) and for concepts themselves. For example, the term or concept of a 'board' as defined earlier in this chapter explains an abstract concept (since it encompasses a variety of units) but it can be used also for indication of a real managerial body.

Second, since management theories arise from data, they suffer a bias resulting from data availability and low data quality. It is believed that a theory and hypotheses testing should guide data collection. Such approach is free of the problem of no-theory analysis charged with the dilemma of what data should be collected. Third, as is widely believed, models may be aimed at prediction but also at explanation. Analyses are also constrained by the possibility to control for endogeneity, organizational and institutional factors. Empirical analyses are also constrained by the data on the board work. It is difficult to separate gender effect from the impact of the given individual.

From a methodological point of view hypotheses may appear biased by the contextual expectations of analysts. For instance, the recent paper by Egan et al. (2017) reveals the existence of double standards for punishing misconduct of men and women in the organizational context. As noticed by van Knippenberg et al. (2007) studies on women on boards could grasp the board dynamics such as process, mechanism and behavioral patterns taking into consideration the complex personal and professional situations of women and men. Other characteristics may have a significant influence on the behavior, strategies and decisions made at work. A paper by Bursztyn et al. (2017) studies marriage market incentives and labor market investments and shows that single female MBA students tend to modify their behaviors to be less ambitious in order not to discourage their male colleagues from being interested in potential relationships.

An interesting and novel solution would be to address the social segregation problem from a data science perspective (Baroni, 2017). Social segregation in this approach refers to the separation of socially defined groups (Massey, 2016) in which people are partitioned into groups on the grounds of personal or cultural traits that can foster discrimination, such as gender, age, ethnicity, income, race, language, religion, political opinion etc. and may be the result of discrimination or homophily (Romei and Ruggieri, 2014). A data science perspective leads to identification of discriminated group objects and in the case of corporate boards is compatible with the observations mentioned in this chapter, encouraging the implementation of this approach more extensively. More precisely, while so far the presence, extent, nature, and trends of social segregation have been investigated by hypothesis testing (Moorhouse, 2017) using segregation indexes for minority groups, Baroni (2017) offers a data-driven approach searching contexts for social groups where *a-priori* unknown segregation factors are quantitatively clearly represented. The segregation-aware data mining framework from relational data and from attributed graphs are used to analyze segregation in company boards in Italian and Estonian companies. The approach employs quantitative segregation indexes adopted from social science literature based on searching sub-groups of population and minorities for which a segregation index is above a minimum threshold. A search algorithm computes a multi-dimensional data cube to be explored then by the analyst. The approach can tackle graph data consisting of bipartite attribute graphs, which model real networks by enriching their nodes with attribute values.

The implementation of the SCube of Baroni (2017) model supports an analyst in discovering the context of social segregation based on identified partitions. In result, an algorithm defines graph partitions. Identified clusters may reveal communities of females/males in a specific sub-graph. The plots reveal the glass ceiling reality for women who are not proportionally represented in top-level job positions. The percentage of female directors over the province of residence ranges from a minimum of 25% in the historically more depressed regions in the south of Italy to a maximum of 43.5% in the more developed regions.

Conclusion

The female participation on boards is a dynamically developing theme in management studies, corporate practice, public debate and regulatory actions. Backed with numerous arguments from various theories and conceptual perspective the topic of women's representation in top positions is tested for the role of institutional environment, organizational determinants, its effect on group dynamics, patterns of behavior and performance. While the socio-political approach emphasizes that females simply make for half of society and this fact should assure their representation in different decision-making bodies, managerial perspective searches for evidence that the presence of women on boards makes a difference for performance, leadership, communication and strategy.

Existing research indicates that the growing stakeholder pressure, changes in legislation and the evidence for efficiency of heterogeneous groups encourage companies to adopt non-discrimination policies and increase gender diversity in boardrooms. Studies reveal the significant increase in female representation on corporate boards, change in leadership and communication patterns.

Undoubtedly, the increasing female representation on boards mirrors social and economic dynamics and changes the way in which organizations operate. It also creates different frameworks for future generations changing the role of stereotypes and contributing to development values. The empirical, theoretical and methodological argument encourages researchers to develop in this area to get a better understanding and thus more effective policies.

References

Acker, J. 1990. Hierarchies, jobs, bodies: A theory of gendered organizations, *Gender and Society*, 4(2), 139–158.

Adams, R., Ferreira, D. 2009. Women in the boardroom and their impact on governance and performance, *Journal of Financial Economics*, 94, 291–309.

Aguilera, R., Jackson, G. 2003. The cross-national diversity of corporate governance: Dimensions and determinants, *Academy of Management Review*, 12(3), 1–19.

Aluchna, M. 2017. Women on boards: The Polish experience within the context of EU recommendations in Caliyurt, K. (ed.), *Women and Sustainability in Business: A Global Perspective*, Oxon: Routledge, 104–120.

Aluchna, M., Krejner-Nowecka, A. 2017. Why do we need women on boards? A synthesis of theories, *Przegląd Organizacji* [Organization Review], 10, 72–80.

Baroni, A. 2017. Segregation aware data mining, PhD. Thesis, at University of Pisa, Department of Computer Science.

BenAmar, W., Francoeur, C., Hafsi, T., Labelle, R. 2013. What makes better boards: A closer look at diversity and ownership, *British Journal of Management*, 24(1), 85–101.

Bear, S., Rahman, N., Post, C. 2010. The impact of board diversity and gender composition on corporate social responsibility and firm reputation, *Journal of Business Ethics*, 97, 207–221.

Bilimoria, D., Wheeler, J. 2000. Women corporate directors: Current research and future directions in Davidson, M., Burke, R. (eds.), *Women in Management: Current Research Issues II*, London: Sage, 138–163.

Blair, M., Stout, L. 2001. Trust, trustworthiness, and the behavioral foundations of corporate law, *University of Pennsylvania Law Review*, 149, 1735–1810.

Bourdieu, P. 1997. The forms of capital in Halsey, A., Lauder, H., Brown, P., Wells, A. (eds.), *Education: Culture, Economy and Society*, Oxford: Oxford University Press, 46–58.

Bourdieu, P., Wacquant, L. 1992. *An Invitation to Reflexive Sociology*, Cambridge: Polity Press.

Britton, D. 2000. The epistemology of the gendered organization, *Gender and Society*, 14(3), 418–434.

Bursztyn, L., Fujiwara, T., Pallais, A. 2017. "Acting wife": Marriage market incentives and labor market investments, NBER Working Paper 23043, www.nber.org/papers/w23043, accessed 29 August, 2017.

Carter, C., Lorsch, J. 2004. *Back to the Drawing Board*, Cambridge, MA: Harvard Business School Press.

Carter, D., D'Souza, F., Simkins, B., Simpson, W. 2010. The gender and ethnic diversity of US boards and board committees and firm financial performance, *Corporate Governance: An International Review*, 18(5), 396–414.Catalyst 2016. 2015 Catalyst census: Women and men board directors, www.catalyst.org/knowledge/2015-catalyst-census-women-and-men-board-directors, accessed 29 August, 2017.

Colaco, H., Myers, P., Nitkin, M. 2011. Pathways to leadership: Board independence, diversity and the emerging pipeline in the United States for women directors, *International Journal of Disclosure and Governance*, 8(2), 122–147.

Cox, T., Blake, S. 1991. Managing cultural diversity: Implications for organizational competitiveness, *Academy of Management Executive*, 5(3), 45–56.

Dahlerup, D. 2006. The story of the theory of critical mass, *Politics and Gender*, 2(4), 511–522.

Dale-Olsen, H., Schone, P., Verner, M. 2013. Diversity among Norwegian boards of directors: Does quota for women improve firm performance?, *Feminist Economics*, 19(4), 110–135.

Dalton, D., Dalton, C. 2009. Women gain (hidden) ground: A business imperative, *Journal of Business Strategy*, 24(5), 8–10.

Dalton, D., Dalton, M. 2010. Women on corporate boards of directors: The promise of increase and substantive, participation in the post Sarbanes-Oxley Era, *Business Horizon*, 53, 257–268.

Dang, R., Vo, L.-Ch. 2014. The influence of top management team characteristics on the presence of women on corporate board, *Reuve Management & Avenir*, 71, 91–110.

Davidson, M., Burke, R. 2004. Women in management worldwide: Facts, figures and analysis – an overview in Davidson, M., Burke, R. (eds.), *Women in Management Worldwide: Facts, Figure and Analysis*, Aldershot: Ashgate.

Davis, G., Cobb, J. 2010. Resource dependence theory: Past and future, *Research in the Sociology of Organizations*, 28, 21–42.

Deloitte 2015. *Women in the Boardroom: A Global Perspective*, Deloitte, https://www2. deloitte.com/content/dam/Deloitte/global/Documents/Risk/gx-ccg-women-in-the-boardroom-a-global-perspective4.pdf, accessed 28 August, 2017.

DiMaggio, P., Powell, W. 1983. The iron cage revisited: Institutional isomorphism and collective rationality in organizational fields, *American Sociological Review*, 48, 147–160.

Dobbin, F., Kalev, A. 2016. Why diversity programs fail, *Harvard Business Review*, July–August, 54–59.

Donaldson, T., Preston, L. 2008. The stakeholder theory of the corporation: Concept, evidence and implications in Crane, A., Matten, D., Spence, L. (eds.), *Corporate Social Responsibility*, London: Routledge, 139–165.

Egan, M., Matvos, G., Seru, A. 2017. When Harry fired Sally: The double standard in punishing misconduct, NBER Working Paper 23242, www.nber.org/papers/w23242, accessed 28 August, 2017.

EgonZehnder 2017. Global Board Diversity Analysis, www.egonzehnder.com/files/2016_ gbda_digital.pdf, accessed 28 August, 2017.

European Commission 2011. Green paper: The EU corporate governance framework, COM 164, http://ec.europa.eu/internal_market/company/docs/modern/com2011-164_en.pdf, accessed 28 August, 2017.

European Commission 2016. Council Directive 2000/43/EC of 29 June 2000 implementing the principle of equal treatment between persons, EU Directive 2000/43/EC Art 13, http://eur-lex.europa.eu/legal-content/EN/TXT/PDF/?uri=CELEX:32000L0043&from =en, accessed 20 August, 2017.

EY. 2015. EY Center for Board Matters, www.ey.com/Publication/vwLUAssets/EY_-_ Women_on_US_boards:_what_are_we_seeing/$FILE/EY-women-on-us-boards-what-are-we-seeing.pdf, accessed 6 February, 2018.

Fama, E., Jensen, M. 1983. Agency problems and residual claims, *Journal of Law and Economics*, 26(2), 327–349.

Fisch, J. 2004. Taking boards seriously in Joo, T. (ed.), *Corporate Governance: Law, Theory and Policy*, Durham: Carolina Academic Press, 329–337.

Foster, A. 2017. A quest to increase women in corporate board leadership: Comparing the law in Norway and the US, *Washington International Law Association*, 26(2), 381–412.

Freeman, R., Reed, L. 1983. Stockholders and stakeholders: A new perspective on corporate governance, *California Management Review*, 25(3), 88–105.

Freidenvall, L., Dahlerup, D., Skjeie, H. 2006. The Nordic countries: An incremental model in Dahlerup, D. (ed.), *Women, Quotas and Politics*, New York and London: Routledge, 55–82.

Gender Diversity Index 2017. 2020 Women on Boards Gender Diversity Index, 2011–2016 Progress of women corporate directors by company size, state and sector, www.2020wob. com/sites/default/files/2016_GDI_Report_Final.pdf, accessed 28 August, 2017.

Hafsi, T., Turgut, G. 2013. Boardroom Diversity and its effect on social performance: Conceptualization and empirical evidence, *Journal of Business Ethics*, 112, 463–479.

Haigh, J. 2008. *Tales from the Glass Ceiling*, London: Piatkus Books.

Hambrick, D., Jackson, E. 2000. Outside directors with a stake: The linchpin in improving governance, *California Management Review*, 42(4), 108–127.

Hambrick, D., Werder, A.V., Zajac, E. 2008. New directions in corporate governance research, *Organization Science*, 19(3), 381–385.

Hillman, A., Shropshire, C., Cannella, A. 2007. Organizational predictors of women on corporate boards, *Academy of Management Journal*, 50(4), 941–952.

Ibrahim, N., Angelidis, J. 1994. Effect of board members' gender on corporate social responsiveness, *The Journal of Applied Business Research*, 10(1), 35–42.

Idemudia, U. 2011. Corporate social responsibility and developing countries: Moving the critical CSR research agenda in Africa forward, *Progress in Development Studies*, 11(1), 1–18.

Jamali, D., Safieddine, A., Rabbath, M. 2008. Corporate governance and corporate social responsibility synergies and interrelationship, *Corporate Governance: An International Review*, 16, 443–459.

Jensen, M., Meckling, W. 1976. Theory of the firm: Managerial behavior, agency costs and ownership structure, *Journal of Financial Economics*, 3(4), 305–360.

Jourová, V. 2016. *Gender Balance on Corporate Boards: Europe Is Cracking the Glass Ceiling*, European Commission, http://ec.europa.eu/justice/gender-equality/files/ gender_balance_decision_making/1607_factsheet_final_wob_data_en.pdf, accessed 20 August, 2017.

Kakabadse, N., Figueira, C., Nicolopoulou, K., Hong Yang, J., Kakabadse, A., Özbilgin, M. 2015. Gender diversity and board performance: Women's experiences and perspectives, *Human Resource Management*, 54(2), 265–281.

Kang, N., Moon, J. 2012. Institutional complementarity between corporate governance and corporate social responsibility: A comparative institutional analysis of three capitalisms, *Socio-Economic Review*, 10, 85–108.

Kim, D., Starks, L. 2016. Gender diversity on corporate boards: Do women contribute unique skills?, *American Economic Review: Papers and Proceedings*, 106(5), 267–271.

Konrad, A., Kramer, V., Erkut, S. 2008. The impact of three or more women on corporate boards, *Organizational Dynamics*, 37(2), 145–164.

Kotiranta, A., Kovalainen, A., Rouvinen, P. 2007. Female leadership and firm profitability, EVA Analysis, no. 3, www.europeanpwn.net/files/eva_analysis_english.pdf, accessed 28 August, 2017.

Larcker, D., Tayan, B. 2011. *Corporate Governance Matters: A Closer Look at Organizational Choices and Their Consequences*, Hoboken, NJ: Pearson Education.

Lee, L.-E., Marshall, R., Rallis, D., Moscardi, M. 2015. *Women on Boards: Global Trends in Gender Diversity on Corporate Boards*, MSCI, https://www.msci.com/ documents/10199/04b6f646-d638-4878-9c61-4eb91748a82b, accessed 28 August, 2017.

Luoma, P., Goodstein, J. 1999. Stakeholders and corporate boards: Institutional influences on board composition and structure, *Academy of Management Journal*, 42(5), 553–563.

Mallin, Ch. 2004. *Corporate Governance*, Oxford: Oxford University Press.

Massey, D. 2016. *Segregation and the Perpetuation of Disadvantage: The Oxford Handbook of the Social Science of Poverty*, Oxford: Oxford University Press, 369–393.

McGuinness, P., Lam, K., Vieito, J. 2015. Gender and other major board characteristics in China: Explaining corporate dividend policy and governance, *Asia Pacific Journal of Management*, 32, 989–1038.

McKinsey & Co. 2009. Women leaders, a competitive edge in and after the crisis, *Women Matter*, 3.

McKinsey & Co. 2010. *Women Matter 2010: Women at the Top of Corporations: Making It Happen*, https://www.mckinsey.de/files/Women_Matter_4_brochure.pdf, accessed 28 August, 2017.

McKinsey & Co. 2016. *Women Matter 2016 Reinventing the Workplace to Unlock the Potential of Gender Diversity*, McKinsey & Co., https://www.mckinsey.com/~/media/mckinsey/global%20themes/women%20matter/reinventing%20the%20workplace%20for%20greater%20gender%20diversity/women-matter-2016-reinventing-the-workplace-to-unlock-the-potential-of-gender-diversity.ashx.

Meyer, J., Rowan, B. 1977. Institutionalized organizations: Formal structure as myth and ceremony, *American Journal of Sociology*, 83, 340–363.

Mizruchi, M., Fein, L. 1999. The social construct of organizational knowledge: A study of the uses of coercive, mimetic and normative isomorphism, *Administrative Science Quarterly*, 44, 653–683.

Monks, R.A., Minow, N. 1996. *Watching the Watchers*, Hoboken, NJ: Blackwell Business.

Monks, R.A., Minow, N. 2004. *Corporate Governance*, Hoboken, NJ: Blackwell Publishing.

Moon, D., Matten, J. 2008. "Implicit" and "explicit" CSR: A conceptual framework for a comparative understanding of corporate social responsibility, *Academy of Management Review*, 33(2), 404–424.

Moon, J., Orlitzky, M., Whelan, G. 2010. *Corporate Governance and Business Ethics*, Northampton: Edward Elgar Publishing.

Moorhouse, E. 2017. Sex segregation by field of study and the influence of labor markets: Evidence from 39 countries, *International Journal of Comparative Sociology*, 49(4–5), 257–281.

Nekhili, M., Gatfaoui, H. 2013. Are demographics attributes and firm characteristics drivers of gender diversity? Investigating women's position of French boards of directors, *Journal of Business Ethics*, 118, 227–249.

Nielsen, S., Huse, M. 2010. The contribution of women on boards of directors: Going beyond the surface, *Corporate Governance: An International Review*, 18(2), 136–148.

Papenfuß, U., Haak, B., Kreig, Th. 2015. Frauen in Top-Managementorganen öffentlicher Unternehmen: Ein deutschlandweiter Städtevergleich, *ZögU – Zeitschrift für öffentliche und gemeinwirtschaftliche Unternehmen*, 38, 335–344.

Pfeffer, J., Salancik, G. 1978. *The External Control of Organizations: A Resource Dependence Perspective*, New York: Harper & Row Publishers.

PWC 2016. Making change happen, What is going to take?, Women on Boards 2015, The Forum of Executive Women, PWC, http://foew.com/wp-content/uploads/2016/01/Women-on-Boards-Report-2015.pdf, accessed 28 August, 2017.

Richard, O.C., Ford, D., Ismail, K. 2006. Exploring the performance effects of visible attribute diversity: The moderating role of span of control and organizational life cycle, *International Journal of Human Resource Management*, 17(12), 2091–2109.

Riyanto, Y., Toolsema, L. 2007. Corporate social responsibility in a corporate governance framework, Department of Economics Working Paper No. 0702, National University of Singapore.

Roe, M. 1994. *Weak Owners, Strong Managers: The Political Roots of American Corporate Finance*, Princeton, NJ: Princeton University Press.

Romei, A., Ruggieri, S. 2014. A multidisciplinary survey on discrimination analysis, *The Knowledge Engineering Review*, 29(5), 582–638.

Rose, C. 2007. Does female board representation influence firm performance? The Danish evidence, *Corporate Governance: An International Review*, 15(2), 404–413.

Sayce, S., Özbilgin, M. 2014. Pension trusteeship and diversity in the UK: A new boardroom recipe for change or continuity?, *Economics and Industrial Democracy*, 35, 49–69.

Seierstad, C. 2016. Beyond the business case: The need for both utility and justice rationale for increasing the share of women on boards, *Corporate Governance: An International Review*, 24(4), 390–405.

Seierstad, C., Warner-Søderholm, G., Torchia, M. 2017. Increasing the number of women on boards: The role of actors and processes, *Journal of Business Ethics*, 141, 289–315.

Shaukat, A., Qiu, Y., Trojanowski, G. 2016. Board attributes, corporate social responsibility strategy, and corporate environmental and social performance, *Journal of Business Ethics*, 135, 569–585.

Sheridan, A. 2001. A view from the top: Women on the boards of public companies, *Corporate Governance*, 1(1), 8–14.

Shleifer, A., Vishny, R. 1997. A survey of corporate governance, *Journal of Finance*, 52, 737–783.

Simpson, W., Carter, D., D'Souza, F. 2010. What do we know about women on boards?, *Journal of Applied Finance*, 2, 27–39.

Singh, V., Terjesen, S., Vinnicombe, S. 2008. Newly appointed directors in the boardroom: How do women and men differ?, *European Management Journal*, 26(1), 48–58.

Sirmon, D., Hitt, M. 2003. Managing resources: Linking unique resources, management, and wealth creation in family firms, *Entrepreneurship Theory and Practice*, 27(4), 339–358.

Smith, N., Smith, V., Verner, M. 2006. Do women in top management firms affect firm performance? A panel study of 2,500 Danish firms, *International Journal of Productivity and Performance Management*, 55(7), 569–593.

Tajfel, H., Turner, J. 1986. The social identity theory of intergroup behavior in Worchel, S., Austin, W. (eds.), *Psychology of Intergroup Relations*, Chicago: Nelson-Hall.

Terjesen, S., Aguilera, R., Lorenz, R. 2015. Legislating a woman's seat on the board: Institutional factors driving gender quotas for board of directors, *Journal of Business Ethics*, 128, 233–251.

Terjesen, S., Sealy, R., Singh, V. 2009. Women directors on corporate boards: A review and research agenda, *Corporate Governance: An International Review*, 17(3), 320–337.

Terjesen, S., Singh, V. 2008. Female presence on corporate boards: A multi-country study of environmental context, *Journal of Business Ethics*, 83(1), 55–63.

van Knippenberg, D., Haslam, S., Platow, M. 2007. Unity through diversity: Value-in-diversity beliefs, work group diversity, and group identification, *Group Dynamics: Theory, Research, and Practice*, 11(3), 207–222.

Verdeyen, V., Put, J., van Buggenhout, B. 2004. A social stakeholder model, *International Journal of Social Welfare*, 13(4), 325–331.

Williams, R. 2003. Women on corporate boards of directors and their influence on corporate philanthropy, *Journal of Business Ethics*, 41(1), 1–10.

Wood, W., Eagly, A. 2012. Biosocial construction of sex differences and similarities in behavior, *Advances in Experimental Social Psychology*, 46, 55–123.

2 Gender diversity on boards in Norway and the UK

A different approach to governance or a case of path dependency?

Rita Goyal, Nada Korac Kakabadse, Filipe Morais and Andrew P. Kakabadse

Introduction

Underutilization of women's talents at the decision-making levels in companies and the need for a change in the approach have been felt by the corporate world and many regulatory regimes (Terjesen et al., 2015). The *Women on boards* report (Whitehead and Normand, 2011, known as the Davies Report) describes three approaches that are adopted in different countries to improve gender diversity on corporate boards. First is legislative intervention or mandatory quotas, as exemplified by Norway, and followed by a few other countries, including Italy, Germany, Spain, France and India (Egon Zehnder, 2014; Sealy et al., 2016; Ahern and Dittmar, 2012). Second, the US and Canada adopt a liberal approach and expect voluntary commitments from private firms (Whitehead and Normand, 2011). The third is a collaborative, business-led approach of recommending targets to improve gender diversity on boards, as adopted in the UK (Sealy et al., 2016; DBIS, 2015). In a regime with a collaborative approach, companies are expected to voluntarily take measures and comply, or explain the failure as recommended by the corporate governance code (FRC, 2016). In this chapter, we focus on two strategies, namely legislative intervention and the collaborative approach, which are adopted in Norway and the UK, respectively.

As a result of Norway's legislative intervention, gender diversity on the boards of its publicly listed companies (PLCs) in 2008, the year of the law's execution with full force (Ahern and Dittmar, 2012), stood at 40%; it now stands at 35% (DBIS, 2015). In the UK, following the traditional 'comply-or-explain' approach to governance and the cooperative approach to board diversity (The Code, FRC, 2016), FTSE 100 companies have achieved Davies's voluntary target of 25% gender diversity on boards. There are no all-men boards in FTSE 100 companies (DBIS, 2015). Dissatisfied with the slow pace of progress and the recent trend of a further slowdown in nominations of women to boards and senior executive positions, there is an increasing clamour for quotas in corporate directorships in the UK (Blackhurst, 2014). Thus we investigate a) possible reasons for adopting different strategies for gender diversity management in boards of these two countries and b) a possible explanation of apparent though partial failure of these strategies in these countries in achieving the objective. We argue that the path dependency perspective in the prevailing legal systems, corporate philosophies, political orientation and socio-cultural practices is responsible for the adoption of different strategies for boards' gender diversity in these countries. We also explain the recent developments which are in contrast to the historical approach adopted in these countries and explain it with the Actor–Network perspective.

Investigations into gender diversity traditionally seek to assess the impact of diversity management strategies and board diversity on firm performance, showing a comparison in the contexts of each respective country (e.g. Terjesen and Singh, 2008; Sweigart, 2012; Terjesen et al., 2015). Grosvold et al. (2007) followed the same pattern in a longitudinal study (seven years in the UK and four years in Norway), exploring different approaches in pre-Davies and pre-quota execution eras in the UK and Norway, respectively. In this chapter, we review and compare some of the antecedents to these diversity management practices in the UK and Norway in order to understand the recent developments.

The rest of the chapter is organized as follows. We first discuss developments in the board gender diversity of listed companies in Norway and the UK and describe the approach adopted for the objective. Then we discuss the impact of enhanced board gender diversity on companies' performance in these countries as discussed in the existing academic literature. Subsequently we present the drivers for promoting gender diversity followed by a theoretical rationale for such contrasting approaches adopted by these countries. We then present the recent reported developments which seem to be a deviation from the legacy in both countries. We suggest that the Actor–Network perspective may be a possible explanation for the trend. In conclusion, we discuss the contribution of the chapter and suggest a few ideas for future research.

Board diversity practices – Norway and the UK

The legislative efforts to make Norwegian corporate boards more gender balanced were initially made in 1999 and 2001 by amending the Gender Equality Act of 1978. The first public announcement of the regulation took place in 2002. The Companies Act of Norway was amended in 2003 and the quota law was applied to state and municipal companies from 2004 (Seierstad, 2015). In 2003, gender diversity on the boards of PLCs in Norway was 9% (Ahern and Dittmar, 2012). A penalty of liquidation for companies failing to adhere to the legal provisions was added in 2005 (Matsa and Miller, 2012; Sweigart, 2012; Randøy et al., 2006). The law was applied to new PLCs from 2006 and existing PLCs from 2008, resulting in 40% gender diversity on non-executive boards (among the shareholder-appointed directors) by January 2008 (Seierstad, 2015). The law was fully adopted in February 2008 (Bøhren and Staubo, 2016). All companies had complied by April 2008 (Matsa and Miller, 2012).

The UK has shown a strong interest in improving gender diversity on corporate boards since 2011, when government, through Lord Davies, took the initiative to encourage voluntary targets among FTSE 100 companies (Chartered Institute of Personnel and Development – CIPD, 2015). The corporate sector in the UK responded favorably, and the target was met amid the political volatility of parliamentary elections and the Brexit vote (DBIS, 2015; Higginbottom, 2015). Lord Davies has now invoked FTSE 350 companies to voluntarily attain 33% gender diversity on their boards by 2020 (DBIS, 2015). In the case of the UK, the promotion of diversity on boards is enshrined in the UK Corporate Governance Code (FRC, 2016) which governs with the spirit of 'comply-or-explain' (Bøhren and Strøm, 2010; Terjesen et al., 2015). The UK government prefers a voluntary approach to improving gender diversity in boardrooms (CIPD, 2015; The Code, FRC, 2016). The UK has not adopted the mandatory quota approach to improving gender diversity on its boards as companies oppose any suggestion of implementation of the quota through the EU (Watson, 2014). Companies often respond positively to a potential warning of legislative intervention if the suggested targets are not met (Gabaldon et al., 2015). It is believed that the success achieved by FTSE 100 companies in 2015 was also achieved due to an implicit looming threat of more intrusive legislative action, should companies fail to comply with voluntary targets (Holehouse, 2015). The prevailing environment in Europe around that time also might have led to the belief that a quota law was imminent in the UK. The justice commissioner at the EU level, Viviane Reding, suggested that the Member States promote gender diversity on boards by 2015 or may face a mandatory quota of 40% women by 2020 (Sweigart, 2012).

Board gender diversity – impact on Norwegian and UK companies

The implementation of the quota law in Norway has been widely analyzed in academic literature since 2008 when the law was implemented with penal provision. Research reports that many listed companies changed their ownership pattern to private companies – possibly to evade compliance with the law (Bertrand et al., 2014). However, scholars argue that the quota law may not have been the sole cause of change of ownership pattern by more than 100 companies, as other legal/regulatory developments could have triggered the change (Sweigart, 2012; Matsa and Miller, 2012; Nygaard, 2011). The companies that didn't change their ownership status improved their board gender diversity to 40% in 2008 (Bertrand et al., 2014). Some studies report a decline in some financial parameters that implemented the law (Ahern and Dittmar, 2012) while others report a stock price increase after 2005 (Nygaard, 2011). Many studies report either a negative or nil impact of increased gender diversity in Norwegian boards on firm performance (e.g. Voß, 2015). In the case of the UK, some studies suggest that improved gender diversity on boards of FTSE 100 companies has resulted in more independence, a greater likelihood of higher and diverse qualifications, and diverse functional background among women (Ferreira, 2010; Singh et al., 2008). The findings of a few comparative studies conducted on board gender diversity in countries including Norway and the UK are presented in Table 2.1.

Table 2.1 Findings of comparative studies conducted in Norway and the UK

Impact of gender diversity on boards	*Country*	*Author(s)*
Women's representation on corporate boards may be influenced by the social, political and economic structures of individual countries. Countries with higher gender diversity on boards may have higher gender diversity in senior management and a narrower gender pay gap	43 countries including Norway and the UK	Terjesen and Singh (2008)
Gender diversity in labor force and other economic and cultural factors impact gender diversity on boards	22 countries including Norway and the UK	Adams and Kirchmaier (2013)
Improved gender diversity on boards of Norwegian and UK companies. No adverse impact on performance of companies. Not the same pool of women directors on multiple boards. No adverse impact on the quality of board directors or number of directorships for women	Norway and the UK	Grosvold et al. (2007)

Source: compiled by the authors

Drivers of board gender diversity

The rationale given for higher gender diversity on boards is twofold (Carter et al., 2003). The economic rationale of a sound business case (Erhardt et al., 2003; Kim et al., 2013) recommends gender diversity for improving the company's bottom-line (Matsa and Miller, 2012; Ahern and Dittmar, 2012; Nygaard, 2011; Grosvold et al., 2007), signaling (Fondas, 2000) and reducing conformity and groupthink (Janis, 1972; Ferreira, 2010; FRC, 2016). The social rationale favors gender diversity on boards for promoting representation of the neglected sections of society (Fairfax, 2011), the consumer communities (Mattis, 2000) and corporate philanthropy (Coffey and Wang, 1998). The former logic suggests that the systematic exclusion of any group from participation in governance will result in the suboptimal performance of the organization (Randøy et al., 2006). The latter rationale believes that it is unethical to deny a group equal opportunities in board positions solely due to their gender (Grosvold et al., 2007). The rationale given for the natural experiment in Norway (Matsa and Miller, 2012) was not of efficiency (i.e. of the sound business case) but of equality (i.e. to promote social order) (Nygaard, 2011; Randøy et al., 2006: 2; Matsa and Miller, 2012). The Code (FRC, 2016) recommends that PLC boards have sufficient diversity to promote and engender an environment of debate and constructive challenge. Thus the driver for promoting gender diversity on boards in the UK is the business case i.e. improving firm/board performance.

Board gender diversity and the path dependency perspective

In this chapter we suggest that the approach adopted by countries when managing gender diversity on their PLC boards may be due to the path dependency of its institutions and processes, which become authoritative guidelines for social behavior, and are adopted over time and space (Scott, 2004). These processes may have an impact on individuals and organizations without actually being incorporated into formal policies (Meyer, 2008). Such rules/institutions are made by state and professional bodies and can be coercive, normative or voluntary in nature (DiMaggio and Powell, 1983; Scott, 2004). They evolve with other institutions and are adopted by organizations, thus becoming institutionalized (Terjesen et al., 2015).

We now present a comparison of the Norway and UK contexts with reference to their legal systems, corporate philosophies, political orientations, socio-cultural practices and their historically diverse management strategies, in support of our argument that the distinction in board gender diversity practice in these countries is due to path dependency. Existing research suggests that the practices adopted by countries for improving board gender diversity in listed companies are influenced by institutional factors, such as the political, social and business environment and philosophies prevailing in these countries. Terjesen and Singh (2008) suggest board gender diversity is influenced by the level of female representation before the quota law, their ratio in senior management positions, and their representation in the political sphere. A country's prevailing institutional structures play an important role in bringing about societal change and economic equity (Korpi, 2001). The institutional theory (Meyer and Rowan, 1977) argues that institutions adopt established structures for legitimacy and survival in the institutional environment. In an empirical study of 15 countries, Crossland and Hambrick (2011) find that formal and informal institutions such as individualism, tolerance of uncertainty, cultural looseness, dispersed firm ownership, a common law legal origin and employer flexibility impact decision-making in corporations. Scholars often present the institutional perspective to explain different gender management approaches (e.g. Terjesen et al., 2015; Grosvold and Brammer, 2011) and rationalize the benefits of the approaches adopted by countries (Iannotta et al., 2016).

Path dependency (Leibowitz and Margolis, 1995) is an important concept in understanding social and political processes (Kay, 2005). We trace path dependency in legal systems (e.g. civil law versus common law), governance approaches (e.g. stakeholder versus shareholder), and development indicators in Norway and the UK to substantiate our argument. Legal, cultural and occupational environments play the most relevant role in determining the participation of women on boards (Adams and Kirchmaier, 2013; Grosvold and Brammer, 2011). We argue that countries adopt board diversity strategies due to the path dependency of the predominant legal, political and socio-economic factors. We argue that Norway and the UK prefer their respective approaches as a result of path dependency of historical acceptance for coercive/mandatory intervention, corporate ownership patterns, prevailing legal systems and the social perceptions of working women. A comparison of some of the institutions that seem to set the path for adopting of diversity management practices for boards follows.

Prevailing legal systems

The implementation of diversity management practices for improving board diversity varies across countries, influenced by the prevailing corporate and legal environment (La Porta et al., 1998). The existing legal systems across countries are originally derived from two legal streams, common law and civil law (La Porta et al., 1998). Common law is of British origin,[1] applied across its erstwhile colonies including the US (Guest, 2008) and is developed through judgements in legal cases (David and Brierley, 1968). Civil law is of Romano-Germanic origin, the oldest and most widely distributed legal tradition across the world (La Porta et al., 1998) and is developed by legal scholars (David and Brierley, 1968). There are three main sub-streams in the civil law: French, German and the Scandinavian. The corporate governance in a country is influenced by the legacy legal system (Cuervo, 2002; Ingley and Van der Walt, 2005). The prevailing legal system in a country impacts other aspects of corporate governance, such as market-oriented or shareholder-oriented, rights of the investors, ownership structure (Babić et al., 2011), ownership concentration, and enforcement of codes, legislation and regulatory practices (La Porta et al., 1998; Cuervo, 2002). The emphasis in common law regimes is on protecting the rights of private shareholders, and thus shareholders' rights are privileged over stakeholders' rights (Crossland and Hambrick, 2011). The civil law regimes endeavor to solidify the power of the state and hence the executives and directors are expected to take into account the interest of all stakeholders, such as employees, customers and the society at large (Crossland and Hambrick, 2011). Thus the mandate of leadership in a country following the civil law is more focused on the 'means' and not an end of "maximize the shareholder wealth" (Crossland and Hambrick, 2011: 803), which is the primary objective in companies working under the common law system (Johnson et al., 2000).

Norway (and the other Scandinavian countries, Denmark, Finland, Iceland and Sweden) follow the civil law system, while maintaining their local characteristics within the legal family of civil law (Bernitz, 2007; Hagstrøm, 2007). On the other hand, the legal system followed in the UK is common law, where the decisions of the senior appellate court become part of the law (McCrudden, 2000).

Corporate structures and philosophies

Both in the UK and Norway, boards are unitary and share similar responsibilities of approving plans, transactions and budgets, and ensuring appropriate accounts and other audit materials are maintained and published as required (Cadbury, 1992; Grosvold et al., 2007). However, unlike in the UK, Norway has mandatory labor representation (Sweigart, 2012; Grosvold et al., 2007). Unlike on UK boards, there is an almost complete absence of executive directors (EDs) from Norwegian boards (Grosvold et al., 2007). Moreover, the ownership pattern is also clearly distinguishable in these countries. Norwegian corporations have diluted and extremely low ownership (Bøhren and Ødegaard, 2001) while the block ownership of the ten highest block owners in UK FTSE 350 companies ranges up to 27% (Abdullah and Page, 2009). Ownership structure again demonstrates the corporate philosophy of a country as block ownership is favored as one of the means to address the agency problem (Agrawal and Knoeber, 2001; Abdullah and Page, 2009). Agency theory of governance (Jensen and Meckling, 1976) supports the primacy of shareholders' rights and claims that boards function to protect and promote shareholders' interests. Thus, while in the UK the prevailing model is a market-based system of corporate governance with an emphasis on shareholder primacy, in Norway and the Nordic region in general, orientation is around stakeholders (Randøy et al., 2006). Moreover, in the UK, an annual general meeting (AGM) is the primary forum for shareholder decision-making on issues impacting long-term value creation and performance. In Norway, corporate councils – which are below the AGM but above boards and have employee representation – play an important role, overseeing both boards and senior management (Grosvold et al., 2007).

Moreover, the approach of mandated intervention which has prevailed in Norway (Sweigart, 2012) is missing from the UK corporate governance system. The approach in Norway's corporate sector has been of mandated participation of employees, but the corporate sector in the UK prefers self-regulation (Lester, 2016; Bartle and Vass, 2005). This factor may have made the acceptance of legislative intervention for board gender diversity more acceptable in Norway. A similar move in the UK may have attracted more resistance from the corporate sector. Companies in the UK often express an aversion to state intervention/legislation in their affairs considering it a "rather blunt instrument" (Stiles, 1993: 122).

Political orientation

The Western countries have been endeavoring to establish a welfare state since the early 19th century to bring about societal change and economic equity, but the approach to implementing those goals has been different (Korpi, 2001). Norway is considered a progressive polity with generous health insurance, the childcare leave, and gender equality, and ranks third in the world in its health, economic, political and educational opportunities for women, as per the World Economic Forum Global Gender Gap Report (Bertrand et al., 2014). Norway adopts the model of a welfare state with a strong commitment to gender equality (Seierstad, 2015). It has a reputation for being a gender sensitive and equitable society (UN Women Committee on Elimination of Discrimination against Women, 2003; World Economic Forum, 2013; Seierstad, 2015). The country was the first to enfranchise women in 1913, is one of the very few countries to have appointed a female premier (in 1981) and has a dedicated seat for a Minister of Children, Equality and Social Inclusion (Sweigart, 2012). Moreover, Norway also has a considerably high ratio of women in its parliament and also follows other progressive legal/commercial practices such as access to each tax-payer's income and making the employment data of its citizens accessible online since 2002 (Sweigart, 2012). Historically (from the Viking period) Norway has been hailed as a haven for gender equality where women have taken multiple responsibilities (Sweigart, 2012). In Norway, the state-owned firms were privatized in the 1980s and 1990s and ever since, due to concerns of ensuring fairness, the government has continued to adopt various measures which have been accepted with a fair amount of compliance (Bertrand et al., 2014).

The UK adopted the concept of welfare state – as against the Nazi warfare state – in the post-world war era, promoting a state's intervention in social provisions (Cox, 1998; Sainsbury, 2008). However, the concept of welfare rights in the UK is systematically undermined in modern times with the idea of conditional entitlements of citizens becoming more common (Dwyer, 2004). Such dismantling of the social welfare state in the UK and other capitalist countries has been reported by many scholars (e.g. Sassen, 1991; Hamnett, 1996). Some suggest that conditionality has always been imposed on welfare measures in the UK model and welfare efforts of the government were never absolute (Powell, 2002). This approach limits government's willingness to intervene to promote the social cause. In the case of gender diversity on boards as well, the argument given is that of business case i.e. improving decision-making in boards (FRC, 2016).

Moreover, in terms of political representation, Norway has 40% female representation in government, while in the UK it hovers around 23%. These factors may have a bearing on Norway deciding to take measures against a glaring gender inequality, which prevailed in boardrooms of listed companies before the implementation of gender-based quotas. In the 1980s, Norway enacted the Equality Act mandating 40% reservation for both genders on public boards and committees – a move that received overwhelming support from the mainstream media, employee organizations and most trade unions (Sweigart, 2012). The UK legal regime prohibits gender-based discrimination under the Equality Act 2010.

Socio-economic and cultural practices

Grosvold et al. (2007) point out a few differences in social and cultural practices prevailing in the UK and Norway. In Norway, non-working women are looked down upon with disdain for not contributing full-time to the welfare of society and for depriving the children of opportunities of growth at kindergartens. In the UK, the trend of mothers staying at home for longer after childbirth and returning to part-time employment has higher acceptability. Moreover, Norway has a significantly expanded childcare system, early childhood-education coverage, and longer and more generous maternity/parental leave since the mid- to late 1980s, even after many neighboring Nordic countries have reduced many of these benefits over the last two decades (Gornick et al., 1997; Henderson and White, 2004). The Norwegian childcare provision system plays a critical role in support of women with professional careers, and the childcare services are extensively used by working mothers (Taguma et al., 2013; Terjesen et al., 2015). The country also has a higher participation of women (around 45%) in the labor force (Sweigart, 2012). Thus a low board gender diversity of 9% (Ahern and Dittmar, 2012) before legislative intervention may have been an aberration, forcing the government and regulatory agencies to intervene. A comparison of the attributes of various institutions and processes in Norway and the UK is presented in Table 2.2 to highlight distinct path dependencies in these two countries.

Thus path dependency of associated environment in Norway and the UK seem to have determined the choice of board diversity strategy in these countries. However, some observations have been made in both countries which warrant explanation.

Table 2.2 The Norway and UK context: path dependency in other institutions/practices

Characteristics	Norway	The UK
Legal system	Civil law	Common law
Predominant corporate philosophy	Stakeholder approach, mandatory employee representation, diluted corporate ownership, almost complete absence of EDs	Shareholder approach, no mandatory employee representation as yet, comparatively concentrated ownership, boards consist of non-executive directors and executive directors
Political orientation	Welfare state with a strong commitment to gender equality and frequent political intervention for promoting gender equity	Adopted the concept of a welfare state in post-war era but welfare rights are not absolute and are diminishing
Social and cultural practices	Society encourages and facilitates early return to full-time work after childbirth, expanded and evolved childcare system. Voluntary sector in Norway consists of 115,000 non-governmental and non-profit organizations. The largest sector is culture and leisure (43%)[i]	Higher acceptability for women staying at home or returning to work later after childbirth, lower participation of women in labor force. There are around 164,000 general charities in the UK. The largest sector is the provision of social services (18%)[ii]
Diversity management practices in other hierarchies	Long tradition of gender-based quotas	Gender-based discrimination is illegal
Income inequality (Gini)	Has the fourth lowest income inequality (Gini coefficient .25) among the OECD countries[iii]	Has the fourth highest income inequality (Gini coefficient .36) among the OECD countries[iv]

Source: compiled by the authors

i www.ngonorway.org/bilateral-partnerships/norwegian-ngos.
ii http://researchbriefings.files.parliament.uk/documents/SN05428/SN05428.pdf.
iii http://hdr.undp.org/en/content/income-gini-coefficient.
iv http://hdr.undp.org/en/content/income-gini-coefficient.

The recent developments in Norway and the UK

The legislative intervention in Norway and the recommendation of voluntary targets in the UK have caused much discussion and a flurry of corporate activity in both countries. However, new developments have been noticed in Norway and the UK on the subject. Davies's five-year review (DBIS, 2015) reports a reduction of gender diversity on boards of listed companies in Norway to 35%. Another recent report puts the gender diversity figure on boards of Norwegian listed companies at 38.7%, down from 40.2% in 2011 (Kollewe, 2016). The report expresses concern that as the clause of 40% quota does not apply to employee representatives, the actual gender representation on Norwegian boards may be even lower. This development is significant as, in Norway, a violation of Norway's Companies Act, including the gender quotas, is punishable by dissolution of the corporation (Sweigart, 2012).

In the UK, the pace of gender diversity improvement is stagnating and, in 2016, UK boards witnessed a particularly low intake of female board directors (Cadman, 2016). Grant Thornton report (2017) reveals that senior business positions held by women have also fallen from 21% in 2016 to 19% in 2017. The percentage of businesses with no women in senior management positions has risen from 36% in 2016 to 40% in 2017, while the global trend shows an upturn (Ali, 2017). Furthermore, support for legal intervention seeking gender-based quotas in corporate directorships (Blackhurst, 2014), judiciary (Proudman, 2015) and parliamentary memberships (Kenny, 2016; Salami, 2017) is becoming more widespread.

Thus the developments observed in both countries defy conventional practices in the respective countries. Hence it is pertinent to seek a possible rationale for the developments.

Actor–Network perspective

We propose an explanation to the recently reported developments and suggest that the Actor–Network theory (Law, 1992; Callon, 1999) may be a possible explanation for the phenomena. The theory propounds that institutions grow and transform along with the networks they exist in, and thus organizations are influenced by network effects. 'Path dependence' explains how organizations are influenced by historical factors and Actor–Network theory explains how such institutions change over time (Greener, 2002). Decision-making structures grow over a period of time, due to the actors and processes involved in institutions and some networks are more durable than others, changing much less in appearance (Greener, 2002).

In increasingly integrated global societies and polities the entities emulate one another. The process can be explained with the Actor–Network perspective as described in the next section. Whether or not the soft law approach (Terjesen et al., 2015) adopted in the UK is effective in achieving the objective is also worth exploring. Thus we propose that it is possible that, with increasing globalization and connectedness in the world, societies and the companies within those societies in Norway and the UK are adopting practices that have been anathema to prevailing philosophies in these regions. The reduction in gender diversity on boards of Norwegian companies despite a legislative injunction with the associated punitive action may be a reflection of their defiance of the state's intervention in their corporate affairs. Similarly, in the UK, a growing demand for the quotas for women is clearly influenced by developments in other countries in Europe and beyond (Pryce, 2015; Davidson, 2015). This proposition may be further investigated in order to obtain a better perspective on gender diversity on boards. Scholars suggest that new developments need to be further explored with comparative studies between countries with empirical evidence (Grosvold and Brammer, 2011; Terjesen and Singh, 2008; Adams and Kirchmaier, 2013), including gender relations and welfare regimes (Orloff, 1996) to supplement the mostly single nation studies (e.g. Huse et al., 2009).

Conclusion

In summary, in this chapter we discuss different board gender diversity strategies adopted by regulatory/legislative authorities in the UK and Norway to promote gender diversity on boards of listed companies. We explain the rationale for the difference in approach with the help of path dependency perspective. Moreover, we give evidence of path dependency in different sectors that may potentially have an impact on diversity management practices in these countries. We also report new developments in both countries, which appear to defy the historical approach and path dependencies. We offer a possible explanation for these developments with the Actor–Network perspective. We propose that the developments warrant detailed academic investigation.

This chapter may contribute towards the better formulation of board diversity regulations by highlighting that any board diversity management approach, as adopted by a country, is more effective if it is adopted with respect to the prevailing path dependency in other related domains. The chapter also explores the potential causes of declining gender diversity on Norway's boards and thus may help the legislative authorities to understand the phenomenon. Lastly, it points out that, in an increasingly interconnected world, corporations may need to evolve a more conciliatory approach to implementing best practices relating to their social welfare measures, such as gender diversity on boards.

This chapter is a conceptual article comparing board gender diversity practices in two countries in Europe, namely the UK and Norway. Both countries have achieved impressive results in improving gender diversity on boards of their listed companies, by adopting two different approaches – collaborative and coercive/mandatory, respectively. However, as institutions and processes vary across the globe, an academic investigation involving a wider set of countries with empirical evidence may improve our understanding of the subject further. We hope that the same can be carried out in future research and the propositions made may be empirically tested. Such a study will make further theoretical and practical contributions to the significant subject of board gender diversity.

Note

1 Encyclopaedia Britannica www.britannica.com/topic/conflict-of-laws#toc276351.

References

Abdullah, A., Page, M. 2009. Corporate governance and corporate performance: UK FTSE 350 companies (Institute of Chartered Accountants of Scotland Report), Edinburgh: ICAS, www.icas.com/__data/assets/pdf_file/0011/10604/69-Corporate-Governance-and-Corporate-Performace-UK-FTSE-350-Companies-ICAS.pdf, accessed 13 February, 2017.

Adams, R.B., Kirchmaier, T. 2013. Making it to the top: From female labor force participation to boardroom gender diversity (ECGI – Finance Working Paper 347), Manchester: Manchester Business School.

Agrawal, A., Knoeber, C.R. 2001. Do some outside directors play a political role?, *The Journal of Law and Economics*, 44(1), 179–198.

Ahern, K.R., Dittmar, A.K. 2012. The changing of the boards: The impact on firm valuation of mandated female board representation, *Quarterly Journal of Economics*, 127(1), 137–197.

Ali, S. 2017. The number of women falls, Grant Thornton report finds Finance Director, www.financialdirector.co.uk/2017/03/08/number-of-women-in-senior-roles-falls-grant-thornton-report-finds/, accessed 8 March, 2017.

Babić, V.M., Nikolic, J.D., Eric, J.M. 2011. Rethinking board role performance: Towards an integrative model, *Economic Annals*, 56(190), 140–162.

Bartle, I., Vass, P. 2005. *Self-Regulation and the Regulatory State: A Survey of Policy and Practice*, Bath, UK: University of Bath School of Management, http://citeseerx.ist.psu.edu/viewdoc/download?doi=10.1.1.553.3190&rep=rep1&type=pdf, accessed 16 March, 2017.

Bernitz, U. 2007. What is Scandinavian law? Concept, characteristics, future, *Scandinavian Studies in Law*, 50(1), 13–30.

Bertrand, M., Black, S.E., Jensen, S., Lleras-Muney, A. 2014. Breaking the glass ceiling? The effect of board quotas on female labor market outcomes in Norway (No. w20256). National Bureau of Economic Research, https://brage.bibsys.no/xmlui/bitstream/handle/11250/217672/workingpaper.pdf?sequence=1&isAllowed=y, accessed 17 March, 2015.

Blackhurst, C. 2014. While men are in charge, gender quotas are the only way to increase the number of women in boardrooms, *The Independent*, January 28, www.independent.co.uk/voices/comment/while-men-are-in-charge-gender-quotas-are-the-only-way-to-increase-the-number-of-women-in-boardrooms-9091582.html, accessed 13 February, 2017.

Bøhren, Ø., Ødegaard, B.A. 2001. Corporate governance and economic performance in Norwegian listed firms, *Research Reports*, 11.

Bøhren, Ø., Staubo, S. 2016. Mandatory gender balance and board independence, *European Financial Management*, 22(1), 3–30.

Bøhren, Ø., Strøm, R.Ø. 2010. Governance and politics: Regulating independence and diversity in the board room, *Journal of Business Finance & Accounting*, 37(9–10), 1281–1308.

Cadbury, A. 1992. The code of best practice (Report of the Committee on the Financial Aspects of Corporate Governance), www.ecgi.org/codes/documents/cadbury.pdf, accessed 10 January, 2015.

Cadman, E. 2016. Female UK board appointments hit five-year low, *Financial Times*, July 7, www.ft.com/content/4a903bb4-4364-11e6-b22f-79eb4891c97d, accessed 13 February, 2017.

Callon, M. 1999. Actor-network theory – the market test, *The Sociological Review*, 47(S1), 181–195.

Carter, D.A., Simkins, B.J., Simpson, W.G. 2003. Corporate governance, board diversity, and firm value, *Financial Review*, 38(1), 33–53.

CIPD 2015. EU briefing: Gender diversity on boards: Do quota systems work?, www.cipd. co.uk/Images/gender-diversity-on-boards-quota-systems-work_june-2015_tcm18-14173.pdf, accessed 28 December, 2016.

Coffey, B.S., Wang, J. 1998. Board diversity and managerial control as predictors of corporate social performance, *Journal of Business Ethics*, 17(14), 1595–1603.

Cox, R.H. 1998. The consequences of welfare reform: How conceptions of social rights are changing, *Journal of Social Policy*, 27(1), 1–16.

Cox, R. 2004. The path-dependency of an idea: why Scandinavian welfare states remain distinct, *Social Policy & Administration*, 38(2), 204–219.

Crossland, C., Hambrick, D.C. 2011. Differences in managerial discretion across countries: How nation-level institutions affect the degree to which CEOs matter, *Strategic Management Journal*, 32(8), 797–819.

Cuervo, A. 2002. Corporate governance mechanisms: A plea for less code of good governance and more market control, *Corporate Governance: An International Review*, 10(2), 84–93.

David, R., Brierley, J.E. 1968. *Major Legal Systems in the World Today: An Introduction to the Comparative Study of Law*, New York: The Free Press.

Davidson, L. 2015. Proof that women in boardrooms quotas work, *The Telegraph*, January 13, www.telegraph.co.uk/finance/newsbysector/banksandfinance/11341816/Proof-that-women-in-boardrooms-quotas-work.html, accessed 28 December, 2016.

Department for Business, Innovation & Skills 2015. Improving the gender balance on British boards: Women on boards – Five-year summary – October 2015 (The Davies Review), www.gov.uk/government/uploads/system/uploads/attachment_data/file/482059/BIS-15-585-women-on-boards-davies-review-5-year-summary-october-2015.pdf, accessed 11 April, 2016.

DiMaggio, P., Powell, W.W. 1983. The iron cage revisited: Collective rationality and institutional isomorphism in organizational fields, *American Sociological Review*, 48(2), 147–160.

Dwyer, P. 2004. Creeping conditionality in the UK: From welfare rights to conditional entitlements?, *The Canadian Journal of Sociology*, 29(2), 265–287.

Egon Zehnder 2014. European board diversity analysis: With global perspective, www.egonzehnder.com/files/2014_egon_zehnder_european_board_diversity_analysis.pdf, accessed 9 September, 2015.

The Equality Act 2010. www.gov.uk/guidance/equality-act-2010-guidance#contents, accessed 23 February, 2017.

Erhardt, N.L., Werbel, J.D., Shrader, C.B. 2003. Board of director diversity and firm financial performance, *Corporate Governance: An International Review*, 11(2), 102–111.

Fairfax, L.M. 2011. Board diversity revisited: New rationale, same old story?, *North Carolina Law Review*, 89, 855–886.

Ferreira, D. 2010. Board diversity in Baker, H.K., Anderson, R. (eds.), *Corporate Governance: A Synthesis of Theory, Research, and Practice*, Hoboken, NJ: John Wiley & Sons, Inc.

Financial Reporting Council 2016. *The UK Corporate Governance Code*, London: Author.

Fondas, N. 2000. Women on boards of directors: Gender bias or power threat? in Burke, R., Mattis, M. (eds.), *Women on Corporate Boards of Directors*, Netherlands: Kluwer Academic Publishers, 171–177.

Gabaldon, P., Anca, C., Mateos de Cabo, R., Gimeno, R. 2015. Searching for women on boards: An analysis from the supply and demand perspective, *Corporate Governance: An International Review*, 24(3), 371–385.

The Gender Equality Act 1978. www.regjeringen.no/en/dokumenter/the-act-relating-to-gender-equality-the-/id454568/, accessed 23 February, 2017.

Gornick, J.C., Meyers, M.K., Ross, K.E. 1997. Supporting the employment of mothers: Policy variation across fourteen welfare states, *Journal of European Social Policy*, 7, 45–70.

Grant Thornton 2017. Women in business: New perspective on risk and reward, www.grantthornton.global/globalassets/1.-member-firms/global/insights/article-pdfs/2017/grant-thornton_women-in-business_2017-report.pdf, accessed 10 April, 2017.

Greener, I. 2002. Theorising path-dependency: How does history come to matter in organisations?, *Management Decision*, 40(6), 614–619.

Grosvold, J., Brammer, S. 2011. National institutional systems as antecedents of female board representation: An empirical study, *Corporate Governance: An International Review*, 19(2), 116–135.

Grosvold, J., Brammer, S., Rayton, B. 2007. Board diversity in the United Kingdom and Norway: An exploratory analysis, *Business Ethics: A European Review*, 16(4), 344–357.

Guest, P.M. 2008. The determinants of board size and composition: Evidence from the UK, *Journal of Corporate Finance*, 14(1), 51–72.

Hagstrøm, V. 2007. The Scandinavian law of obligations, *Scandinavian Studies in Law*, 50, 117–123.

Hamnett, C. 1996. Social polarisation, economic restructuring and welfare state regimes, *Urban Studies*, 33(8), 1407–1430.

Henderson, A., White, L.A. 2004. Shrinking welfare states? Comparing maternity leave benefits and child care programs in European Union and North American welfare states, 1985–2000, *Journal of European Public Policy*, 11(3), 497–519.

Higginbottom, K. 2015. FTSE100 firms on track to make 25% target for women on boards, *Forbes*, www.forbes.com/sites/karenhigginbottom/2015/03/25/ftse100-firms-on-track-to-make-25-target-for-women-on-boards/#47a67f22202d, accessed 20 December, 2016.

Holehouse, M. 2015. Britain seeks to halt EU gender quota plan, *The Telegraph*, December 4, www.telegraph.co.uk/news/worldnews/europe/eu/12034462/Britain-seeks-to-halt-EU-gender-quota-plan.html, accessed 20 February, 2017.

Huse, M., Nielsen, S.T., Hagen, I.M. 2009. Women and employee-elected board members, and their contributions to board control tasks, *Journal of Business Ethics*, 89(4), 581–597.

Iannotta, M., Gatti, M., Huse, M. 2016. Institutional complementarities and gender diversity on boards: A configurational approach, *Corporate Governance: An International Review*, 4(24), 406–427.

Ingley, C., Van der Walt, N. 2005. Do board processes influence director and board performance? Statutory and performance implications, *Corporate Governance: An International Review*, 13(5), 632–653.

Janis, I.L. 1972. *Victims of Groupthink: A Psychological Study of Foreign-Policy Decisions and Fiascos*, Boston: Houghton Mifflin Company.

Jensen, M. C., Meckling, W. H. 1976. Theory of the firm: Managerial behavior, agency costs and ownership structure. *Journal of Financial Economics*, 3(4), 305–360.

Johnson, S., La Porta, R., Lopez-de-Silanes, F., Shleifer, A. 2000. Tunneling, *American Economic Review*, 90, 22–27.

Kay, A. 2005. A critique of the use of path dependency in policy studies, *Public Administration*, 83(3), 553–571.

Kenny, M. 2016. Why aren't there more women in British politics? (Political Studies Association), www.psa.ac.uk/insight-plus/why-arent-there-more-women-british-politics, accessed 10 February, 2017.

Kim, I., Pantzalis, C., Park, J.C. 2013. Corporate boards' political ideology diversity and firm performance, *Journal of Empirical Finance*, 21, 223–240.

Kollewe, J. 2016. Women occupy less than a quarter of UK board positions, *The Guardian*, April 27, www.theguardian.com/business/2016/apr/27/women-uk-board-positions-gender-equality-europe, accessed 11 February, 2017.

Korpi, W. 2001. Contentious institutions an augmented rational-action analysis of the origins and path dependency of welfare state institutions in western countries, *Rationality and Society*, 13(2), 235–283.

La Porta, R., Lopez-de-Silanes, F., Shleifer, A., Vishny, R.W. 1998. Law and finance, *Journal of Political Economy*, 106(6), 1113–1155.

Law, J. 1992. Notes on the theory of the actor-network: Ordering, strategy, and heterogeneity, *Systems Practice*, 5(4), 379–393.

Leibowitz, S.J., Margolis, S.E. 1995. Path dependence, lock-in, and history, *Journal of Law, Economics and Organization*, 11(1), 205–226.

Lester, S. 2016. The development of self-regulation in four UK professional communities, *Professions and Professionalism*, 6(1), 1–14.

Matsa, D.A., Miller, A.R. 2012. A female style in corporate leadership? Evidence from quotas. Evidence from quotas, *American Economic Journal: Applied Economics*, 5(3), 136–169.

Mattis, M.C. 2000. Women corporate directors in the United States in Burke, R., Mattis, M. (eds.), *Women on Corporate Boards of Directors*, Netherlands: Kluwer Academic Publishers, 43–56.

McCrudden, C. 2000. A common law of human rights? Transnational judicial conversations on constitutional rights, *Oxford Journal of Legal Studies*, 20(4), 499–532.

Meyer, J.W. 2008. Reflections on institutional theories of organizations, *The Sage Handbook of Organizational Institutionalism*, 790–811, https://pdfs.semanticscholar.org/4cd5/f132350cf4f3268f4e1c88e8d7570de478f4.pdf, accessed 14 December, 2016.

Meyer, J.W., Rowan, B. 1977. Institutionalized organizations: Formal structure as myth and ceremony, *American Journal of Sociology*, 83(2), 340–363.

Nygaard, K. 2011. Forced board changes: Evidence from Norway, Discussion Paper, https://core.ac.uk/download/pdf/6400402.pdf, accessed 3 September, 2015.

Orloff, A. 1996. Gender in the welfare state, *Annual Review of Sociology*, 22(1), 51–78.

Powell, M. 2002. The hidden history of social citizenship, *Citizenship Studies*, 6(3), 229–244.

Proudman, C. 2015. Quotas are the only way to combat sexism in the workplace, and we shouldn't be afraid to demand them, *The Independent*, November 10, www.independent.co.uk/voices/quotas-are-the-only-way-to-combat-sexism-in-the-workplace-and-we-shouldnt-be-afraid-to-demand-them-a6728426.html, accessed 10 November, 2015.

Pryce, V. 2015. Why we need quotas for women on boards, *The Guardian*, November 23, www.theguardian.com/women-in-leadership/2015/nov/23/why-we-need-quotas-for-women-on-boards, accessed 23 November, 2015.

Randøy, T., Thomsen, S., Oxelheim, L. 2006. A Nordic perspective on corporate board diversity, www.nordicinnovation.org/Global/_Publications/Reports/2006/The%20performance%20effects%20of%20board%20diversity%20in%20Nordic%20Firms.pdf, accessed 30 October, 2015.

Sainsbury, D. 2008. Gendering the welfare state in Goertz, G., Mazur, A. (eds.), *Politics, Gender, and Concepts: Theory and Methodology*, Cambridge: Cambridge University Press, 94–103.

Salami, M. 2017. On parliamentary equality the UK is 48th: It could learn from No 1: Rwanda, *The Guardian*, January 17, www.theguardian.com/commentisfree/2017/jan/12/female-mps-britain-rwanda-senegal-parliamentary-gender-equality, accessed 12 January, 2017.

Sassen, S. 1991. *The Global City: New York, London, Tokyo*, Princeton, NJ: Princeton University Press.

Scott, W.R. 2004. *Institutional Theory, Encyclopedia of Social Theory*, Thousand Oaks, CA: Sage.

Sealy, R., Doldor, E., Vinnicombe, S. 2016. Women on boards: Taking stock of where we are (The Female FTSE Board Report), www.cranfield.ac.uk/~/media/images-for-new-website/centres/school-of-management-centres/global-centre-for-gender-and-leadership/female-ftse-board-report-2016.ashx?la=en, accessed 21 February, 2017.

Seierstad, C. 2015. Beyond the business case: The need for both utility and justice rationales for increasing the share of women on boards, *Corporate Governance: An International Review*, 24(4), 390–405.

Singh, V., Terjesen, S., Vinnicombe, S. 2008. Newly appointed directors in the boardroom: How do women and men differ?. *European Management Journal*, 26(1), 48–58.

Stiles, P. 1993. The future for boards: Self-regulation or legislation?, *Long Range Planning*, 26(2), 119–124.

Sweigart, A. 2012. Women on board for change: The Norway model of boardroom quotas as a tool for progress in the United States and Canada, *Northwestern Journal of International Law & Business*, 32(4), 81A–105A.

Taguma M., Litjens, I., Makowiecki, K. 2013. Quality matters in early childhood education and care: Norway 2013, OECD, www.oecd-ilibrary.org/education/quality-matters-in-early-childhood-education-and-care-norway-2012_9789264176713-en, accessed 6 February, 2018.

Terjesen, S., Aguilera, R.V., Lorenz, R. 2015. Legislating a woman's seat on the board: Institutional factors driving gender quotas for boards of directors, *Journal of Business Ethics*, 128(2), 233–251.

Terjesen, S., Singh, V. 2008. Female presence on corporate boards: A multi-country study of environmental context, *Journal of Business Ethics*, 83(1), 55–63.

UN Committee on the Elimination of Discrimination against Women 2003. Report of the committee on the elimination of discrimination against women, https://documents-dds-ny.un.org/doc/UNDOC/GEN/N03/468/20/PDF/N0346820.pdf?OpenElement, accessed 25 April, 2017.

Voß, J. 2015. The impact of gender diverse boards on firm financial performance in Norway, Bachelor's thesis, University of Twente. Paper presented at the 5th IBA Bachelor Thesis Conference, July 2, Enschede, the Netherlands.

Watson, K. 2014. Gender diversity on corporate boards, *Journal of the Australian Law Teachers Association*, 7(1, 2), 1–9, https://papers.ssrn.com/sol3/papers.cfm?abstract_id=2586354, accessed 15 May, 2016.

Whitehead, H., Normand, C. 2011. Women on boards (The Davies Report), www.gov.uk/government/uploads/system/uploads/attachment_data/file/31480/11-745-women-on-boards.pdf, accessed 17 April, 2015.

World Economic Forum 2013. The global gender gap report, www3.weforum.org/docs/WEF_GenderGap_Report_2013.pdf, accessed 27 April, 2017.

3 Regulation of the gender composition of company boards in Europe

Experience and prospects

Kevin Campbell and Leszek Bohdanowicz

Introduction

The desire to increase the share of women on corporate boards in Europe has led to the incorporation of voluntary targets into corporate governance codes of best practice in some European countries and the introduction of board gender quota laws in others. Taking affirmative action by imposing a quota can create a critical mass of women on boards that is sufficient to sustain greater numerical equality once the quota is removed (Kogut et al., 2014). A quota law for company boards, set at 40% for each gender, was first proposed in Norway in 2002, to the surprise of many (Bøhren and Staubo, 2016). At the time women held only 9% of board seats (Ahern and Dittmar, 2012). Passed by the Norwegian Parliament one year later, the quota became mandatory in 2008 and sparked public debate in other countries about the possibility of using quotas to increase the representation of women on corporate boards. The European Commission, with the support of the European Parliament and a number of Member States, decided in 2012 that legislative action was necessary to improve gender balance on corporate boards and put forward the proposal for a Directive that sets a 40% target for the presence of the under-represented gender among non-executive directors of companies listed on stock exchanges by 2020.

In this chapter we evaluate the advantages and disadvantages of the enforcement approach proposed by the European Commission. Our review draws on evidence about the mandatory quota system in Norway. We explore the circumstances in which this kind of approach can have either positive or negative outcomes, as well as the unintended consequences that could follow. We explore the different factors that affect the success of quotas, such as the nature of the sanctions against non-compliant companies, and their enforcement. The UK has adopted a voluntary approach to improving board gender diversity, seeking to increase boardroom gender diversity using voluntary targets for listed companies included in the FTSE 100 and 250 indices. We review the success of this approach, and related initiatives in other European countries. These contrasting approaches (hard versus soft law) raise a crucial question for board diversity: which approach, compulsory quotas or a voluntary approach, is the most effective way of improving the representation of women in senior roles?

A catalyst for change: the Norwegian gender quota law

Nordic countries have long been at the forefront of advancing policies to reduce social inequality, with Norway playing a leading role (Borchorst, 2009). Since the early 1970s female participation in the Norwegian labour market has been on the increase, in part stimulated by generous welfare state provision, and is among the highest in the OECD (Johnsen, 2012). Whether a gender balance naturally arises from such a trend is debatable. Karvonen and Selle (1995) suggest that the increased integration of women into leadership positions in Nordic society would eventually result in gender parity as they become increasingly mobilized and active, but with an uncertain time lag. Frustration at the slow pace of change in the private sector eventually led to the enactment of the mandatory gender quota law in 2008 and follows on from a tradition of Norwegian state involvement in advancing the rights of women (Teigen, 2012). Gender quotas have been used by Norwegian political parties since the 1970s and they have been applied in the Norwegian public sector since the 1980s, with the result that women hold a relatively equal share of management positions in publicly owned enterprises (Bolsø and Sørensen, 2013). Despite the high rate of working women, and women active in politics and in positions of influence in the Norwegian public sector, women in positions of power in private businesses was paradoxically low (Storvik, 2011).

By the end of the 1990s it became clear that the private sector was lagging behind the public sector and this began to capture political attention. By 2002 less than 10% of the board members of the largest listed Norwegian companies were female directors (Eckbo et al., 2016). A review of the *Gender Equality Act* in 1999 proposed that the gender quota applicable to the public sector also be applied to corporate boards. At this stage the argument for this extension was based on the principle of gender equality: that women should have equal representation in all positions of power and influence, including corporate boards. The proposal was criticized by the corporate sector and did not initially cause too much concern. However, this all changed in 2002 when the conservative politician and Minister of Trade and Industry, Ansgar Gabrielsen, announced that he wanted to impose a 40% quota on the boards of directors of Norway's listed firms. The language used by Gabrielsen was controversial, reflected in the headline in Norway's largest newspaper, *Verdens Gang*: "The Minister of Trade and Industry is Sick and Tired of the Men's Club: Wants to Force Women into Boardrooms". Gabrielsen argued that the low representation of females on corporate boards stemmed from ingrained cultural attitudes and that a quota was the only way to prevent discrimination against women (Nygaard, 2011; Strøm, 2015).

The proposal led to a wide-ranging debate in Norway, with most business executives opposed to the proposed legislation on the grounds that it was punitive and restricted their freedom to conduct business as they saw fit (Fouche and Treanor, 2006). Arguments were also advanced that the new law would lead to stereotyping and produce a negative view of women since their appointments to boards would be seen to be due to their gender rather than their competences (Casey et al., 2011). To counter resistance from the corporate sector and convince skeptics that the quota law should be supported the government shifted its argument away from gender equality towards more strict economic reasoning, emphasizing the "business case": that competitive advantages arise from greater female board participation and lead to better corporate governance and increased profitability. This re-framing turned out to be successful and the Norwegian Parliament passed the law in 2003. It initially required public limited firms to apply the quota on a voluntary basis, but after voluntary compliance failed the law became compulsory on 1 January, 2006, with a two-year transition period backed by a sanction that firms not in compliance by January 2008 faced the penalty of liquidation. Notices to comply were issued to 77 delinquent firms in January 2008, but by April all public limited firms were in compliance with the law (Ahern and Dittmar, 2012). The law increased the average fraction of directorships filled by females from 11% when it was passed to 42% when it became mandatory (Bøhren and Staubo, 2016).

An important part of the story about the imposition of the gender quota in Norway is that the law applied only to limited liability firms that are classed as public limited firms (known or *allmennaksjeselskap* or ASA firms). However, Norwegian firms with limited liability can choose an alternative organizational form known as AS (*aksjeselskap*) which is equivalent to a private limited firm. ASA firms can make public offering of stock and list on the Oslo Stock Exchange whereas AS firms can only raise equity finance from private placements. There are both listed and non-listed ASAs, and the quota applies equally to both groups. Prior to the implementation of the quota rule in 2008 half of the ASA firms altered their organizational form to AS and so the quota law had the unintended consequence of impacting only half of the firms targeted (Bøhren and Staubo, 2014).

Furthermore, as can be observed from Figure 3.1, the female share of board representatives in Norwegian public limited companies has not increased to any great extent beyond the statutory minimum of 40% since the enactment of the quota law in 2008. In contrast the female share of board representatives in private limited companies has hardly changed since 2008 and stood at 18% in January 2017. It would thus appear that the quota law has not strengthened female board representation beyond the catchment area of the law.

Furthermore, as Figure 3.2 shows, the share of females holding general manager positions in Norway is actually higher in private limited companies than in public limited companies. While the share of females holding general manager positions in the latter has increased slightly since 2008 it still lies below that of the share in private limited companies and there is no sign of this gap narrowing. Taken together, these statistics raise questions about the ability of the board gender quota law to increase the number of Norwegian women in decision-making positions in economic life in general.

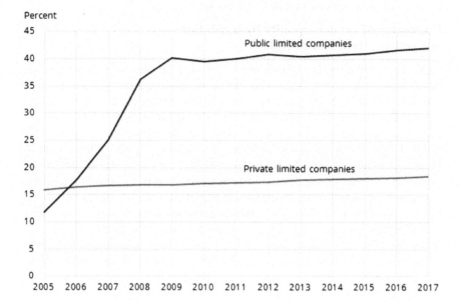

Figure 3.1 Share of female board representatives in public and private limited companies in Norway (2005–2017)

Source: Statistics Norway

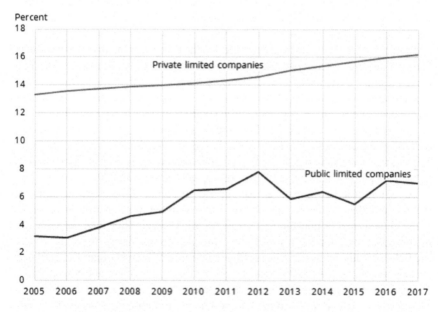

Figure 3.2 Share of female general managers in public and private limited companies in Norway (2005–2017)

Source: Statistics Norway

Promotion of gender equality by legislation and self-regulation in Europe

Against a backdrop of low female representation on boards in EU countries, the Norwegian experiment energized the debate on gender quotas. In 2003 the average share of female board members was only 9% (Armstrong and Walby, 2012). Several European countries have since introduced hard or soft laws to improve the gender balance on company boards. Following the Norwegian lead some have adopted similar legislative actions based on mandatory quotas: Spain in 2007; Belgium, France, Italy and the Netherlands in 2011; and Germany in 2016. These laws differ in terms of the rules governing targeted firms, the size of the gender quota, and the severity of sanctions for non-compliers. Other countries, such as the UK and Sweden, have adopted a voluntary approach that has involved the inclusion of targets in corporate governance codes for listed companies.

The available data indicate that mandatory quotas have succeeded in increasing the proportion of women on boards. Apart from Spain, in all countries with mandatory quotas between 2004 and 2014, the proportion of women on boards increased sharply after the date of the introduction of the legislation, and it is well beyond the EU average (Comi et al., 2016). The share of women on company boards in the 28 EU countries, and the national measures in place to encourage board gender diversity, has been investigated by Jourová (2016) and the results are shown in Table 3.1, the data for which is sourced from the European Institute for Gender Equality (EIGE) *Gender Statistics Database*.[1] As of April 2016, the average share of women on boards across the EU-28 average was 23.3%. In column 2 of Table 3.1, those countries with performance above the EU-28 average are shown in bold.

Despite the progress evident from Table 3.1, the European Commission proposed a Directive in 2012 to accelerate progress in improving the gender balance on corporate boards within EU Member States (European Commission, 2012b). The Directive sets a quantitative objective of a 40% presence of the under-represented gender among non-executive directors of companies listed on EU stock exchanges by 2020, and by 2018 in public sector companies. The Directive requires companies to issue annual reports on the composition of their boards and for sanctions to be imposed in the event of negative evaluations. The European Parliament voted with a strong majority to back the proposed Directive in 2013 (European Commission, 2013).

Despite a broad consensus across the EU in favour of measures to improve the gender balance on company boards, some Member States would prefer either national measures or non-binding measures at EU level. They take the view that the proposal does not comply with the principle of subsidiarity, which holds that the EU may only intervene if it is able to act more effectively than EU countries at their respective national or local levels. At the Employment and Social Policy Council meeting in June 2015, Croatia, Denmark, Estonia, Germany, Hungary, Slovakia, the Netherlands and the UK expressed reservations regarding the Commission's proposal and formed a blocking minority. In March 2017, in a resolution on equality between women and men in the EU in 2014–2015, the European Parliament urged the Council for a swift adoption of the Directive. As of January 2018 no agreement had been reached on its adoption (European Parliament, 2018).

Table 3.1 Share of women on company boards and national measures in place in EU countries to encourage board gender diversity

Member State	Share of women on boards(*) EU-28 average: 23.3%	Quotas in place	Other national measures in place
Austria	20.1%	Yes: only state-owned companies (35% for supervisory boards by 2018)	Self-regulation: the Corporate Governance Code of 2009 recommends representation of both genders in appointments to supervisory boards
Belgium	**26.6%**	Yes: 33% for executives and non-executives in state-owned and listed companies by 2017 and in listed SMEs by 2019	Self-regulation: the Corporate Governance Code of 2009 recommends that the composition of a board is determined on the basis of gender diversity
Bulgaria	17.9%	No	No
Croatia	22.2%	No	No
Cyprus	10.9%	No	No
Czech Republic	8.8%	No	No
Denmark	**27.0%**	No	Boards in state-owned companies should 'as far as possible' have an equal gender balance; a man and a woman nominated for every vacancy (executives and non-executives). From 2013 – obligation to all companies (listed and non-listed) to self-regulate and set their own targets. A company can be fined if it hasn't set any target figures or hasn't submitted any reporting
Estonia	8.2%	No	No
Finland	**29.9%**	No	State-owned companies are required to have an 'equitable proportion of women and men'. The corporate governance code for listed companies contains recommendation that 'boards shall consist of both sexes'

(*Continued*)

Table 3.1 (Continued)

Member State	Share of women on boards(*) *EU-28 average: 23.3%*	Quotas in place	Other national measures in place
France	**37.1%**	Yes: from 2011 – 40% by 2017. Applicable to non-executive directors in large listed and non-listed companies	The AFEP-MEDEF Corporate Code: recommendation containing same quotas as in the Law of 2011, applicable to all board members
Germany	**27.2%**	Yes: from 2016 – 30% for supervisory boards of the listed companies that are submitted to parity co-determination (the roughly 110 biggest listed companies)	Other companies that are either listed or fall under parity co-determination have to set individual quantitative objectives of women on boards with regard to non-executive and executive board members and senior managers below board level and deadlines to achieve them
Greece	9.4%	Yes, 33% – only companies fully or partially owned by the state. Applicable to all board positions (executives and non-executives)	Soft positive action measures in public sector
Hungary	11.2%	No	Soft positive action measures in public sector
Ireland	16.0%	No	A policy target of 40% female participation on all state boards and committees. Soft positive action measures in public sector employment
Italy	**30.0%**	Yes: 33% by 2015 for listed companies and state-owned companies. Applicable to management boards and supervisory boards (i.e. executives and non-executives)	Yes
Latvia	**27.7%**	No	Soft positive action measures in the public sector
Lithuania	13.0%	No	No
Luxembourg	12.9%	No	Soft positive action measures. The Corporate Code of 2009 recommends the board to have an appropriate representation of both genders. The rule is applicable to all board members

Member State	Share of women on boards(*) EU-28 average: 23.3%	Quotas in place	Other national measures in place
Malta	5.0%	No	No
Netherlands	**28.1%**	Target of 30% in the executive boards and supervisory boards of large companies – 'comply-or-explain' mechanism, no sanctions. Measure to expire in 2016	Self-regulation: diversity clauses in the Dutch Corporate Governance Code of 2009, applicable to both executives and non-executives. Voluntary Charter with targets for more women in management
Poland	19.9%	No	The executive ordinance of Minister of State Treasury obliges state-owned companies to 'choose adequately prepared members of supervisory boards, taking into account the balanced participation of women and men'. The Code of Good Practice attached to that ordinance establishes a target of 30% for 2015 and a priority rule for equally qualified women. No sanctions are envisaged
Portugal	14.2%	No	A government resolution of 2015 encourages listed companies to attain 30% of the under-represented sex at their administrative bodies by 2018
Romania	10.1%	No	Soft positive action measures in public sector employment
Slovakia	14.3%	No	No
Slovenia	**23.9%**	No	Regulation on state-owned companies: a principle of 40% representation of each sex applies to the nomination or appointment of government representatives to management and supervisory boards of state-owned enterprises (executives and non-executives). No sanctions apply if the principle is not respected

(Continued)

Table 3.1 (Continued)

Member State	Share of women on boards(*) *EU-28 average: 23.3%*	Quotas in place	Other national measures in place
Spain	20.2%	Yes: 40% (both executives and non-executives) by 2015 (but no sanctions, thus rather a recommendation by nature) in state-owned companies with 250 or more employees. New possible models under discussion	Soft positive action measures in public sector employment
Sweden	**36.1%**	No	Self-regulation: the Corporate Governance Code of 2004 has a voluntary goal of parity for listed companies – 'comply-or-explain' mechanism
United Kingdom	**27.1%**	No	Self-regulation – from 2012 on the basis of principles of UK corporate governance code (following the Lord Davies's recommendation). The recommended target for listed companies in FTSE 100: 25%, by 2015 is applicable to all board members. FTSE 350 companies recommended setting their own aspirational targets to be achieved by 2013 and 2015

Source: V. Jourová, *Gender Balance on Corporate Boards: Europe Is Cracking the Glass Ceiling*, European Commission, Directorate-General for Justice and Consumers, Fact Sheet, July 2016

Note: * performances above the EU average are in bold

The promotion of gender equality in Europe using quotas

We now turn our attention to research on the promotion of gender equality and the introduction of gender quotas in Europe. We focus on studies of the impact of the mandatory gender quota law in Norway. The introduction of this law provides a "natural experiment" that allows researchers to examine the impact of female directors on firm performance free from the problem of endogeneity (Hermalin and

Weisbach, 2003). Despite this, no clear conclusion has emerged from the studies that examine the effect of the law on firm performance (Ferreira, 2015).

Before it was introduced, Norwegian firms affected by the law decided how many women to hire as directors and so the fraction of female directors was endogenous (internally specified by firms). Researchers could not conclude with certainty whether firms that performed well did do *because* of the proportion of women on their boards, or whether firms that performed well were able to then hire more female directors. To determine causality the proportion of female directors needs to be exogenously determined, meaning that it must be specified the same way for all firms. What the Norwegian gender quota law did was to force all publicly listed firms to have 40% of their board seats occupied by women and so the proportion of female directors became an exogenously determined variable (decided by forces external to firms) and thus free from the endogeneity problem.

Ahern and Dittmar (2012) employ an event study method to examine the immediate stock market reaction to the first report of the quota in the *Verdens Gang* newspaper on 22 February 2002. As the announcement affected all public limited liability firms they calculate industry-adjusted abnormal returns by subtracting the average return of US firms in the same industry as firms listed on the Oslo Stock Exchange in the five days surrounding the announcement. Data for US rather than Scandinavian industry returns are used on the grounds that global investors were unlikely to anticipate that the law would directly affect US firms, whereas they may have anticipated that similar laws would be passed in other Scandinavian countries. The authors find significant negative abnormal returns around the announcement date, and these are significantly larger for firms with no women on the board (−3.54%) compared to firms with at least one woman on the board (−0.02%). In contrast to these findings, another event study by Nygaard (2011) finds a significantly positive stock market reaction, but in this case the date chosen is when the quota was mandated by the Norwegian Parliament and liquidation was established as the penalty for noncompliance, on 9 December 2005.

The difference in the results of these two studies is partly due to what Ferreira (2015) calls the "timing problem" as the exact date of the "quota shock" is subject to interpretation. The gender quota was first discussed in 1999, the intention of the government to introduce a law was revealed in 2002, a law proposing the 40% quota was passed in 2003 without a penalty for noncompliance, in 2005 liquidation was established as the penalty for noncompliance, with firms given two years to adjust, and full compliance was only achieved in 2008. There is thus a great deal of freedom to define the shock: is it when the Norwegian government first announced that it planned to legislate (Ahern and Dittmar, 2012) or is it when the Norwegian Parliament made clear that it was serious in its intent by establishing liquidation as the penalty for noncompliance (Nygaard, 2011)? Ultimately, this is a matter of judgement. Another reason for the different event study results is the absence of a natural control group against which to compare firms (Ferreira, 2015). Normally stock returns of firms affected by an event are compared to some measure of the market average, but because the quota law applies to all Norwegian listed firms there is no obvious comparator. While Ahern and Dittmar (2012) use the returns of US firms in the same industry, Nygaard (2011) uses the returns on firms that comprise the Morgan Stanley Capital International (MSCI) World Index.

In addition to examining the stock market reaction to the quota law, researchers have also examined its longer-term financial impact. Ahern and Dittmar (2012) focus on the market-based performance measure Tobin's Q rather than accounting-based measures, such as ROA, because the adoption by Norwegian firms of International Financial Reporting Standards (IFRS) during the transition period of the quota makes accounting performance measures less reliable. They find that the value of Tobin's Q in 2007 through 2009 was substantially lower than in 2003 for those firms most impacted by the quota. They also investigate how the quota impacted the characteristics of boards of directors and find that the new female directors were substantially different from retained male directors: they had significantly less CEO experience, were younger, more highly educated, and more likely to be employed as non-executive managers. They also found that board size did not change as a result of the quota. Thus, rather than meet the quota by simply adding new female directors, firms maintained the size of the board at the cost of replacing male directors.

As noted earlier, a major side-effect of the introduction of the mandatory quota law was that its effect could be avoided by firms altering their form of legal organization from public limited to private limited (Bøhren and Staubo, 2014). Another means of avoiding the law was to incorporate in another country or be acquired by a private or foreign firm. Ahern and Dittmar (2012) provide evidence that both changes occurred following the introduction of the law. Overall the number of public limited firms in Norway in 2009 was less than 70% of the number in 2001 while the number of private limited firms (not affected by the quota) increased by just over 30%. Ahern and Dittmar (2012) also find a strong negative relationship between the probability of delisting after the quota is passed and the number of women on the board before the quota is passed, after controlling for firm size, risky investments and industry effects.

A significant decline in financial performance following the introduction of the quota law is also detected by Matsa and Miller (2013). They find that the ratio of operating profits to assets among affected firms decreased from 2003 to 2009 by about 4% compared with a matched sample of unlisted firms in Norway, and listed and unlisted firms in other Nordic countries. They attribute this deterioration to differences in employment policies: firms affected by the quota laid off fewer employees, causing an increase in relative labour costs and a reduction in short-run profits. The strongest effects were found among firms that were required to add the most women in order to comply with the law. The reduced layoffs are not attributable to changes in board strategy as boards affected and unaffected by the quota were equally willing to initiate mergers, acquisitions and joint ventures. They also find no evidence that the impact of the gender quota was driven by changes in board member characteristics other than gender, such as age or experience. Although the new female directors were younger on average, they replaced younger men and did not decrease the average age of the boards.

Research into the financial performance consequences of the gender quota law is also undertaken by Dale-Olsen et al. (2013). They find that the change in the ROA of non-financial public limited companies affected by the law is negligible compared to that of private limited companies unaffected by the law over the period from 2003 to 2007. They also find that the reform had no significant impact on the operating revenues or on the operating costs of the affected firms, and that although these firms accumulated more capital after the reform, either by raising debt or equity, this is more likely due to a shortage of capital on financial markets as the financial crisis approached rather than a greater appetite for risk by the additional female board members.

Bøhren and Staubo (2016) also examine the impact of the gender quota law on the financial performance of listed and non-listed Norwegian firms. They compare ROA in 2003, when the gender law was passed by the Norwegian Parliament, to the average ROA in the subsequent period from 2004 until 2008, when the law became mandatory. They find that firms that needed to hire more female directors (as they had fewer women on the board prior to the quota) have significantly lower ROA, while no such relationship is found for the unexposed, non-listed firms. They also measure board independence, defined as the fraction of outside directors, and find that this increased significantly, which they attribute to independence being a much more common characteristic among female director candidates than among males. Bøhren and Staubo (2016) argue that there is a trade-off between the value of monitoring provided by independent directors and the value of advice provided by inside directors and that board quality declined when the introduction of the mandatory quota tipped boardroom independence above its optimal level. It is also possible that board independence increased because of the influence of the Norwegian corporate governance code, which was introduced two years before the gender quota law became mandatory in 2008 and which recommends that half of the board members are independent. However, while the gender quota law applies to both listed and non-listed firms, the code applies only to listed firms, and Bøhren and Staubo (2016) find the same upward shift in independence regardless of listing status. Thus, they conclude that increased independence is due to the gender quota law rather than the corporate governance code.

The Norwegian approach to implementing gender quotas has not been repeated in other countries. In Germany a law requiring that women hold 30% of supervisory board seats of the top 100 or so publicly traded companies went into effect in January 2016. A March 2016 study from the Hans Böckler Foundation reports that only about 22% of supervisory board seats at Germany's top companies were occupied by women (Weckes, 2016). Although the share of women in top board positions doubled over a five-year period, the legally mandated quota was not met. This is most probably related to the fact that the quota law in Germany has no teeth, unlike quota laws in other European countries, such as Norway and France, where companies face fines and other sanctions for not complying. It may also be related to negative perceptions of quota-based selection policies in Germany, as revealed in an experimental study by Shaughnessy et al. (2016) based on recruits from German social networking sites. Their findings show that quota-based selection policies negatively influence applicant evaluations of an organization and ultimately their decision to pursue employment. Nevertheless, the identification of non-compliant companies is having some impact as German companies wish to avoid being viewed as a negative example, which suggests that the number of compliant companies is likely to rise over time (Weckes, 2016).

Most studies of the impact of gender diversity initiatives focus on a single country, but there is some evidence from multi-country studies. Casey et al. (2011) compare the hard and soft policies used, respectively, by Norway and New Zealand to achieve board gender equality using qualitative data collected between 2004 and 2005 on women's experiences of governance participation. Their study involved interviews with 35 women: 18 in Norway and 17 in New Zealand. They find evidence of a perception in Norway that some women were 'quota-filling' and lacked competence in a forced compliance situation, while in New Zealand there is evidence of a view that the voluntary approach enabled some boards to insulate themselves entirely from gender equality issues. Labelle et al. (2015) use a multi-country research design to examine how gender diversity is related to firm performance in countries that apply an "enabling approach" based on regulation and those that use a "voluntary approach" where there is no enforcement mechanism. They exclude Norway as the only country using what they term a "coercive approach" based on affirmative action. Their sample comprises 719 firms from 17 countries at the beginning of 2009 and 2011. Nine countries are classified as adopting a voluntary approach in 2009 (Canada, France, Germany, Greece, Italy, Portugal, Switzerland, the UK and the US) while eight countries are classified as adopting an enabling approach (Austria, Belgium, Denmark, Finland, the Netherlands, Ireland, Spain and Sweden). As changes to corporate governance codes promoting gender diversity came into effect by 2011 in France, Germany, the UK and the US, these countries shifted to the group following a regulatory approach. The authors find that gender diversity is positively related to firm performance, measured by ROA, in countries using the voluntary approach, but negatively related in countries adopting the regulatory approach. While their research can be criticized for using an unbalanced panel of data over a limited time period, their result is nevertheless in line with the intuition that an accelerated increase in demand for more female directors in countries following the regulatory approach can result in firms appointing less experienced women to the board.

The voluntary approach to the promotion of gender equality in Europe

Across many EU countries a range of voluntary initiatives have been developed to address under-representation of women at board level. National corporate governance codes encourage, to varying degrees, gender diversity on company boards, and in some countries these are complementary to quotas (see Table 3.1).

The UK has adopted a purely voluntary approach to the promotion of gender equality on company boards following the recommendation of an independent review by Lord Davies of Abersoch into how obstacles to the participation of women on boards could be removed (Davies, 2011). The Davies Report *Women on Boards* recommended that the UK's comply-or-explain corporate governance code be amended to require listed companies to establish boardroom diversity policies, and this was duly implemented the following year in a revised version of *The UK Corporate Governance Code* (Financial Reporting Council, 2012). It also set a target of 25% female representation on the boards of FTSE 100 listed companies by 2015. Smaller companies comprising the FTSE 250 index were recommended to set their own aspirational targets. In a review of progress four years later, Lord Davies was able to report that the target for FTSE 100 companies had been met, with female representation more than doubling since 2011 to stand at 26.1% (Davies, 2015). The FTSE 250 firms started their journey from a lower base and more than doubled female representation on their boards: in 2011 only 17 companies had 25% or more women on their boards compared to 79 companies by 2015. He also notes there were no all-male boards in the FTSE 100 in 2015, compared with 21 in 2011, and characterizes the UK as "a leader and role model on the international stage for having made such good progress under an entirely voluntary regime" (Davies, 2015: 10). He also notes that the UK was sixth in Europe in terms of female boardroom representation, behind Norway, Sweden, France, Finland and Belgium, all of which had largely introduced legislative quota regimes.

Acknowledging the need to maintain momentum, the UK government set up another independent review on female representation at board level with a remit to continue improving the proportion of women on the boards of FTSE 350 companies, and also to improve their representation below board level in the senior layers of management. Chaired by Sir Philip Hampton, with Dame Helen Alexander as deputy chair, the *Hampton-Alexander Review* set a new target of 33% female representation on boards of FTSE 100 companies by 2020, with the same voluntary target for FTSE 350 companies (Hampton and Alexander, 2016). It also set a target of 33% female representation by 2020 for board executive committees of FTSE 100 companies and for those who directly report to these executive committees. In targeting board executive committees and the layers beneath the Board, the *Hampton-Alexander Review* is setting a more ambitious agenda that will require companies to increase reporting of data about their executive pipeline that has hitherto not been subject to disclosure requirements. Whether the *Hampton-Alexander Review* targets can be met by 2020 and whether momentum for increased female representation can be sustained more generally has arguably been affected by the UK decision to exit the EU following the referendum in 2016. A company chairman quoted anonymously by Davies states that his report encouraged businesses to work together to avoid quotas being imposed by Europe. It is thus possible that UK businesses may feel less inclined to meet targets in a post-Brexit environment. That said, another company chairman was quoted by Davies (2015: 14) saying that

nobody wants to be left out, so once it becomes a direction of travel then people climb on board because they don't want to appear to be the odd ones out. The more people that did it, the more people saw that actually the boardroom dynamics improved.

It is therefore feasible that the culture of change has become embedded and that achievement of targets will be unaffected by Brexit.

Some EU countries chose to promote greater female board representation using charters to which companies can sign up. In the Netherlands, the charter *Talent to the Top* requires companies to establish quantitative goals for the representation of women in senior management positions, to measure their achievements against these goals and to report annually to a monitoring committee each year on the progress they have made. The 110 largest Dutch companies signed the charter, including many large household names such as Shell, Phillips, Heineken, Reed Elsevier and Unilever (Branson, 2012). By 2010 the share of women in senior positions in companies that signed the charter in 2008 and 2009 had grown by 7.5% and, overall, 72% of companies recorded an increase over this period (European Commission, 2012a).

In Denmark, a similar pledge initiative was developed in 2008 by the Danish Ministry of Gender Equality in the form of a *Charter for More Women in Management*. No sanctions were included in the Charter and it was criticized for a lack of evident results (Agustín and Siim, 2015). It was followed in 2010 by another initiative called *Operation Chain Reaction – Recommendation for more women on supervisory board* which encouraged companies to recruit more female managers to the supervisory boards of Danish limited liability companies. By 2012, only 55 companies had adopted *Operation Chain Reaction* and so the Danish Parliament legislated in 2013 to require companies to set target figures and prepare a policy if either gender represents less than 40%. Although the new rules are flexible in the sense that no specific quotas are set, given that companies are subject to a reporting duty it can be argued that the rules introduce a form of quota through the back door.

Conclusion

Most European countries that have considered gender balance regulation at board level have opted for a voluntary rather than a mandatory approach, while some have adopted a hybrid approach that combines self-regulation alongside quotas. Norway provides the clearest example of the mandatory approach with a quota backed by sanctions while the UK best exemplifies the self-regulation route based on the comply-or-explain principle. The experience of the UK suggests that substantial progress can be made using a voluntary approach. Against the backdrop of the European Commission's proposed Directive that sets a 40% board seat target, the experience of Norway provides the clearest example of what might lie ahead. The ability of some Norwegian companies to evade the quota, alongside evidence that gender diversity did not improve among those Norwegian companies not subject to the quota, suggests that a one-size-fits-all approach is not necessarily the best approach to follow.

Note

1   The European Institute for Gender Equality, an EU Agency located in Vilnius, Lithuania, is the host of the Gender Statistics Database. The reference is to a source of data available on a website, and not to a specific, dated publication. However, I have now included the European Institute for Gender Equality in the References and included the url and the date accessed. http://eige.europa.eu/gender-statistics/dgs/browse/wmidm.

References

Agustín, L.R., Siim, B. 2015. Dilemmas in the Danish approach to equality without gender quota, European University Institute Working Paper, Department of Law, 2015/27. The European University Institute is located in Florence, Italy.

Ahern, K.R., Dittmar, A. 2012. The changing of the boards: The impact on firm valuation of mandated female board representation, *Quarterly Journal of Economics*, 127(1), 137–197.

Armstrong, A., Walby, S. 2012. Gender Quotas in Management Boards: Note to the European Parliament, http://www.europarl.europa.eu/document/activities/cont/201202/2012 0216ATT38420/20120216ATT38420EN.pdf, accessed 16 February, 2018.

Bøhren, Ø., Staubo, S. 2014. Does mandatory gender balance work? Changing organizational form to avoid board upheaval, *Journal of Corporate Finance*, 28, 152–168.

Bøhren, Ø., Staubo, S. 2016. Mandatory gender balance and board independence, *European Financial Management*, 22(1), 3–30.

Bolsø, A., Sørensen, S.Ø. 2013. How the quota law came about in Tutchell, E., Edmonds, J. (eds.), *Made in Norway: How Norwegians Have Used Quotas to Increase the Number of Women on Company Boards*, London: Labour Finance and Industry Group and the Fabian Women's Network, 1–10.

Borchorst, A. 2009. Women-friendly policy paradoxes? Childcare policies and gender equality visions in Scandinavian in Melby, K., Ravn, A.-B., Wetterberg, Ch.C. (eds.), *Gender Equality and Welfare Politics in Scandinavia: The Limits of Political Ambition?*, Bristol: The Policy Press, 27–42.

Branson, M. 2012. Pathways for women to senior management positions and board seats: An A to Z list, *Michigan State Law Review*, 5, 1505–1585.

Casey, C., Skibnes, R., Pringle, J.K. 2011. Gender equality and corporate governance: Policy strategies in Norway and New Zealand, *Gender, Work, and Organization*, 18(6), 613–630.

Comi, S., Grasseni, M., Origo, F., and Pagan, L. 2016. Quotas have led to More Women on Corporate Boards in Europe, http://www.globalpolicyjournal.com/blog/06/10/2016/quotas-have-led-more-women-corporate-boards-europe, accessed 16 February, 2018.

Dale-Olsen, H., Schøne, P., Verner, M. 2013. Diversity among directors – the impact on performance of a quota for women on company boards, *Feminist Economics*, 19(4), 110–135.

Davies, M. 2011. *Women on Boards*, London: Department for Business, Innovation and Skills.

Davies, M. 2015. *Improving the Gender Balance on British Boards: Women on Boards Davies Review Five Year Summary*, London: Department for Business, Innovation and Skills.

Eckbo, B.E., Nygaard, K., Thorburn, K.S. 2016. Do board gender quotas reduce firm value?, Working Paper, https://ssrn.com/abstract=2746786, accessed 22 July, 2017.

European Commission 2012. Women in economic decision-making in the EU: Progress report, https://publications.europa.eu/en/publication-detail/-/publication/8832ea16-e2e6-4095-b1eb-cc72a22e28df, accessed 16 February, 2018.

European Commission 2012. Proposal for a Directive of the European Parliament and of the Council on improving the gender balance among non-executive directors of companies listed on stock exchanges and related measures, COM(2012) 614 final, http://eur-lex.europa.eu/legal-content/EN/TXT/?uri=CELEX:52012PC0614, accessed 16 February 2018.

European Commission 2013. Cracking Europe's Glass Ceiling: European Parliament backs Commission's Women on Boards proposal, Press Release database, 20 November 2013, http://europa.eu/rapid/press-release_IP-13-1118_en.htm, accessed 16 February 2018.

European Parliament 2018. Legislative Train Schedule, Area of Justice and Fundamental Rights: Gender Balance on Boards, 20 January 2018, http://www.europarl.europa.eu/legislative-train/theme-area-of-justice-and-fundamental-rights/file-gender-balance-on-boards, accessed 16 February, 2018.

European Institute for Gender Equality, http://eige.europa.eu/gender-statistics/dgs, accessed 16 February, 2018.

Ferreira, D. 2015. Board diversity: Should we trust research to inform policy?, *Corporate Governance: An International Review*, 23(2), 108–111.

Financial Reporting Council 2012. The UK Corporate Governance Code, Financial Reporting Council, London.

Fouche, G., Treanor, J. 2006. In Norway, a woman's place is in the boardroom, *The Guardian*, January 9, www.guardian.co.uk/money/2006/jan/09/business.workandcareers, accessed 19 July, 2017.

Hampton, P., Alexander, H. 2016. Hampton-Alexander review: FTSE women leaders improving gender balance in FTSE Leadership, https://ftsewomenleaders.com, accessed 20 July, 2017.

Hermalin, B.E., Weisbach, M.S. 2003. Boards of directors as an endogenously determined institution: A survey of the economics literature, *Federal Reserve Bank of New York Economic Policy Review*, 9(1), 1–20.

Johnsen, S. 2012. Women in work: The Norwegian experience, *OECD Observer*, 293(Q4), 6–7.

Jourová, V. 2016. Gender balance on corporate boards: Europe is cracking the glass ceiling, European Commission, Brussels, Belgium. Directorate-General for Justice and Consumers, Fact Sheet, July.

Karvonen, L., Selle, P. (eds.) 1995. *Women in Nordic Politics: "Closing the Gap"*, Aldershot: Dartmouth.

Kogut, B., Colomer, J., Belinky, M. 2014. Structural equality at the top of the corporation: Mandated quotas for women directors, *Strategic Management Journal*, 35, 891–902.

Labelle, R., Francoeur, C., Lakhal, F. 2015. To regulate or not to regulate? Early evidence on the means used around the world to promote gender diversity in the boardroom, *Gender, Work and Organization*, 22(4), 349–363.

Matsa, D., Miller, A. 2013. A female style in corporate leadership? Evidence from quotas, *American Economic Journal: Applied Economics*, 5(3), 136–169.

Nygaard, K. 2011. Forced board changes: Evidence from Norway, Norwegian School of Economics, Bergen, Norway. Department of Economics Research Paper Series No. 5/2011.

Shaughnessy, B., Braun, S., Hentschel, T., Peus, C.V. 2016. Diverse and just? The role of quota-based selection policies on organizational outcomes, *European Journal of Social Psychology*, 46, 880–890.

Storvik, A. 2011. Women on boards – experience from the Norwegian quota reform, *Cesifo DICE*, 9(1), 34–41.

Strøm, R.Ø. 2015. Gender discrimination before mandated quotas? Evidence from Norway: 1989–2002, *Scandinavian Journal of Management*, 31, 303–315.

Teigen, M. 2012. Gender quotas on corporate boards: On the diffusion of a distinct national policy reform in Engelstad, F., Teigen, M. (eds.), *Firms, Boards and Gender Quotas: Comparative Perspectives*, Bingley: Emerald Group Publishing Limited, 115–146.

Weckes, M. 2016. Beginning cultural change or foreseeable stagnation at 30%? The gender distribution in the supervisory board of the four leading indices, MBF Report No. 21, Hans-Böckler-Stiftung, March.

Part III
Regulation and compliance

4 Gender balance in Australian boardrooms

The business case for quotas

*JF Corkery, Madeline Elizabeth Taylor
and Melanie Hayden*

Introduction

Can corporations still rely on merit to facilitate change in favor of female membership in the boardroom? Leaving aside the issues of board structure, how does diversity (and thus board composition) affect corporate governance? And will quotas fundamentally change the position of women in corporate leadership?

> Merit by its very nature is subjective. It is a combination of experience and a subjective judgment of potential. If we accept that, we accept that relying on merit to overcome systemic gender inequality is fundamentally flawed.
>
> (Baird, 2013 citing Julie McKay, executive director
> of the Australian National Committee for
> UN Women at the time of publication)

In 2010, the ASX Corporate Governance Council introduced recommendation 1.5 advising ASX companies to establish and disclose its corporate diversity policies. The recommendation mandates the board to set measurable objectives for achieving gender diversity and to assess diversity objectives annually:

> At the end of each reporting period [disclose] the measurable objectives for achieving gender diversity set by the board or a relevant committee of the board in accordance with the entity's diversity policy and either the respective proportions of men and women on the board, in senior executive positions and across the organization or if the entity is a relevant employer under the Workplace Gender Equality Act, the most recent Gender Equality Indicators.
>
> (ASX Corporate Governance Council, 2014: 11)

Despite this, ASX female board members in Australia has increased by only 4% from 2004–2017. As at 2015, women represented 8.2% of directors, 4.9% of senior executives, 4.2% of CEOs and 13.0% of CFOs (Diversity Council of Australia, 2015). The number of female directors on Australian boards remains low by international standards. The Diversity Council of Australia Report in 2017 noted that a corporate chair or CEO in an Australian company is more likely to be named 'Peter' or 'John' rather than to be female, and,

> In the ASX 200, there are nine female CEOs, being 4.5% of all ASX 200 CEOs. The rest are males – 13 CEOs are named Andrew and another 13 named Peter, 10 are named John, nine are named David and eight are named Michael.

(Khadem, 2017a)

Further, the number of culturally diverse female ASX CEOs represented only 15 of all 1482 CEOs, 44 of all 2327 senior executives, 188 of all 7491 directors and 55 of all 1350 CFOs. Therefore, just 2.5% of all 7491 ASX directors were culturally diverse women (compared to 5.7% who were non-culturally diverse women).

In 2015, the Australian Institute of Company Directors (AICD) released its 30% target of female board representation by 2018 for ASX 200 companies. By 2016, 51 ASX 200 companies had reached the 30% target; however 20 ASX 200 boards do not have any female representation. In 2016, the AICD chairman, Elizabeth Proust, declared the promotion of women to boards and senior management in Australia had happened at a "glacial pace. . . . The trajectory is not fast enough . . . My maths tells me it [rate of board appointments] needs to be higher than current rate in order to reach 30% by 2018" (Khadem, 2016). A failure to hit the AICD target by 2018 will likely spark the renewed debate for the government to mandate legislative gender quotas. Proust agrees: "quotas will have to be on the table. We will have to have a debate and I would like to broaden it from being about gender to all aspects of diversity" (Khadem, 2016).

This chapter examines the current Australian policy position of 'soft regulatory intervention' (Klettner et al., 2016: 340) to increase women in corporate leadership positions and assesses the potential benefits of enacting mandatory gender quota legislation. The first section of this chapter examines the global context of gender diversity. Many governments in Europe have put in place mandatory quotas for women on corporate boards backed by legal sanctions. Others, including Australia, have taken a softer voluntary approach by recommending that companies set targets and/or disclose policy on gender diversity. Our chapter draws on relevant literature both supportive and opposed to gender diversity on boards falling within two broad categories of arguments, namely fairness, equity and psychology in the context of responsible business practices and value in the context of firm performance (Vafaei et al., 2015). Boardroom diversity effects on performance of firms will then be analyzed as an evolving argument for legislative quotas.

The second part of this chapter explores the importance of improving corporate culture to be more inclusive of women in leadership positions and diminishing male-dominated groupthink in corporations, before examining the gender of leaders and executives in the political and academic sectors. Finally, this chapter concludes in arguing that despite progress of increasing gender diversity in Australia via the soft policy and regulatory approach by ASX, the need for a long-term plan is evident, owing to the complexities of the issue and the current slow progress for women on Australian boards. Therefore, coercive legislative measures in the form of mandatory legislated diversity quotas are needed as an adjunct to the current 'soft regulatory' measures in Australia. It is clear the appetite for change persists, as demonstrated by the volume of literature and reports examining the issue of increasing board diversity in Australia.

Global boardroom diversity

Many countries are now adopting mandatory regulatory positions and specifying either targets or quotas to aid in increased gender diversity. The most significant change in diversity strategy is the popularity of quotas. In May 2013, GMI Ratings *Women on Boards* report (using data from 6,000 companies across 45 countries) reported a slow progression of women in the boardroom (Gladman and Lamb, 2013). Globally, female representation on boards has risen just eight-tenths of one percentage point since 2009 (Noked, 2013).

KPMG's report on *ASX Corporate Governance Council Principles and Recommendations on Diversity* disclosure statistics in 2016 highlighted the continued 'imbalance' on Australian boards (KPMG, 2016a). The report concluded that in ASX 501+ companies only 6% of board members were women, down from 9% in 2013. However, for S&P/ASX 200 companies, 22% of board members were women, up from 18% in 2013; while for ASX 201–500 companies, 15% of board members were women, up from 10% in 2013 (KPMG, 2016a: 5).

While the top ASX 200 companies are improving in gender diversity, Australian companies are far from reaching gender parity, and the percentage of women in CEO and COO/deputy CEO roles has remained stagnant since 2015. Female representation at CFO level actually reduced. In both 2011 and 2016, just 5% of CEOs and 10% of COOs were women; the proportion of CFOs fell from 8% in 2011 to 6% in 2016. (Interestingly, US companies are far more likely to appoint female COOs or CFOs – 17%.)

The KPMG report also noted that, despite 99% of ASX 200 companies holding a diversity policy, "very few companies set or disclosed transparent quantitative objectives such as 30% of director seats to be held by women by 2018" (KPMG, 2016b). The majority of the diversity objectives focused on implementing diversity programs or initiatives such as undertaking a pay equity review, implementing programs in unconscious bias or undertaking an all-employee satisfaction survey. These are all necessary steps to ensure greater diversity, however as the report highlights, "there continued to be a number of entities reporting more 'aspirational' objectives such as achieving a culture of inclusion, making it difficult for these entities to measure progress against their objectives both now and in future years" (KPMG, 2016b).

In comparison, European countries show leadership in boardroom gender diversity. Norway was the first jurisdiction to implement a gender quota of 40% in 2005. This model has been replicated by a number of developed and developing countries. A failure to have at least 40% of female company board members in Norway leads to the company being delisted. Norway now has the highest proportion of female non-executive directors in the world. In 2011, Belgium, Italy, France, Malaysia and the Netherlands followed suit by implementing quotas of 30% or 40% female representation on corporate boards. Germany implemented its 30% gender diversity quota in 2015 (Choobineh, 2016). Norway, Sweden and Finland lead the developed world in their high percentage of female directors, with Norway at 36.1%, Sweden at 27.0% and Finland at 26.8% (Choobineh, 2016).

The US and the UK have, along similar lines to Australia's ASX *Corporate Governance Principles and Recommendations*, instituted voluntary corporate gender diversity guidelines, within the *Sarbanes-Oxley Act* and the Higgs Review. All three jurisdictions encourage but do not require greater diversity on boards. The effectiveness of these 'soft law' internal targets provisions remains to be seen. The majority of firms in the US, UK and Australia that do have female directors have only one female director. Branded as 'tokenism', this has limited impact on the firm (Branson, 2006).

In the UK, female board membership has crept to 4% since 2009 and, although they have published guidelines, the UK government remains opposed to a legislated quota, despite the European Parliament call for EU wide legislation requiring 40% quotas by 2020. The *2009 Securities and Exchange Commission proxy disclosure rules to enhance US corporate diversity requirements* states:

> Companies are required to disclose whether diversity is considered by the nominating committee in nominating directors, and if so, how it impacts the nomination process. Additionally, if the nominating committee or the board has a policy with regard to the consideration of diversity in identifying director nominees, the rules require disclosure of how this policy is implemented and how the nominating committee or the board assesses the effectiveness of its policy.
>
> (Krus et al., 2012: 7)

In the US, section 342 of the *Dodd-Frank Wall Street Reform and Consumer Protection Act 2010* requires "all financial regulators undertake significant efforts to recruit and promote employees from all backgrounds" (Krus et al., 2012: 8). In the absence of a legislative quota, US boards have also seen little progress towards gender diversity for more than a decade, with the increase of merely 5% of female board members since 2001. Similarly, Canada's progress on boardroom diversity has been stagnant at 13.1% since 2013 (Noked, 2013). Meanwhile, some Asian countries come in much lower in progressing towards an increase in gender diversity: for example, in Japan, just 3.5% of board members are female. Qatar hardly makes a ripple – 0.9%, while the UAE is marginally better – 1.1% (Noked, 2013).

Nonetheless, the influence of quotas is now reaching the developing world. India passed The Companies Bill in December 2012. Chapter XI requires "public companies must have at least one woman director and minimum of three directors in total" (Deloitte, 2013: 13). India currently has the fastest growing number of female board members, with a 5.5% increase since 2010 amounting to 11.2% of female board members (Noked, 2013). In 2011, the Malaysian

Cabinet approved a quota to ensure at least "30% representation of women in decision-making positions in the private sector to promote gender equality by 2016" (Deloitte, 2013: 15). Women now comprise 10% of boards in Malaysia, up from 6% in 2010.

A recent study of boardroom gender diversity in Brazilian businesses found 4.5% of Brazilian board members are female (Lazzaretti et al., 2013). The lack of female participation in Brazilian boardrooms has been linked to the "image of good management culturally attributed to men" (Lazzaretti et al., 2013: 105). The Brazilian Senate argues a legislative quota must be enacted to require a 40% female representation on boards by 2020 to aim for the level of gender diversity within some EU nations (Lazzaretti et al., 2013). Without doubt, countries enacting quota legislation lead the push for increased boardroom diversity.

Credit Suisse says women held 14.7% of board seats in 2015, after an examination of over 3,000 global companies in 2016. 73.5% had at least one woman director, while just 20.1% held at least three female board members (Credit Suisse, 2016: 2).

The equity argument

A call for gender equity is a call for fairness to women and men. This implies there should be equal access to resources and equal opportunities. Women have been historically disadvantaged and they have different life experiences, goes the argument. Thus, they should be compensated and any inequality of resources and opportunities redressed, so that there is a level playing field. Equity is required to enable equality to take place.

Mari Teigen uses the word justice instead of fairness. She lists arguments and counter-arguments on gender quotas: improving individual justice, utilitarianism and social justice in "shifting the question of affirmative action for women from 'why women?' to 'why not women' "? (Teigen, 2000: 65). Individual justice is grounded within the concept of the right to equal opportunities and non-discrimination for individuals and, she argues, the merit criterion should dominate in governance decisions (Teigen, 2000). Utilitarianism emphasizes the direct effect of gender inclusion and diversity on company boards and its positive effects on the economy and the firm generally. Social justice favors a more egalitarian society representing women's rights as a collective. Consequently, women's influence in the workplace, a more equal distribution of labor between the sexes, and a balanced representation on company boards is necessary for a democratic egalitarian society.

The resource dependency theory postulates that firms are viewed as open systems that are dependent on the external environment's unpredictability (Pfeffer and Salancik, 1978). Pfeffer's and Salancik's research has shown that women bring different knowledge to the industry that can enable the organization to reduce risk stemming from its dependence on the environment. In this vein, women have been shown to be more willing to engage in higher-quality analysis (Pfeffer and Salancik, 1978). This leads to a higher rate of efficiency in decisions made at a board level. Further, a woman's predisposition to be risk-averse has been shown to prevent boards from entering risky projects (Byrnes et al., 1999). While this is not always beneficial, this is generally perceived as the safer option. A more risk-averse team would arguably have saved several major corporations and the economy from rapid collapse in 2007–2008.

Women are also more likely to hold CEOs accountable and to ensure CEOs are replaced when corporations are becoming insolvent. The capability of a board to take the initiative to encourage CEO turnover due to a fall in stock performance has proven vital in recent years during the Global Financial Crisis. Research undertaken by Adams and Ferreira in 2009 has shown women to be tougher, finding that for a firm with no female directors, a one-standard deviation fall in the stock performance (-0.47) increased the probability of CEO turnover by 9.87% (Adams and Ferreira, 2009). Contrasting this proposition, the same study found that if female directors encompass 40% of board positions, this probability increases to 15.23% (Adams and Ferreira, 2009). This indicates that women are more risk-averse and willing to make difficult calls to ensure the consistent profitability of the company. As stated by KPMG's 2017 ASX 300+ report, "Female CEOs in the ASX 300+ delivered a 9% increase in revenue in 2016, compared to the group-wide average of 0.5%" (KPMG, 2017: 4).

Pfeffer and Salancik argue that the three most important resources for a firm are advice and counsel, legitimacy, and channels for communicating information between the firm and external organizations (Pfeffer and Salancik, 1978). The institutional theory suggests that an organization can only be perceived as legitimate when its means and ends appear to conform to social norms, values and expectations. Legitimacy can be sought through either substantive or symbolic management. Increasing women on boards will be a substantive change to management as it creates a real change in the organizational structure. Studies have also proposed that directors have a duty to increase the firm's standing, and increasing its perception of legitimacy is therefore a necessity (Lim et al., 2007). Accordingly, promoting women will satisfy stakeholders and increase workplace motivation (Bear et al., 2010).

In contrast, counter-arguments to quotas within the literature argues that the quota system should not replace a 'merit-based' system, as women who receive boardroom seats by a mandate will be unlikely to be as successful as those women who were voluntarily given seats based solely on merit. It is also argued that quota systems tend to be seen as a blunt tool to solve a complex and tangled problem, as stated by Lansing and Chandra: "The concern being that this system will force firms to either pad their boardrooms with token non-executive female directors, or, allocate real power on the basis of sex rather than merit" (Lansing and Chandra, 2012: 3). These concerns are reinforced in the Norwegian example via the 'Golden Skirts'; women who sit on multiple different boards are tokenistic and this limits opportunities for other women to rise to leadership positions (Lansing and Chandra, 2012).

Rhode and Packel state that the under-representation of women on corporate boards is due to "a lack of prioritisation within companies, under-representation of women and minorities in the traditional pipeline, in-group bias, gender stereotypes regarding competence and leadership and lack of interest from women" (Rhode and Packel, 2014: 402). However, as Dhir points out, just 20% of new independent board members appointed in 2015 met the criteria of necessary executive-level or board experience, and far more of those newly appointed independent directors were men (137) rather than women (95) of S&P 500 companies (Dhir, 2015: 11). Further, Dhir argues that as board nomination processes rely heavily on social networks of existing directors, newly appointed directors tend to hold similar socio-demographic characteristics of existing directors. The 'pool problem' criticism of quotas argues the lack of a large pool of women to appoint as directors means that board appointments tend to draw from the same small pool of female talent (Dhir, 2015: 38).

Dhir also finds some boardroom challenges created by quota legislation in Norway, citing that decision-making processes may be longer, there may be less initial bonding among directors, and boards may experience some additional conflicts arising from the introduction of different perspectives. However, when interviewing directors on this criticism, Dhir found some directors saw the prolonged decision-making as either a positive or as a fault of the management, rather than due to quota legislation. Overall, Dhir's finding suggests gender diversity due to quota legislation in Norwegian boardrooms as:

> quota-induced diversity has positively affected boardroom work and firm governance . . . the quota compelled directors to look beyond their social networks and the traditional pipeline . . . quota law has helped to redistribute power in society by giving so many women access to a coveted site of corporate leadership.
>
> (Dhir, 2015: 101)

Boardroom diversity quotas have emerged as one of the critical corporate governance reforms of the last two decades. The global nature of the development of boardroom diversity and its impact on firm performance, corporate social responsibility and organizational health has sparked scholarly and political debate in gender quota designs and its long-term effect on firms. This has led to recognition by corporate actors of the positive role of increased female representation due to legislative quotas spurring dramatic increases in women elected to corporate boards around the world.

The psychology case

As women participate more in management in meaningful numbers, it is asked what each gender contributes or adds to the leadership of groups and companies. Do the genders offer different qualities? Should the boardroom be selected, rather like a sports team, to meet defined managerial needs of corporations?

The answers from psychological research is unclear. There is the stereotypical response: that, according to the research, men and women are equally effective in some settings, less so in others – their effectiveness depending on their typical skills: For example, women's typically more mentoring, coaching style is more favorably received in female-dominated professions; men's more typically 'command-and-control' style is well received in male-dominated professions. As stated by Paustain-Underdahl et al.,

> According to the research, while men and women are equally effective in some settings, more often effectiveness depends on the fit between the setting and management gender. For example, women's typically more mentoring, coaching style is more favorably received in female-dominated professions.
>
> (Paustian-Underdahl et al., 2014)

Some research shows that women are more effective in middle and senior management than men. If so, then the slowness to promote more women into higher levels of management and the inequality of pay between men and women on the same job requires further research. There appears to be a dual standard of competence, where women have to prove themselves more competent to get to the top and earn the top pay compared to expectations on men.

It is noteworthy that psychologically men and women reduce the behavioral differences between the genders, and in some of their management behaviors, in the more urgent society of today, women prove to be more adaptable. The global digital economy demands more mental power and less might, "as organizations have become fast-paced, globalized environments, some organizational scholars have proposed that a more feminine style of leadership is needed to emphasize the participative and open communication needed for success" (Paustian-Underdahl et al., 2014).

Research suggests that women have come to symbolize increased competence in the boardroom and this "new cultural symbolism may be fuelled in part by exposure of the illegal and unethical business practices of Enron and other businesses led by men" (Eagly and Carli, 2003: 809). At the least, management selection now comes from an enlarged pool of talent that women's emergence has created. This of itself increases companies' abilities to find leaders who are effective in the modern economy.

The business case

Statistics from the last decade support a business case for employing women. A 2001 study of Fortune 500 companies found that "those with a high number of women executives outperformed median competitors in their industry, and that companies that scored best in terms of promoting women were consistently more profitable" (Adler, 1998: 3). The *McKinsey Quarterly Report* of 2011 found that even on a small scale there are direct correlations among large numbers of senior women, financial performance and organizational health. An enhanced return on equity, combined contributions of a more diverse skill-set and the holistic consideration of issues through the implementation of more diverse boards, will provide long-term benefits through greater boardroom diversity.

As Julie McKay implies in the opening quotation to this chapter, the current subjective judgment of potential used to assess merit is only going to continue to see men selected by men at the top levels. One of the most concerning organizational factors holding women back is the perceived lack of a mentor. Women argue that this reduces their credibility and legitimacy, and that they are disadvantaged without access to a sponsor's network. Further, mentors can overcome stereotypes, male hierarchies and lack of informal networks (Tharenou, 1999). Corkery and Taylor discusses the merit issue and questions the sincerity of the renewed enthusiasm for merit in the selection of board members: "[I]t's as if merit has always been the basis for appointments" (Corkery and Taylor, 2012: 2).

Even if it is considered that appointments are based on merit, researchers and academics still find it difficult to believe that with more women graduates than men, women still are not equally worthy of board appointments. In a 2011 UK review of the actions being taken to encourage women on boards, Lord Davies wrote in the Foreword:

> [G]iven the long record of women achieving the highest qualifications and leadership positions in many walks of life, the poor representation of women on boards, relative to their male counterparts, has raised questions about whether board recruitment is in practice based on skills, experience and performance.
>
> (Lord Davies, 2015: 2)

Despite increased graduate numbers at entry level, women are lagging behind. There are more women than men at entry level. This is surprising; as statistics from most Western developed countries have increasingly shown that there are consistently more female law and MBA graduates than male. In 2011–2014, in the US there have been one million more female graduates than male, a reversal from ten years before.

Further, in Australia since 1989 there have been more females entering higher education in Australia than men and more females complete their degrees successfully than men. Young Australian women are still less likely than men to transition into full engagement in work, study or a combination of the two. This gap between men and women narrowed over time until 2002, but has since remained unchanged. There are certainly societal changes encouraging more women to get an education, but as Carter and Silva insist, more should be done to encourage women to stay in the workforce and participate at higher levels.

Another ongoing concern is the 'work–life balance' issue. Despite the significant growth in wage equality and the surge in education of women, according to economists Justin Wolfers and Betsey Stevenson, women are less 'happy' today than women were in 1972 – both in absolute terms and also relatively compared to men (Stevenson and Wolfers, 2009: 190). This presents a further struggle for female leaders that are pushing one another – we need to find a way to encourage women to have a choice and make their own choice; but still improve the overall statistics.

Leading women's organization Chief Executive Women partnered with Bain & Company in 2011 to provide strategic advice on what can be done to encourage greater levels of female empowerment. The research followed a 2011 survey completed by Bain & Company which found that 75% of members of the Australian business community felt that gender diversity should be a 'strategic imperative' for their organization. The paper 'What stops women from reaching the top? Confronting the tough issues' found that 83% of surveyed respondents felt that women's careers are disrupted by the work–life balance; and that women's choice played a large role, with 69% of respondents agreeing that women choose a more balanced lifestyle instead of their own career progression (Sanders et al., 2011).

There are already considerably fewer women than men at first-level manager. By the time both genders reach middle managerial roles, there is at least two times the amount of men in managerial positions. So, with CEOs and senior executives, it is not surprising that the percentage of women in C-level roles is still in single digits in all developed nations. Globally, investors, regulators and other market participants continue to have a growing focus on the need for board gender diversity and greater transparency of corporate initiatives.

While encouraging, growth in recent statistics is too slow to ensure significant numbers and positive change in the next decade. As Sandberg writes, women hold only 17% of total board seats in the US, only a minor increase from 14% ten years ago. Growth in female graduate numbers, shown through linear programming, will only have a very marginal impact on women's representation on governing bodies. At the current rate of growth in the US, it would take at least 70 years for women to reach parity with men on Fortune 500 boards (Joy, 2008). The same statistic is disclosed in Lord Davies's 2011 paper 'Women on boards review' from the UK (Lord Davies, 2011).

Dobbin and Jung cite the 'reverse causation' argument as evidence that boardroom quotas are not needed. They argue that strong corporate performance leads to increased board diversity, rather than diverse boards. Dobbin and Jung's later research supported the finding of Adams and Ferreira "that the cross-sectional positive relationship found between board diversity and corporate performance is likely spurious – a consequence of reverse causation" (Dobbin and Jung, 2011: 820). Similarly, Reskin, McBrier and Kmec argue that quota legislation leads to 'tokenism' whereby the interests of women in boardrooms as a minority group is promoted for political reasons, rather than diversity being embraced as an opportunity based upon individual merit (Reskin et al., 1999).

Despite counter-arguments and resistance to the implementation of quotas, it makes little business or economic sense to resist diversity. Diversity on boards is not only fair morally and socially, evidence suggests that it improves corporate performance. Rodriguez-Dominguez et al. assert that "a more diverse work team will evince a better preparation for more appropriate decisions and problem solving" (Rodriguez-Dominguez et al., 2012: 618). Baroness Mary Goudie, a senior member of the British House of Lords and a founder of the *30% Club*, believes having gender-varied boards "deters groupthink . . . improves the decision-making process, ensures talent is functioning optimally, and helps businesses redefine CSR policies" (Quast, 2013).[1]

Lisa Fairfax is co-director of the *Direct Women Board Institute* promoting board diversity and advocates the economic, moral and social justifications to diversify the corporate boardroom (Fairfax, 2011). A 2014 study indicates that boardrooms with greater gender diversity spend less on capital, development and acquisitions. They were more risk-averse, which may lower the long-term results for the company. While their shares show lower volatility in price, "firms with more diverse boards are more likely to pay dividends as well as pay greater amount of dividend per share than those with less diverse boards" (Casey, 2014). Despite numerous reports, opinions and academic literature pointing to women on the board increasing equality, business advantages and profits, 49% of Fortune 1000 companies have one or no women on their boards (Casey, 2014).

WIM and PWC UK concluded in 2013 that the mining industry has the lowest number of women on boards of any industry in the world. Women occupy just 5% of board seats in the top 500 mining companies (van Dyke and Dallmann, 2013). The research indicated that:

> 18 mining companies with 25% or more female board members had an average net profit margin in 2011 financial year 49% higher than the average net profit margin for top 500 mining companies . . . mining companies with female board members had a higher average profit margin overall (23%) than the average net profit margin of the top 100 mining companies (20%).
>
> (van Dyke and Dallmann, 2013: 9)

Data linking improved financial performance to board diversity in the mining industry are consistent with numerous reports from Catalyst, Credit Suisse and McKinsey.

Groupthink and cultural change

Corporate governance literature suggests diverse boards better "fulfil their conformance and performance roles, because diversity is seen as a way to combat the group-thinking problem" (Bohdanowicz, 2012: 10). A diversified board changes the strongly homo-centric structure of boards that can lead to groupthink. Zelechowski's and Bilimoria's work demonstrates that "three women are required to change boardroom groupthink dynamics and a 'critical mass' of 30% or more women at board level produces the best financial results" (Zelechowski and Bilimoria, 2004: 339).

Internationally, led by the Norwegian legal requirements to appoint women on corporate boards, progress with women on boards has become a measure of progressive corporate culture. The move towards gender diversity is frequently welcomed by shareholders and various stakeholders. It tends to strengthen the value of the company brand and its value on the share market. The *FidAR WoB Index*, which provides public ranking of companies, suggest that gender diversity cements a corporation's image as a progressive firm, as a female-friendly employer and as a socially responsible organization (Machold et al., 2013). Agencies such as Bloomberg and Reuters now routinely compile indices for socially responsible investors, including women's representation on boards as a good governance measure. To build a sustainable reputation, companies' top-ranking must be secured by a well-founded governance and HR strategy over a long-term horizon. Morley reiterates the need for women on boards: "In these challenging times, the stakes are too high to keep the status quo . . . It is time to act now in order to speed up progress and achieve more concrete results" (Morley, 2010: 28).

Two of the largest corporation collapses this century – Enron and HIH Insurance – occurred at a time where there were few women on boards and a prevalence of groupthink, where there is such conformity in a group that independent thinking and innovation are all but impossible. Pioneering writer in this field, O'Connor, identified groupthink as a major boardroom villain. She considered that greater board diversity would mean less group paralysis, better ethical outcomes and reduced fraud. But while women executives' behavioral traits may foster honesty in the workplace, it is more important to emphasize how these cognitive differences also impede women's progress in climbing the corporate ladder. In general, she argues, "businesswomen must master a high-wire act that manoeuvres around the 'double bind' – a woman executive cannot be too masculine or feminine" (O'Connor, 2006: 468).

Another societal hurdle is the key lack of women who support women in the industry. The perception is still that incumbent women are reluctant to form the same collegial ties that many men in the same industries have formulated. The drift towards excessive bureaucracy brings on "the metaphysical pathos of much of the modern theory of group organisation . . . that of pessimism and fatalism" (Gouldner, 1955: 498). Strategic choice by both female and male leaders can overcome organizational paralysis, though, and strategic change in the participation of women in leadership can come if they are convinced of the need and devote the required time and resources (Aguilera et al., 2007: 844).

Thomson et al. see three key stages to effect cultural change and increase boardroom diversity:

> Senior people become convinced that gender balance on their boards, and among their senior executives, is advantageous. Organisations begin actively to promote gender diversity through their recruitment, promotion, talent management and succession planning policies. Gender-balanced boards and executive committees become the norm.
>
> (Thomson et al., 2015: 224)

Having diversity targets alone does not lead to improvement of firm performance. The culture of the organization from the top down is what matters. This starts with boards appointing the right CEO, and firms being "really committed to it [diversity], not just reading the lines" (Khadem, 2017b) as OZ Minerals' chairman Neil Hamilton puts it. Telstra chairman John Mullen believes "men tend to be more set in their ways. . . . The women I have worked with are more ready to challenge their own assumptions" (Khadem, 2017b).

Australian organizations must change their corporate culture, starting from the recruitment process in ensuring female-centric recruiters and removing any biases in interview questioning to workplace policies such as paid parental leave and flexible working to support and promote women gaining the necessary skills to move from managerial roles to senior executives. As highlighted by Du Plessis, O'Sullivan and Rentschler:

> A change in cultural attitudes, so that the advantages of diversity are recognised and female participation encouraged, will increase the quantity of qualified, experienced female directors in a sustainable and productive manner.
>
> (du Plessis et al., 2014: 27)

Extensive research has been undertaken on the proposition that women are, or are seen to be, intrinsically less suited to management. The *Heidi Roizen* case study at Columbia Business School was instructive. The students were asked to appraise the resume and background of *Howard* Roizen, who had industry experience at top companies including Apple, entrepreneurial skills, and a powerful network of contacts. The case study also described the opinion of Howard from colleagues as a 'captain of industry' and a 'catalyst' in the market (Muir, 2012). Half the class were given exactly the same data but attached to the name *Heidi* Roizen. Students found Heidi to be selfish and someone who they did not want to hire. In contrast, students with Howard's paper found him to be efficient and likeable.

The *Heidi v Howard Roizen* case study was reflected in a 2011 study surveying 60,000 workers in the US. The conclusions reached in this research supported the proposition that women are not perceived equally by their peers and subordinates. Seventy-two percent of respondents (out of the 46% that expressed a preference for their boss's gender) stated a preference for a male manager (Elsesser and Lever, 2011). The NSW government referred to the *Heidi v Howard* study in a 2012 paper and Australian sex discrimination commissioner, Elizabeth Broderick, says this societal 'belief barrier' has a damaging impact on women and an ability to progress in the workplace. Her perception of Australian society, and its belief that a good mother must be with her children and therefore cannot be available more than five days a week, is consistent with the McKinsey finding that the dominant model used in businesses continues to hold women back.

The gender of executives in differing sectors

Politics

The roots of gender parity in elected office is enshrined in the *Universal Declaration of Human Rights 1948*, which protects the equal rights of men and women, including the right to participate in government.[2] As at 1 October 2013, women occupy only one-fifth of all seats in national legislatures worldwide. In a global study of gender political quota laws, Schwindt-Bayer concludes:

> If a 30% quota has a placement mandate and strong enforcement mechanisms, women make up 27% of the national legislature, on average. If a 30% quota, however, does not have a placement mandate and no enforcement mechanisms, then women make up 10% of the national legislature, on average.
>
> (Schwindt-Bayer, 2009: 6)

In 1995, a report by the UN Development Programme concluded that 30% was the 'critical minority' required for "women as a group to exert a meaningful influence in legislative assemblies" (Inter-Parliamentary Union, 2005). As of 2012, ten African countries adopted a gender quota law for national legislative elections. However, the percentage of female representations after legislative enactment varies between African countries. In Algeria, Angola, Burundi and Senegal, women constituted 30% or more of the national legislature following the adoption of the gender quota law. Conversely, in Burkina Faso, Djibouti and Niger women represent less than 17% of the national legislatures (Hoodfar and Takali, 2011).

Nordic countries excel in holding the highest participation of women in politics at 42% in the lower houses. In contrast, the Pacific region (including Australia) holds the lowest percentage at 15.9% with both houses combined (Joy, 2013). Gender quotas in politics, as in other sectors, depend upon the prevailing culture to increase female representation. Adoption of gender quotas has reframed gender equality from a formalistic elucidation as equality before the law, towards the broad equality in opportunities and outcomes (Meier, 1998).

NGO advocacy promoting political leadership equality is an increasing phenomenon. For example, the Running Start program's mission is to engage young women in politics by introducing secondary school girls to the importance of women in leadership and equipping them with training in public speaking, networking and media training (Running Start, 2014). Despite the evident NGO advocacy for female participation in politics, many parties around the globe reject or resist the idea of a legislative quota within politics. In lieu of formal quotas, however, some parties have introduced voluntary targets to encourage the selection of female candidates.

In New Zealand, after the rejection of a party quota system (Dahlerup, 2006: 197) the NZ Labour Party constitution includes a principle of 'gender balance' for all selection procedures. Australia is one of ten Commonwealth countries in which one or more major political parties has adopted a voluntary political party quota system. The Australian Labor Party adopted a voluntary political party quota in 1994 (McCann, 2013),[3] and in 2012 the Party's constitution set out an affirmative action model of 40:40:20, whereby a minimum of 40% of relevant positions must be held by each gender. The Coalition parties (Liberals and Nationals) reject gender quotas and instead 'support and encourage participation'. The greatest increases in women's parliamentary representation have occurred in those countries with legislated quotas.

Academia

There is consistently low representation of women in senior positions of academia in countries within divergent geopolitical contexts. *The Association of Commonwealth Universities* reports that in 23 of the 35 countries in the Commonwealth, universities are led by men only (ACU, 2009). Women comprise 15.3% of professors and 29.1% of associate professors and senior lecturers across the Commonwealth, according to Morley (Morley, 2010: 29). As stated by the European Commission, "Inequality must be addressed by taking measures to systematically introduce the gender perspective in human resource development and in future research. This includes training the decision makers" (European Commission, 2008).

Among Commonwealth countries, women's participation in management and academic leadership is higher than average in developed countries including Australia, Canada and the UK. In contrast, few women are heads of administration in South Asian or African countries (Morley, 2010: 28). Enacting a quota for academic employment has been advocated by commentators since the 1970s. Kay believes:

> In a work environment in which intellectual and collegial interaction and respect is highly prized, the voluntary adoption of such a policy would go far towards alleviating the present strains caused by past societal neglect of the qualities and aspirations of women and minority group members.
>
> (Kay, 1979: 149)

Further, Lipton identifies the embedded gender biases in research output reporting, such as within the Australian government's Excellence in Research for Australia (ERA) initiative. Her study finds that the "ERA is a tool of neoliberal corporate new managerialism, which has significant gendered consequences for women in higher education. It is a quality assurance measure that, in its current form, does not benefit women in academia" (Lipton, 2015: 67). While the implementation of quality assurance was created as an opportunity to make visible women's contributions in academia, it is clear management positions of women in academia within this framework "are often a horizontal sidestep away from centralised executive leadership and positions of influence, which may limit the impact such roles have on university strategy and decision making" (Lipton, 2015: 68). White et al. finds that women occupy more junior positions in academia, while promotional panels and interview committees remain dominated by senior academic men (White et al., 2011). As such, women in academia continue to be redirected from pathways to influential leadership positions. Consequently, in Australian higher education, women leadership capability is still considered to be of 'soft' management skills, which are undervalued in a management culture focused on research output.

Conclusion: a holistic approach to board diversity

This chapter argues that we need solutions as research has shown that typically CEOs 'pass the baton' onto an inside director already within the firm and women are currently not in the pool of candidates. It may be that all we need to do is to recruit more female directors, and then the problem will resolve itself. Catalyst reports:

> A clear and positive correlation exists between the percentage of women board directors in the past and the percentage of corporate officers in the future. The more women board directors the company has in its past, the more women corporate officers it will have in the future.
>
> (Catalyst, 2008: 3)

Some commentators argue that quotas will not assist the morale of women, nor gain any respect from the men already on boards. While a mandated requirement for women on boards would increase diversity, this alone does not necessarily lead to better board performance. It is crucial that any mandated change ensures that merit is still the primary factor for selection.

A flaw in the free market argument is the subjectivity of merit, and the potential presence of structural bias. The free market approach has, at least to this point, failed. Implementing mandatory quotas is not a risk-free endeavor – women may not be treated as equals, especially by embittered sexists who believe that women obtained their positions out of legislative sympathy. Their opinions might not be valued. This in turn could cause discomfort and dissatisfaction, as well as board-room tension, forcing women back out.

Catalyst hypothesizes that companies with two or more female board members in 2000 would have 28% more female board members in 2005 than companies with one female board member in 2000 (Catalyst, 2008). A legislative quota system would, by example, enable an increased number of women on boards and the system will trickle down to the next generation of female leaders. The implicit appeal of the quota is the positive future for female corporate leaders; as Fine suggests, "although the first generation of women leaders may encounter significant prejudice, their experience can pave the way for others to go further" (Fine, 2012). The concerns cited previously may be ameliorated by a larger, supportive female presence.

Quotas need not be permanent measures. Sunset dates could be set for them. But they would be the jumpstart required to overwhelm the biases that inhibit greater female representation. The question then becomes, do the rewards of diversity outweigh the risks? Some countries, such as Norway, have taken the gamble and it seems to be paying off. Less controversial measures than quotas might be taken. These could include a greater acceptance of the need for females at senior management level, and collaboration in our top companies to ensure effective management of career-life transitions. This is only possible in organizational cultures where diversity is valued, and where a variety of leadership styles and skills are rewarded.

McKinsey's (2007) report contemplated a variety of factors that would provide women with greater accessibility to board roles, and other senior industry roles, without necessitating a quota in all developed societies. Companies need to provide greater support services and facilities to avoid the 'work–life balance' barrier that placates women from their first entry-level interviews. In particular, this should include increasing the availability of career progression programs and providing tailored career plans for all staff at entry level in the firm. Providing mentoring programs for women has continually shown to be a leading factor that not only provides women with necessary skills, but increases their confidence and perception that they are suitable for the job. Mentoring more junior women throughout the development of their career is expected to have an influence on the number of women who choose to stay in the business industry and progress to director roles.

The most encouraging development in Australia has been a rising awareness of the inequity and intractability of the imbalance. When that sits beside the evidence of enhanced profitability that diversity can bring, the case for gender equity becomes powerful. It benefits the company to have both genders properly represented there – we have come to see the economic benefits of diversity.

In March 2013, the ASX Group released a diversity report that indicated 196 of the ASX 200 have now adopted a diversity policy, or provided reasons to the ASX to explain why they do not deem it necessary to have one. This level of transparency is critical, and further accountability for inaction from the ASX is necessary, at this time, for any effects to stabilize long term. As this chapter has demonstrated, just as important as the recruitment of qualified professional women for Australia's boards is maintaining a high level of participation by women in senior executive and governance roles throughout major Australian listed companies. It is clear from our research that there is no simple solution. A legislative quota appears to be the most realistic interim solution, but will only be effective in conjunction with strong corporate leadership, enhanced company cultures that support gender equality at all levels, and continued ongoing promotion and sponsorship of Australia's greatest potential women leaders.

Notes

1 Baroness Mary Goudie believes that women are more pro-active in pursuing CSR policies associated with education, food security and human trafficking policies.
2 Other UN documents rectified promoting gender parity in politics including the *World Plan of Action* in Mexico City in 1975, *the Convention on the Elimination of All Forms of Discrimination against Women* in 1979 and the *Nairobi Forward-Looking Strategies* in 1985 which lead to the creation of the *1995 Beijing Platform for Action*, signed by all Member States at the UN to a specific target of 30% women in decision-making positions.
3 Women preselected for 35% of winnable seats.

References

ACU 2009. Annual Report, www.acu.ac.uk/about-us/council-senior-management/acu-annual-report-2009-2010, accessed 12 January, 2017.
Adams, R.B., Ferreira, D. 2009. Women in the boardroom and their impact on governance and performance, *Journal of Financial Economics*, 94, 291–309.

Adler, R. 1998. Women in the executive suite correlate to high profits, www.csripraktiken. se/wp-content/uploads/adler_web.pdf, accessed 4 February, 2017.

Aguilera, R., Rupp, D., Williams, C., Ganapathi, D. 2007. Putting the S back in corporate social responsibility: A multilevel theory of social change in organizations, *Academy of Management Review*, 32(3), 836–863.

ASX Corporate Governance Council 2014. CGC principles and recommendations, www. asx.com.au/documents/asx-compliance/cgc-principles-and-recommendations-3rd-edn. pdf, accessed 10 April, 2016.

Baird, J. 2013. Cabinet vs community. Marie Claire, www.marieclaire.com.au/article/news/ diversity-in-cabinet, accessed 8 August, 2016.

Bear, S., Rahman, N., Post, C. 2010. The impact of board diversity and gender composition on corporate social responsibility and firm reputation, *Journal of Business Ethics*, 97, 207–221.

Bohdanowicz, L. 2012. Ownership structure and female directors on two-tier boards: Evidence from Polish listed companies, https://papers.ssrn.com/sol3/papers.cfm?abstract_ id=2117870, accessed 10 August, 2016.

Branson, D. 2006. *No Seat at the Table: How Corporate Governance Keeps Women Out of America's Boardrooms*, New York: New York University Press.

Byrnes, J., Miller, D., Schafer, W. 1999. Gender differences in risk taking: A meta-analysis, *Psychological Bulletin*, 125(3), 367–383.

Casey, M. 2014. Study finds a diverse corporate boards rein in risk, good for shareholders, *Fortune*, July 30, http://fortune.com/2014/07/30/study-finds-a-diverse-corporate-boards-rein-in-risk-good-for-shareholders/, accessed 3 February, 2017.

Catalyst 2008. Advancing women leaders: The connection between women board directors and women corporate officers, www.catalyst.org/system/files/Advancing_Women_ Leaders_The_Connection_Between_Women_Board_Directors_and_Women_Corporate_ Officers_0.pdf, accessed 8 March, 2017.

Choobineh, N. 2016. Gender quotas for corporate boards: A holistic analysis, http:// repository.upenn.edu/joseph_wharton_scholars/21, accessed 10 May, 2017.

Corkery, J., Taylor, M. 2012. The gender gap: A quota for women on the board, *Corporate Governance eJournal*, 27, 1–14.

Credit Suisse 2016. The CS gender 3000: The reward for change, www.tribunafeminista. org/wordpress/wp-content/uploads/2016/09/csri_gender_3000.pdf, accessed 8 May, 2017.

Dahlerup, D. 2006. *Women, Quotas and Politics*. London: Routledge.

Deloitte 2013. Women in the boardroom, www.deloitte.com/assets/Dcom-Global/ Local%20Assets/Documents/dttl_Women%20in%20the%20boardroom2_2013.pdf, accessed 12 August, 2016.

Dhir, A. 2015. *Challenging Boardroom Homogeneity: Corporate Law, Governance and Diversity*, Toronto: Cambridge University Press.

Diversity Council of Australia 2015. Capitalising on culture and gender in ASX leadership, www.dca.org.au/dca-research/capitalising-on-culture-and-gender-in-asx-leadership. html#sthash.70MQLwtV.dpuf, accessed 8 January, 2017.

Dobbin, F., Jung, J. 2011. Corporate board gender diversity and stock performance: The competence gap or institutional investor bias?, *North Carolina Law Review*, 89, 809–819.

du Plessis, J., O'Sullivan, J., Rentschler, R. 2014. Multiple layers of gender diversity on corporate boards: To force or not to force?, *Deakin Law Review*, 19(1), 1–50.

Eagly, A., Carli, L. 2003. The female leadership advantage: An evaluation of the evidence, *The Leadership Quarterly*, 14, 807–834.

Elsesser, K., Lever, J. 2011. Does gender bias against female leaders persist? Quantitative and qualitative data from a large-scale survey, *Human Relations*, 64(12), 1555–1578.

European Commission 2008. Mapping the maze getting more women to the top in research, http://ec.europa.eu/research/science-society/document_library/pdf_06/mapping-the-maze-getting-more-women-to-the-top-in-research_en.pdf, accessed 11 March, 2017.

Fairfax, L. 2011. Revisiting justifications for board diversity, www.conference-board.org/retrievefile.cfm?filename=TCB-DN-V3N22-11.pdf&type=subsite, accessed 8 March, 2017.

Fine, C. 2012. Status quota, *The Monthly*, March, www.themonthly.com.au/issue/2012/march/1330562640/cordelia-fine/status-quota, accessed 10 January, 2017.

Gladman, K., Lamb, M. 2013. GMI ratings' 2013 women on boards survey, www.calstrs.com/sites/main/files/file-attachments/gmiratings_wob_042013-1.pdf, accessed 16 October, 2016.

Gouldner, A.W. 1955. Metaphysical pathos and the theory of bureaucracy, *American Political Science Review*, 49(2), 496–507.

Hoodfar, H., Takali, M. 2011. Electoral politics making quotas work for women, www.wluml.org/sites/wluml.org/files/Electoral%20Politics%20-%20Making%20Quotas%20Work%20for%20Women%20%28final%29_0.pdf, accessed 2 February, 2017.

Inter-Parliamentary Union 2005. Parliament and democracy in the 21st century preliminary report by the inter-parliamentary union, www.ipu.org/splz-e/sp-conf05/democracy-rpt.pdf, accessed 14 February, 2017.

Joy, L. 2008. Women board directors in the united states: An eleven year retrospective in Vinnicombe, S. (ed.), *Women on Corporate Boards of Directors: International Research and Practice*, Cheltenham, UK: Edward Elgar Publishing, 15–25.

Joy, M. 2013. Electoral quotas for women: An international overview, www.aph.gov.au/About_Parliament/Parliamentary_Departments/Parliamentary_Library/pubs/rp/rp1314/ElectoralQuotas, accessed 14 November, 2016.

Kay, H. 1979. The need for self-imposed quotas in academic employment, *Symposium: The Quest for Equality*, 1, 137–145.

Khadem, N. 2016. Australia will not hit 30% women on boards by 2018, time for quotas: Elizabeth Proust, *The Sydney Morning Herald*, June 8, www.smh.com.au/business/workplace-relations/australia-will-not-hit-30-women-on-boards-by-2018-time-for-quotas-elizabeth-proust-20160607-gpdd80.html, accessed 25 March, 2017.

Khadem, N. 2017a. No corporate diversity: Captains of Australian business likely to be named Peter or John, *The Sydney Morning Herald*, March 27, www.smh.com.au/business/workplace-relations/no-corporate-diversity-captains-of-australian-business-likely-to-be-named-peter-or-john-20170301-gunw4s.html, accessed 30 March, 2017.

Khadem, N. 2017b. Australia's top chairmen came to support quotas, when will we?, *The Sydney Morning Herald*, March 30, www.smh.com.au/business/workplace-relations/australias-top-chairmen-came-to-support-quotas-when-will-we-20170329-gv8vx8.html, accessed 30 March, 2017.

Klettner, A., Clarke, T., Boersma, M. 2016. Strategic and regulatory approaches to increasing women in leadership: Multilevel targets and mandatory quotas as levers for cultural change, *Journal of Business Ethics*, 133, 395–419.

KPMG 2016a. ASX corporate governance council principles and recommendations on diversity report, May 24, https://assets.kpmg.com/content/dam/kpmg/pdf/2016/05/

asx-corporate-governance-council-principles-recommendations-diversity-jan-dec-2015. pdf, accessed 15 November, 2016.

KPMG 2016b. Diversity: ASX corporate governance council principles and recommendations, https://home.kpmg.com/au/en/home/insights/2016/05/asx-corporate-governance-council-principles-recommendations-diversity.html, accessed 20 December, 2016.

KPMG 2017. Secrets to success of the ASX 300: Six priorities of opportunity and challenge, https://assets.kpmg.com/content/dam/kpmg/au/pdf/2017/secrets-to-success-asx-300-mid-market-enterprises.pdf, accessed 25 January, 2017.

Krus, C., Morgan, L., Ginsberg, T. 2012. Board diversity: Who has a seat at the table?, *The Corporate Governance Advisor*, 20(2), 1–7.

Lansing, P., Chandra, S. 2012. Quota systems as a means to promote women into corporate boardrooms, *Employee Relations Law Journal*, 38(3), 3–10.

Lazzaretti, K., Godoi, C., Camilo, S., Marcon, R. 2013. Gender diversity in the boards of directors of Brazilian businesses, *Gender in Management: An International Journal*, 28(2), 94–110.

Lim, S., Matolcsy, Z., Chow, D. 2007. The association between board composition and different types of voluntary disclosure, *European Accounting Review*, 16(3), 555–587.

Lipton, B.A. 2015. New era of women in leadership: The gendered impact of quality assurance in Australian higher education, *The Australian Universities' Review*, 57(2), 60–70.

Lord Davies, E. 2011. Women on boards, www.gov.uk/government/uploads/system/uploads/attachment_data/file/31710/11-745-women-on-boards.pdf, accessed 4 October, 2016.

Lord Davies, E. 2015. Improving the gender balance on British boards, www.gov.uk/government/uploads/system/uploads/attachment_data/file/482059/BIS-15-585-women-on-boards-davies-review-5-year-summary-october-2015.pdf, accessed 12 April, 2016.

McKinsey, 2007.Women Matter: Gender Diveristy, a Corporate Performance Driver, https://www.mckinsey.com/~/media/McKinsey/Business%20Functions/Organization/Our%20Insights/Gender%20diversity%20a%20corporate%20performance%20driver/Gender%20diversity%20a%20corporate%20performance%20driver.ashx, accessed 10 April, 2016.

Hold, S., Huse, M., Hansen, K., Brogi, M. 2013. *Getting Women on to Corporate Boards: A Snowball Starting in Norway*, Cheltenham, UK: Edward Elgar Publishing.

McCann, J., 2013. Electoral quotas for women: An international overview, Parlimentary Library Researach Paper http://parlinfo.aph.gov.au/parlInfo/download/library/prspub/2840598/upload_binary/2840598.pdf;fileType=application/pdf, accessed 13 February, 2017.

Meier, P. 1998. Paritaire democratie: Over een nieuw concept en oude wonden, *Ethiek & Maatschappij*, 1(4), 9–23.

Morley, L. 2010. Hyper modernisation and archaism: Women in higher education internationally in Riegraf, B., Aulenbacher, B., Kirsch-Auwärter, E., Müller, U., Morley, L. (eds.), *Gender Change in Academia: Re-Mapping the Fields of Work, Knowledge, and Politics from a Gender Perspective*, Verlag: Springer VS, 27–42.

Muir, S. 2012. Heidi versus Howard perception barrier to be hurdled, www.dpi.nsw.gov.au/archive/agriculture-today-stories/ag-today-archive/march-2012/heidi-versus-howard-perception-barrier-to-be-hurdled-commissioner, accessed 30 February, 2017.

Noked, N. 2013. 2013 Women on boards survey, May, http://blogs.law.harvard.edu/corpgov/2013/05/20/2013-women-on-boards-survey/, accessed 4 April, 2017.

O'Connor, M. 2006. Women executives in gladiator corporate cultures: The behavioral dynamics of gender, ego, and power, *Maryland Law Review*, 65(2), 465–505.

Paustian-Underdahl, S., Walker, L., Woehr, D. 2014. Study: Women leaders perceived as effective as male counterparts, www.apa.org/news/press/releases/2014/04/women-leaders. aspx, accessed 24 March, 2017.

Pfeffer, J., Salancik, G. 1978. *The External Control of Organisations: A Resource Dependence Perspective*, New York: Harper & Row Publishers.

Quast, L. 2013. The importance of women in the boardroom: Q and A with Baroness Mary Goudie, www.forbes.com/sites/lisaquast/2013/05/20/the-importance-of-women-in-the-boardroom-qa-with-baroness-mary-goudie/, accessed 10 March, 2017.

Reskin, B., McBrier, D., Kmec, J. 1999. The determinants and consequences of workplace sex and race composition, *Annual Review of Sociology*, 25, 335–347.

Rhode, D., Packel, A. 2014. Diversity on corporate boards: How much differences does difference make?, *Delaware Journal of Corporate Law*, 39(2), 377–426.

Rodriguez-Dominguez, L., Garcia-Sanchez, I.-M., Gallego-Alvarez, I. 2012. Explanatory factors of the relationship between gender diversity and corporate performance, *European Journal of Law and Economics*, 33(3), 603–620.

Running Start 2014. Young women's political leadership, http://runningstartonline.org/programs/young-womens-political-leadership, accessed 10 March, 2017.

Sanders, M., Hrdlicka, J., Hellicar, M., Cottrel, D., Knox, J. 2011. What stops women from reaching the top? Confronting the tough issues, www.bain.com/offices/australia/en_us/publications/what-stops-women-from-reaching-the-top.aspx, accessed 27 March, 2017.

Schwindt-Bayer, L. 2009. Making quotas work: The effect of gender quota laws on the election of women, *Legislative Studies Quarterly*, 31(4), 5–28.

Stevenson, B., Wolfers, J. 2009. The paradox of declining female happiness, *American Economic Journal: Economic Policy*, 1(2), 190–225.

Teigen, M. 2000. The affirmative action controversy, *Nordic Journal of Feminist and Gender Research*, 8(2), 63–77.

Tharenou, P. 1999. Gender differences in advancing to the top, *International Journal of Management Reviews*, 1(2), 111–132.

Thomson, P., Laurent, C., Lloyd, T. 2015. *The Rise of the Female Executive*, Germany: Springer.

Vafaei, A., Ahmed, K., Mather, P. 2015. Board diversity and financial performance in the top 500 Australian firms, *Australian Accounting Review*, 25(4), 413–427.

Van Dyke, A., Dallmann, S. 2013. Mining for talent a study of women on boards in the mining industry, www.womenonboards.org.au/pubs/reports/2013-mining-for-talent.pdf, accessed 15 February, 2017.

White, K., Carvalho, T., Riodran, S. 2011. Gender, power and managerialism in universities, *Journal of Higher Education Policy and Management*, 33(2), 179–188.

Zelechowski, D., Bilimoria, D. 2004. Characteristics of women and men corporate inside directors in the US, *Corporate Governance: An International Review*, 12(3), 337–342.

5 Women on corporate boards in Poland and Estonia in the context of the EU gender equality policy[1]

Marta Pachocka, Aleksandra Szczerba-Zawada and Diana Eerma

Introduction

Implementation of equal opportunities for women and men necessitates both legal and socio-economic encouragement. This holds true for female representation on decision-making positions in politics, economy and society. There are several factors which hinder women's presence in this area that differ among European countries. However, some common tendencies are visible. To identify them, the authors study the cases of Poland and Estonia, which have both been EU Member States since 2004. The aim of the chapter is to analyze and discuss women's presence in decision-making positions illustrated by an example of their representation on corporate boards in Poland and Estonia, while taking into consideration a broader background of the EU gender equality policy. For this reason, the chapter draws from the perspective of the EU and its approach to gender equality as a reference frame and inspiration for the developments in the discussed EU Member States. In this context, the following research questions were formulated. What is the situation in both states? Do they and, if yes, how do they respond to the EU efforts aiming to guarantee gender equality in politics, economy and society? Are there any good practices to follow? Therefore, qualitative research methods were broadly used in this chapter, including: the analysis of acts of law and other official documents at the EU and national levels, the content analysis, the case study approach and the comparative perspective. These were supplemented with the analysis of quantitative data.

Women on boards – the EU as a gender equality promoter

The issue of female participation in economy, finance and business, including their involvement in corporate boards, is gaining importance in recent years in the EU and its Member States. It is often discussed in the much broader context of gender equality, gender balance, gender diversity and related issues. It is well reflected in the increasingly rich literature of the subject and the publications provided by international organizations, the EU and its different bodies as well as by other – often national – institutions and scholars.

The EU pays great attention to the principle of gender equality. The require-ment of equal treatment of women and men with respect to remuneration was the first aspect of equality principle codified in the *Treaty Establishing European Economic Community* (TEEC) (EU, 1957). Article 119 TEEC – now art. 157 of the *Treaty on the Functioning of the European Union* (TFEU) (EU, 2012a) – that obliged Member States to ensure and maintain the application of the principle of equal pay for equal work as between men and women workers, was introduced due to economic reasons, i.e. to prevent Member States from gaining a competi-tive advantage through cheap female work that could distort the functioning of the internal market (More, 1999: 518). This Treaty provision was transformed into a complex set of rules on equal treatment of women and men in employment and social security, and subsequently into EU antidiscrimination law (see Zawidzka-Łojek and Szczerba-Zawada, 2015). This evolution was a result, to a great extent, of the judicial activity of the Court of Justice of the European Union (CJEU) (Szczerba-Zawada, 2011).

The Court recognized the direct effect of art. 119 TEEC and decided that the protection against gender discrimination includes protection against discrimination based on gender reassignment, and thus expanded the notion of discrimination to different forms of unequal treatment and permitted a shift in the burden of proof from the complainant to the respondent (Bell, 2011: 615). First and foremost, the CJEU decided that discrimination based on sex endangers a part of the fundamen-tal rights, constituting general principles of the EU law, the observance of which it has a duty to ensure (CJEU, 1978: para. 2). The general principle of gender equality plays a crucial – even constitutional – role in the EU legal system as it is used as a standard to review the legality of actions taken both by the Member States and the EU.

The obligation of the EU to respect gender equality has been codified by art. 8 TFEU that stipulates that the Union shall aim to eliminate inequalities, and to promote equality, between men and women in all its activities and by art. 10 TFEU according to which "in defining and implementing its policies and activities, the Union shall aim to combat discrimination based on sex, racial or ethnic origin, religion or belief, disability, age or sexual orientation" (EU, 2012a). Thus, the Treaty clearly highlights the obligation of gender mainstreaming for the Union that the EU undertook vividly in 1996. After an initial positive assessment of the EU's effort to insert a gender equality perspective into all the levels of public policy, uneven results started to appear (Hafner-Burton and Pollack, 2009: 115).

The main reason is the division of power between the EU and Member States – the implementation of gender equality in practice through the EU binding instru-ments requires the consent of the Member States under subsidiarity principle. However, they do not seem to be interested enough in contributing to the EU gender equality legislation. This can be exemplified by the *Proposal for a Directive of the European Parliament and of the Council on improving the gender balance among non-executive directors of companies listed on stock exchanges and related measures* (EU, 2012b) that has been blocked by some Member States both at the stage of the consultation procedure (six Member States, including Poland, submitted reasoned opinions alleging that the proposal is inconsistent with subsidiarity principle) and the Council meetings that resulted in a lack of qualified majority on this dossier despite changes introduced to the proposal (CEU, 2017: 1–5).

As the EU Member States are more willing to improve gender balance on company boards through national measures or EU non-binding measures rather than through applying EU legislation, the list of EU official documents devoted to gender equality, although pretty long, is exemplified mainly by soft law, as it encompasses apart from directives also communications (see Aluchna, 2017: 105–106; EC DG JUST a), recommendations, reports, strategies and conclusions. Among them the most up to date are the following:

1   *Strategic engagement for gender equality 2016–2019* (EC, 2015b)
2   *Report from the Commission to the European Parliament, the Council and the European Economic and Social Committee Report on the application of Council Directive 2004/113/EC implementing the principle of equal treatment between men and women in the access to and supply of goods and services* (EC, 2015a)
3   *Directive 2014/95/EU of the European Parliament and of the Council of 22 October 2014 amending Directive 2013/34/EU as regards disclosure of non-financial and diversity information by certain large undertakings and groups* (EU, 2014)
4   *Commission Recommendation of 7.3.2014 on strengthening the principle of equal pay between men and women through transparency (text with EEA relevance)* (EC, 2014)
5   *Council conclusions on women and the economy: economic independence from the perspective of part-time work and self-employment* (CEU, 2014)
6   *Report from the Commission to the European Parliament and the Council on the application of Directive 2006/54/EC of the European Parliament and of the Council of 5 July 2006 on the implementation of the principle of equal opportunities and equal treatment of men and women in matters of employment and occupation (recast)* (EC, 2013)
7   *Council conclusions on the European Pact for gender equality for the period 2011–2020, 3073th Employment, Social Policy, Health and Consumer Affairs Council meeting* (CEU, 2011a)
8   *Review of the implementation of the Beijing Platform for Action – Women and the Economy: reconciliation of work and family life as a precondition for equal participation in the labour market – Council Conclusions* (CEU, 2011b)
9   *Strategy for equality between women and men 2010–2015* (EC, 2011b)

One of the most recent documents concerning gender equality-related issues made available by the European Commission (EC) is *Strategic engagement for gender equality 2016–2019* (EC, 2015b), which is a continuation of the *Strategy for equality between women and men 2010–2015* adopted in September 2010

(EC, 2011b). According to Věra Jourová, commissioner for justice, consumers and gender equality in the EU:

> While Europe has made step-by-step progress over recent years, thanks to hard work at local, national and European level, gender equality still remains unfinished business. We are far from reaching equality, in particular in areas such as participation in the labour market, economic independence, pay and pensions, equality in leadership positions, fighting gender-based violence, and gender equality in our external action.
>
> (EC, 2015b: 5)

The new strategic document from 2015 refers broadly to the previous strategy. The five key areas for actions aiming at providing the gender equality in the EU and beyond it are rooted in the existing priorities (see EC, 2011b) and they are as follows (EC, 2015b: 9):

1   increasing female labour-market participation and the equal economic independence of women and men;
2   reducing the gender pay, earnings and pension gaps and thus fighting poverty among women;
3   promoting equality between women and men in decision-making;
4   combating gender-based violence and protecting and supporting victims;
5   promoting gender equality and women's rights across the world.

In the years 2010–2015 progress assumed in the EC strategy was achieved only partially, so the efforts have to be continued in the coming years with the involvement of different stakeholders and implementation of special actions to guarantee equality between women and men. In this context, the issue of women's involvement in decision-making processes and positions, especially in the economy and business, seems very important. Taking it into consideration, it is worth having a closer look at how the Commission has declared to approach this topic in its strategy devoted to gender equality between 2016 and 2019.

Women on boards – EU's wasted effort?

Promoting equality between women and men in decision-making is one of the priorities of the EU gender equality policy until 2019. This priority corresponds to the five objectives set in *Strategic engagement for gender equality 2016–2019* that stipulate (EC, 2015b: 27):

1   "continue efforts to improve the gender balance in economic leadership positions, in particular among the non-executive directors of companies listed on stock exchanges (at least 40% of the under-represented sex);
2   improve the gender balance among executive directors of major listed companies and in the talent pipeline;

3   improve data collection and gender balance in decision-making positions in research organizations;
4   improve the gender balance in political decision-making and public life, including sports;
5   reach the target of 40% women in senior and middle management positions in the Commission by the end of 2019".

In order to meet these objectives, dedicated actions were scheduled for which different bodies within the European Commission are responsible (Table 5.1). In addition, the progress is to be monitored by seven indicators relating to the EU average (Table 5.2).

Table 5.1 EU actions scheduled for the years 2016–2019 in relation to the objectives under the priority "Promoting equality between women and men in decision-making"

No.	Action	Responsible body/ies within the European Commission	Timing
1	Continue to support adoption of the 2012 proposal for a Directive on improving the gender balance among non-executive directors of companies listed on stock exchanges by 2016; closely monitor its transposition and implementation; support other targeted initiatives to improve the gender balance in decision-making, including guidance for Member States	Directorate-General for Justice and Consumers (DG JUST)	Ongoing
2	Continue to collect and disseminate further data on the representation of women and men in high decision-making positions, in close cooperation with the EIGE	Directorate-General for Justice and Consumers (DG JUST), European Institute for Gender Equality (EIGE)	Ongoing
3	Consider measures to improve the gender balance in political decision-making and continue to encourage Member States and support national authorities' activities promoting gender balance in political and public decision-making positions	Directorate-General for Justice and Consumers (DG JUST)	2018
4	Provide guidance to Member States on a common approach to implementing quantitative targets for decision-making positions in research	Directorate-General for Research and Innovation (DG RTD)	2016
5	Reach the target of 40% women in senior and middle management in the Commission by the end of its mandate	Directorate-General for Human Resources and Security (DG HR)	Ongoing

Source: EC (2015b: 27)

Table 5.2 Indicators monitoring progress under the priority "Promoting equality between women and men in decision-making"

No.	Indicators	Average in the EU (year)
1	Proportion of women among members of the highest decision-making body of the largest nationally registered companies listed on the national stock exchange	21.2% (April 2015)
2	Proportion of women among presidents and CEOs of the largest nationally registered companies listed on the national stock exchange	Presidents: 7.1%, CEOs: 3.6% (April 2015)
3	Proportion of women among executive and non-executive members of the two highest decision-making bodies of the largest nationally registered companies listed on the national stock exchange	Non-executive directors: 22.5%, Senior executives: 13.7% (April 2015)
4	Proportion of women heads of higher education institutions	15.5% (2010)
5	Proportion of women in the single/lower houses of the national/federal parliaments of the Member States and in the European Parliament	29% (May 2015) EP: 37%
6	Proportion of women in the single/lower houses of national/federal governments and the European Commission	27% (May 2015) EC: 32%
7	Proportion of women in Commission senior/ middle management	28% / 32% (February 2015)

Source: EC (2015b: 28)

The EU through its institutions, networks and different initiatives has done a lot to promote equality between women and men in decision-making in different life areas, including politics and economy, not only with respect to 2015 EC strategy but also earlier. These efforts and their results are illustrated by such documents and publications as i.a. (EC DG JUST b):

1 *Gender balance on corporate boards: Europe is cracking the glass ceiling* (EC DG JUST, 2016)
2 *Women and men in leadership positions in the European Union 2013* (EC DG JUST, 2013)
3 *Positive Action Measures to Ensure Full Equality in Practice between Men and Women, including on Company Boards* (Senden and Selanec, 2012, 2013)
4 *Working Paper: how to engage senior men to promote women to senior decision-making positions in their organizations* (European Commission's Network to Promote Women, 2012)
5 *Women in economic decision-making in the EU: progress report. A Europe 2020 Initiative* (EC DG JUST, 2012)
6 *Special Eurobarometer 376: Women in Decision-Making Positions – Report* (EC, 2012)

 7   *Commission Staff Working Paper: The Gender Balance in Business Leader-ship* (EC, 2011a)
 8   *More women in senior positions – key to economic stability and growth* (EC DG ESAEO, 2010)
 9   *Women in European politics – time for action* (EC DG ESAEO, 2009)
10   *Women and men in decision-making 2007 – analysis of the situation and trends* (EC DG ESAEO, 2008)
11   *Decision-making: exchange of good practice* (EC DG ESAEO, 2007a)
12   *Opinion on EU Network of Women in Economic and Political Decision-Making Positions* (EC DG ESAEO, 2007b)

It is clear from the above list that the EU supports gender balance in decision-making, including corporate boards, using mainly soft law instruments. Thus, this kind of tool could be considered an incentive for Member States as they do not prescribe legal responsibility for non-compliance with the gender equal-ity principle. The newest EU legislation supporting gender equality on corporate boards – *Directive 2014/95/EU of the European Parliament and of the Council of 22 October 2014 amending Directive 2013/34/EU as regards disclosure of non-financial and diversity information by certain large undertakings and groups* (OJ L 330, 15.11.2014) (EU, 2014) – follows this logic. First, it poses an obligation to disclose diversity policies in relation to the administrative, management and supervisory bodies with regard to aspects such as gender only on certain large undertakings. Second, it requires that the disclosure of the diversity policy should be part of the corporate governance statement, as laid down by Article 20 of Direc-tive 2013/34/EU, yet if no diversity policy is applied, there should not be any obli-gation to put one in place, but the corporate governance statement should include a clear explanation as to why this is the case. Because of such attitude there is a great divergence of national measures on gender balance on corporate boards and of progress achieved between Member States.

As of September 2015, when the EC strategy was adopted, the situation in the field of development of the gender equality policies among the EU Member States was uneven. This was strongly conditioned by socio-economic, cultural and legal differences across these countries. However, a positive manifestation was an increasing number of EU members implementing the national strategies and/ or national actions plans focused on the gender equality issues (EC, 2015b: 20).

Table 5.3 summarizes briefly the situation in Estonia and Poland in the dis-cussed period. In general, the national gender equality strategies and/or action plans could encompass different key fields that were divided into: social inclu-sion and poverty, education and training, access to health, gender-based vio-lence, economy and labor market, gender stereotypes, reconciliation of working and family life, decision-making. As stated in the strategy from 2015, all of these areas were covered that time at the national level in Poland. In the case of Estonia, three out of eight areas were not addressed in national strategies/

Table 5.3 The state of play in the development of the gender equality policies in Estonia and Poland (as of September 2015)

EU MS	Actions – the state of play	Notes
Estonia	• Action plan to reduce the pay gap between women and men (2012–2016) – AG • Development plan for children and families (2012–2020) – AG • Development strategy for preventing violence (aimed at reducing domestic violence, violence against children, gender-based violence and trafficking in human beings) (2015–2020) – AG • Development plan for welfare (covering labor, employment, social security, social inclusion, gender equality and equal opportunities) (2016–2023) – D	
Poland	• National Programme of Activities for Equal Treatment 2013–2016 (NAP) – AG • National Programme Counteracting Violence in the Family (2006–2013, updated for 2014–2020) – AG • Human capital development strategy (2020) – AG	The preparation of the NAP is required by the 2010 Act on the Implementation of Certain Provisions of the European Union in the Field of Equal Treatment (Anti-discrimination Act, Journal of Laws from 2010 No. 245 item 1700 as amended)

Notes: AG: approved by government; D: draft.

Source: own elaboration on EC (2015b: 42, 44)

plans, i.e. social inclusion and poverty, access to health and decision-making (EC, 2015b: 47–48).

In April 2016, the shares of women on the corporate boards in Poland (19.9%) and Estonia (8.2%) (see Aluchna et al., 2016; Kupts and Rell, 2015) were still below the EU-28 average share of women on the boards of the largest publicly listed companies registered in the EU Member States (23.3%). The EU average corresponded to an increase of 11.4 percentage points between 2010 and 2016. Despite the overall improvement, the Member States with percentage of women on corporate boards above the EU-28 average were still less numerous than these below the threshold. According to the EC factsheet on *Gender balance on corporate boards: Europe is cracking the glass ceiling* (EC DG JUST, 2016), they were as follows: France (37.1%), Sweden (36.1%), Italy (30%), Finland (29.9%), the Netherlands (28.1%), Latvia (27.7%), Germany (27.2%), the UK (27.1%), Denmark (27%), Belgium (26.6%) and Slovenia (23.9%).

Most of these best achievements were, unfortunately, below the "critical mass" of 30%, which the EU finds necessary in order to have a sustainable impact on gender equality, including board performance (EU, 2012b: 5). In addition, this is much below the EC target of 40% set in the *Proposal for a Directive of the European Parliament and of the Council on improving the gender balance among non-executive directors of companies listed on stock exchanges and related measures* (EU, 2012b) and in the *Strategic engagement for gender equality 2016–2019* (EC, 2015b).

Gender equality on boards: cases of Poland and Estonia

For better understanding the situation in the field of gender inequality in decision-making in economy, finance and business in Estonia and Poland, it is important to have a general overview of the state of art in both countries in a broader context of the gender mainstreaming. It is understood as

> a strategy towards realising gender equality. It involves the integration of a gender perspective into the preparation, design, implementation, monitoring and evaluation of policies, regulatory measures and spending programmes, with a view to promoting equality between women and men, and combating discrimination.
>
> (EIGE c)

The comparison of key aspects of gender mainstreaming in Estonia and Poland based on the data provided by European Institute for Gender Equality (EIGE) and additional sources are presented in Table 5.4.

An overall assessment of the multidimensional situation concerning the gender equality in Poland and Estonia is offered by the European Institute for Gender Equality in the form of the Gender Equality Index (GEI). So far, the GEI includes the results for the years 2005, 2010 and 2012 allowing comparison. The index is calculated on the basis of detailed indicators assigned to eight domains. Consequently, work, money, knowledge, time, power and health are combined to give a core index supplemented by two satellite areas, i.e. violence and intersecting inequalities (EIGE, 2015a: 11–12).[2] Within the core part of the GEI each domain encompasses some sub-domains within the conceptual framework (Ibidem: 12, 18), e.g.:

1   work – participation, segregation, quality of work,
2   money – financial resources, economic situation,
3   knowledge – educational attainment, segregation, lifelong learning,
4   time – economic activities, care activities, social activities,
5   power – political, social, economic,
6   health – status, behavior, access.

Table 5.4 Gender mainstreaming in Estonia and Poland

Aspect	Estonia	Poland
General information	Gender issues started to receive attention in Estonia in the late 1990s upon the ratification of international conventions and with preparation for accession to the EU. The legal framework for gender equality is contained in both the Estonian constitution, which provides, inter alia, that everyone is equal before the law and that no one shall be discriminated against on the grounds of sex, and in the Gender Equality Act 2004, which defines equality of women and men as a fundamental human right and provides for gender equality to be mainstreamed into all areas of social life. It was at the start of the 2000s that the first gender-mainstreaming initiative, organized by the Ministry of Social Affairs, took place. The aim of the project was to improve understanding of gender equality and to use the dual-track approach to achieve equality and develop specific methods and tools, in particular on gender impact assessment, for the promotion of gender mainstreaming. In the following years, several EU-funded projects focusing on gender mainstreaming were developed and continue to be implemented. The financial support under the European Social Fund (ESF) has been relevant in Estonia (e.g. "Promotion of gender Equality in 2008–2010" and "Promoting Gender Equality 2011–2013").	The first governmental commitment to gender mainstreaming in Poland was made in the National Action Plan for Women (NAP) 1997–2000. Due to a political shift in the 1997 election, the NAP was not implemented. The second National Action Plan for Women (2003–2005) was successfully launched with the aim to mainstream gender equality into government policies at all levels, thanks to the efforts of the Government Plenipotentiary for the Equal Status of Men and Women, established in 2001. However, the gender-mainstreaming process was somewhat interrupted in 2005, when the Plenipotentiary was dissolved after parliamentary elections, and no new national program was put into effect in that respect. Several subsequent offices responsible for preventing discrimination have followed. After the dissolution of the Plenipotentiary, its competences were taken over by the Department of Women, Family and Counteracting Discrimination within the Ministry of Labour and Social Policy. The department was responsible for the coordination of implementing the gender-mainstreaming perspective but was dissolved in January 2010. However, in order to implement the task of providing equal opportunities to women and men in the labor market, the Division for Gender Equality in the Labour Market was created in the Department of Economic Analyses and Forecasts. In 2008 a new institution was established – the Government Plenipotentiary for Equal Treatment. Among its tasks, described in the Anti-discrimination Act, was drafting the first "National Action Plan for Equal Treatment for the Years 2013–2016". Despite it being expired, a new NAP has not been drawn up at the time of publication of this book.

(Continued)

Table 5.4 (Continued)

Aspect	Estonia	Poland
		Overall, the EU's influence on gender mainstreaming in Poland has been relatively significant because of the EU funding. For instance, all projects co-financed within the European Social Fund (ESF) framework must have a gender impact assessment. Moreover, gender mainstreaming itself has been the focus of a number of projects funded by the ESF. Although NAP sets one of its aims as enhancement of gender equality with respect to decision-making (aim 1.4.), the Polish attitude towards (EU) instruments on gender equality is exemplified by reasoned opinion on the European Commission's proposal for a directive on gender balance among non-executive directors claiming its inconsistency with the principle of subsidiarity.
Structures	The permanent body for dealing with gender equality issues was established in December 1996 as the Gender Equality Bureau within the Department of International Cooperation and European Integration. It was reorganized into the Gender Equality Department in December 2003 and since 2005 it has been in charge of developing gender-mainstreaming processes and methodologies. In 2011, a Gender Mainstreaming Working Group, composed of representatives from Estonian government ministries and coordinated by the Ministry of Social Affairs, was re-formed with the aim of providing training for a range of government employees on gender mainstreaming and drafting gender-mainstreaming strategies in various policy areas. In general, it is the Ministry of Social Affairs that designs the appropriate policy for the achievement of gender equality and implements policies that directly promote gender equality in Estonia. Moreover, it is responsible for the coordination of equal treatment (concerning sexual orientation, age, disability) and the preparation of the respective draft legislation. Within its structure it is the Equality Policies Department devoted to the previously mentioned tasks.	The Government Plenipotentiary for Equal Treatment was established in 2008 as a non-ministerial equal treatment agency, integrated within the structures of the Chancellery of the Prime Minister but headed by a secretary of state. Its main responsibility was to promote the equal treatment of all persons without discrimination based on gender or other grounds. It filled the institutional vacuum left after the dissolution, in 2005, of the Government Plenipotentiary for the Equal Status of Men and Women. Nowadays, according to art. 18 of Anti-discrimination Act, "Performance of tasks related to the implementation of the principle of equal treatment shall be entrusted with the Commissioner for Human Rights (Ombudsman) and the Government Plenipotentiary for Equal Treatment". While ombudsman is an independent body, the Plenipotentiary is a governmental body. The commissioner for human rights guards the human and citizen rights and freedoms, specified in the Constitution of the Republic of Poland and other normative acts, and also guards the implementation of the principle of equal treatment.

Furthermore, a Gender Equality and Equal Treatment Commissioner works on discrimination issues as an independent and impartial expert, monitoring compliance with the requirements of the Gender Equality Act and Equal Treatment Act. Gender Equality and Equal Treatment Commissioner is a national equality body representing Estonia in the European Network of Equality Bodies (Equinet).

Proceeding from the law, the Gender Equality Council, advising the government of the Republic of Estonia, was established in 2013.

With regard to the implementation of the principle of equal treatment, the scope of responsibilities of the ombudsman comprises i.a. examining motions addressed to him, including complaints about the infringement of the principle of equal treatment and undertaking appropriate activities, in accordance with the Act on the Commissioner for Human Rights, analysis, monitoring of and support for equal treatment of all persons, execution of autonomous studies and research concerning discrimination and development and issue of independent reports, and issue of recommendations regarding problems related to discrimination. The commissioner is the Polish member in the European Network of Equality Bodies (Equinet).

The Plenipotentiary has several important competences. He prepares and presents to the Council of Ministers the NAP for Equal Treatment and then reports on its execution annually. Other competences include preparing draft laws related to equal treatment and preparing opinions about such drafts; a number of analytical and monitoring competences; the promotion of equal treatment; international cooperation; and implementing projects that support equal treatment and counteracting discrimination. The Plenipotentiary may establish special research teams, call for specific research or expert analysis and provide reports based on this research. It may also issue recommendations.

Since 2016 the Office of the Government Plenipotentiary for Equal Treatment is held concurrently with the Office of the Government Plenipotentiary for Civil Society (under the name Government Plenipotentiary for Civil Society and Equal Treatment).

(Continued)

Table 5.4 (Continued)

Aspect	Estonia	Poland
		Additionally, each Minister is responsible for combating discrimination and enhancing equality in his/her scope of competences. To realize this duty, ministries shall nominate coordinators for equal treatment. Moreover, a national advisory body on equal treatment has been established in 2015 as foreseen in the National Programme for Equal Treatment for the years 2013–2016. The advisory body consisted of high level representatives of all ministries.
		One of the actions set forth by the NAP for 2013–2016 was the development and implementation of the regional network of plenipotentiaries of equal treatment coordinating the implementation of the equal treatment principles (including gender-mainstreaming issues) at the level of voivodeships.
Law and policies	Gender equality issues are mainly regulated by the Gender Equality Act of 2004. The act stipulates that state and local government agencies are required to promote gender equality systematically and purposefully; that public authorities are required to address conditions and circumstances that hinder the achievement of gender equality; and that agencies must take into account gender equality when planning, implementing and assessing national, regional and institutional strategies, policies and action plans. The act also established the institution of the Gender Equality and Equal Treatment Commissioner.	There is no national law dedicated exclusively to gender equality in Poland. The law addressing the issue is the Equal Treatment Act of 2010, which includes gender among the other protected characteristics in the fields of protection required by the equality directives and the Labour Code, implementing certain EU provisions on equal treatment in employment. The previously mentioned laws, to a varying extent, specify areas and methods for counteracting discrimination, points out the grounds on which unequal treatment is unlawful – among them gender – and also defines the responsibilities and competences of the Government Plenipotentiary for Equal Treatment, including the obligation to develop and implement the National Action Plan for Equal Treatment 2013–2016. This Action Plan anticipates activities in all areas, including (but not limited to) the further general implementation of anti-discrimination policies.
	Until September 1, 2009, the Commissioner's institution was responsible only for gender equality. The mandate of the Commissioner was broadened with the coming into force of the Equal Treatment Act (2009). Since then the Commissioner deals with all discrimination grounds listed in the two Acts.	

There are no articles about law enforcement supervision in the GEA and in the ETA. Law enforcement is a challenge. The GEA and the ETA have a small number of articles about implementation and define duties of respective bodies, but no state supervision is foreseen. In 2015, the Ministry of Justice expressed the opinion that there is no need for amendments to the GEA and the ETA in this respect because state supervision takes place regarding the implementation of other legal acts (Employment Contracts Act, Civil Service Act, Health Insurance Act etc.) in which equality requirements are stipulated.

According to the expert from the European network of legal experts in gender equality and non-discrimination (European Commission), in 2016, there has been a serious backlash compared with previous years in the work of the Gender Equality and Equal Treatment Commissioner. In 2013–2016 the Norway Grants program supported the Office of the Commissioner. This was due to a poor state's budget being allocated to the Office of the Commissioner and the influence of party policies on the appointment of the Commissioner in 2015. The promotion of gender equality has mainly relied on foreign funding. The state's budget has stayed modest for gender equality bodies and for the Equality Policies Department at the Ministry of Social Affairs. At the same time, the workload has increased. There were no resources in the Ministries for gender experts for assisting decision-makers for gender mainstreaming

Although a gender-mainstreaming strategy is absent at national level, several programs on gender equality and gender mainstreaming have been carried out, as well as projects financed by EU or external funds.

It also established a national advisory body on equal treatment, which has gender equality and women's rights within its scope. One of the actions set forth by the National Action Plan for Equal Treatment for 2013–2016 was the development and implementation of the regional network of plenipotentiaries of equal treatment, which should coordinate the implementation of the equal treatment principles (including gender-mainstreaming issues) at the level of voivodeships.

The report on implementation of the NAP for equal treatment points to the following problems with its realization:
• Lack of vertical and horizontal cooperation between bodies of public authority resulting in lack of complementarity of actions undertaken under the same objectives;
• Inability of part of obliged institutions to undertake prescribed actions;
• Actions delayed as compared to the timetable;
• Low engagement of non-governmental organizations in implementation of actions envisaged by NAP.

(Continued)

Table 5.4 (Continued)

Aspect	Estonia	Poland
	In order to increase awareness and improve the implementation of the GEA and the ETA, it is necessary for gender equality and equal treatment to be clearly highlighted in policies at the national level. The gender equality strategy and action plan could offer a solution in this respect. Opposing statements argue that for the public good it would be better to work with a smaller number of strategies and to incorporate gender equality in every strategy as a horizontal measure. Unfortunately, gender mainstreaming has not been a successful approach to move towards a more gender-balanced society in Estonia. In 2016, the Welfare Development Plan 2016–2023 enters into force, and the improvement of gender equality in some spheres of life (employment, health and social protection) is expected to follow.	According to the country report on gender equality in Poland for the period from July 2015 to April 2016, prepared within the framework of the European network of legal experts in gender equality and non-discrimination of the EC DG JUST, the implementation of the EU gender equality acquis in Poland is rather satisfactory, even if some provisions and solutions still require amendments.

Nevertheless, some worrying changes have been made or have been at least discussed that can affect the state of equality policy in Poland, including the dissolution of the Council for the Prevention of Racial Discrimination, Xenophobia and Intolerance or the proposal for stricter anti-abortion laws. |
| State of affairs | According to the country report on gender equality in Estonia for the period from July 2015 to April 2016, prepared within the framework of the European network of legal experts in gender equality and non-discrimination of the EC DG JUST, the transposition of the EU equality directives into Estonian legislation has been satisfactory. However, law enforcement is a challenge as there are no articles about law enforcement supervision in the GEA and in the ETA. Both Acts have a small number of articles about implementation and define duties of respective bodies, but no state supervision is foreseen. | |

In addition, serious problems remain: economic inequality, the gender pay gap, gender segregation in the labor market, rigid gender roles and gender stereotypes, and the big difference in the average life expectancy of women and men.

The main requirement of the GEA and the ETA for state and local governments, educational institutions and employers to promote gender equality is poorly implemented. There are no gender equality promotion programs or gender equality plans. Discrimination claims on grounds of gender are made to the gender equality and equal treatment commissioner who could give a non-binding written opinion. The Competence Centre for Equality was established in 2015 to increase the equality outcomes in planned projects of the Structural Funds.

Methods and tools

Few gender-mainstreaming methods are being deployed. Training and capacity-building has been provided to officials from the Ministry of Social Affairs and other public servants. In addition, a range of support materials exist, such as publications or awareness-raising efforts that have been made over the past few years. Statistics and data are disaggregated by sex.

The EU is the driver of gender mainstreaming in Poland. Gender-mainstreaming methods are applied almost exclusively within programs implemented with the support of EU funding, e.g. a project titled "*Gender mainstreaming jako narzędzie zmiany na rynku pracy*" ("Gender mainstreaming as a tool for changes in the labor market") realized under Progress Program 2007–2013.

Some changes have been made, nevertheless, also outside EU funds, although rather limited in number. For example, it can be used the regulation of the Ministry of Science and Higher Education dated as of 25 October, 2015 stipulating that the Ministry appoints members of the Science Policy Committee taking into account balanced representation of women and men (§ 6.2, Journal of Laws from 2015 item 1879).

(*Continued*)

Table 5.4 (Continued)

Aspect	Estonia	Poland
Good practices	Examples: • Equal Treatment Network (since 2013) unites NGOs, whose main activities include protecting the equal rights of their target groups. The objective of the Network is to support its members (i.a. Estonian Human Rights Centre (EHRC), Estonian Women's Associations Roundtable (EWAR), Estonian Centre of Disabled Persons (EPIK), Estonian LGBT Association (ELGBTA), Estonian National Youth Council (ENL), Ida-Viru County Integration Centre (IVI), Tallinn Human Rights Information Centre) across specific target groups and cooperate in finding common interests, speak up jointly to achieve this and organize other activities. The Network collaborates with national institutions within the common interest and promotes the institutions to better follow and value the principle of equal treatment. The Equal Treatment Network was developed in a project, supported by the Open Estonia Foundation through the NGO Fund. In 2015, the Network's activity was sponsored by the Council of Gambling Tax through the Ministry of Social Affairs. • Contest for family friendly firms: "Pere-ja Töötajasõbralike firmade konkurss" – a contest to select the most family and employee-friendly companies in Estonia (since 2001).	Examples: • "Budżet Równych Szans. Gender Budgeting Dla Samorządów" ("Equal Opportunity Budget. Gender Budgeting for Local Governments"), Biuro Programu Narodów Zjednoczonych ds. Rozwoju w Warszawie (UNDP Office in Poland), (2012) • A multi-pronged national campaign on the father's role: "Etat Tata. Lubię to!" ("Full-time Dad – I Like It!") (2012) • Gdańsk Gender Budget Initiative, The Network of East-West Women NEWW-Polska (2005) • Project "Aktywizacja społeczno-ekonomiczna kobiet na poziomie lokalnym i regionalnym" ("Socio-economic activization of women at local and regional levels") (2008–2013)

Source: own elaboration based on Bałandynowicz-Panfil and Opac (2005); Bojarski (2016: 1–2); Budżet Równych Szans; Commissioner for Human Rights (in Poland); EIGE a; European Network of Equality Bodies (Equinet); Gender Equality and Equal Treatment Commissioner (in Estonia); Human Rights Center (in Estonia); Laas (2016a: 6–7, 59) and Laas (2016b: 1–2); MNiSW (2015); MPiPS DAEP; MSA; MUW (2015); PRdsSOiRT; Riigikogu (2004, 2008); Sejm (2010); and Zielińska (2016: 6–7, 60–61)

Power is a domain that covers the decision-making-related issues. Political power is expressed by the women and men representation among ministers, members of Parliament and members of regional assemblies. Economic power is about women and men representation among members of boards in the largest quoted companies (supervisory board or board of directors) and members of central banks. In both cases the power is measured as share and referred to the population aged 18 years old and over. Social power is unmeasured due to lack of appropriate gender indicators (Ibidem:14, 18, 53). The scores for the GEI and its domains and sub-domains range from 1 to 100. 100 represents the best situation

> in terms of levels of achievements and full gender equality. It should be interpreted with caution since it measures both how far women and men are from each other, but also the relative positions of Member States to the best achieved situation (the highest level achieved by Member States). As such it is not a "pure" measure of gender equality as it also captures the level of social cohesion across Member States. The score for the EU on average needs to be interpreted slightly differently: it measures gender gaps in relation to the level of cohesion across the Member States. The EU score rises in line with a closing of the gender gaps on average and fewer differences in levels between the Member States (i.e. higher levels of cohesion).
>
> (EIGE, 2015b: 1)

Taking these conceptual and methodological details into account, we can briefly compare the results of the GEI and the power domain for Estonia and Poland in the context of the EU average situation. Each year for which the scores are available – 2005, 2010 and 2012 – the GEI values for Poland and Estonia were below the EU average, but with Estonia ranked higher than Poland (Table 5.5). Between 2005 and 2012, both the EU and the two states improved their performance, with the largest positive change for Estonia from 45.3 to 49.8 points out of 100. Assuming the EU consisting of 28 countries for the purposes of comparing in the whole period under review (2005–2012), the value of the Gender Equality Index improved for 20 out of 28 EU members, with the highest increase for Italy and the lowest for Greece. The countries for which the results have deteriorated included Slovakia, the UK, Bulgaria, Lithuania, Romania, Croatia, Austria and Denmark (Figure 5.1).

Table 5.5 Overall scores of the Gender Equality Index for EU Member States (2005, 2010 and 2012)

No.	EU MS	Abbreviation	2005	2010	2012
1	Austria	AT	50.5	49.1	50.2
2	Belgium	BE	55.6	58.3	58.2
3	Bulgaria	BG	42.3	38.1	38.5
4	Croatia	HR	41.6	40.1	39.8

(Continued)

Table 5.5 (Continued)

No.	EU MS	Abbreviation	2005	2010	2012
5	Cyprus	CY	38.5	42.6	44.9
6	Czech Republic	CZ	40.3	42.1	43.8
7	Denmark	DK	71.1	72.7	70.9
8	**Estonia**	**EE**	**45.3**	**49.7**	**49.8**
9	Finland	FI	70	71.4	72.7
10	France	FR	52.5	55.9	55.7
11	Germany	DE	49.7	49.9	55.3
12	Greece	EL	38.2	39.8	38.3
13	Hungary	HU	37.2	42	41.6
14	Ireland	IE	50.8	55.1	56.5
15	Italy	IT	34.6	39.6	41.1
16	Latvia	LV	44	45.3	46.9
17	Lithuania	LT	43.6	42.2	40.2
18	Luxembourg	LU	53.7	50.1	55.2
19	Malta	MT	43.4	42.4	46.8
20	Netherlands	NL	63.6	69.1	68.5
21	**Poland**	**PL**	**42.7**	**43**	**43.7**
22	Portugal	PT	37.4	40.1	37.9
23	Romania	RO	36	35	33.7
24	Slovakia	SK	41.5	39.8	36.5
25	Slovenia	SI	52.7	54.9	57.3
26	Spain	ES	48.7	53.7	53.6
27	Sweden	SE	72.8	74.4	74.2
28	United Kingdom	UK	62	58.9	58
	European Union (28 countries)	**EU28**	**51.3**	**52.4**	**52.9**

Source: own elaboration based on EIGE b (accessed on 27 August, 2017)

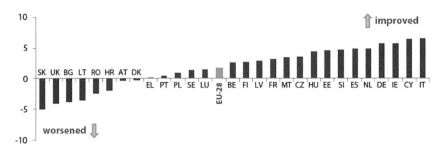

Figure 5.1 Scores of the Gender Equality Index for EU Member States (differences between 2005 and 2012)

Source: EIGE (2015a: 76)

If we look only at the situation in 2012 (Figure 5.2), the year with the most recent GEI calculations, we can observe that despite the progress compared to 2005, both states – Poland and Estonia – are below the EU average (52.9). In general, Estonia occupies 14th place (49.8) and Poland 19th (43.7) in terms of gender equality; moreover, Estonia follows Austria (50.2) and Poland is in a similar situation as the Czech Republic (43.8). The leader of the ranking is Sweden (74.2) and the last one is Romania (33.7). Of the 28 EU Member States, only 12 are above the EU average, and only one of the countries joining the EU in 2004 or later is included in this group, i.e. Slovenia, ranked seventh with the score of 57.3.

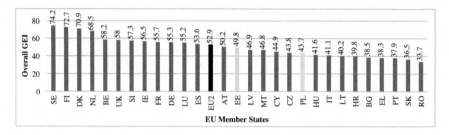

Figure 5.2 Overall scores of the Gender Equality Index for EU Member States (2012)
Source: own elaboration based on EIGE b (accessed on 27 August, 2017).

While discussing the state of art for the domain of power,

> in the EU, on average, progress is more marked in the sub-domain of politi-cal decision-making (up 11 points) than in the sub-domain of economic decision-making (up by 6.3 points) between 2005 and 2012. Progress is very uneven across (and within) Member States, with countries such as Germany or Spain experiencing a marked increase in one and a large decrease in the other sub-domain, while still seeing an overall improvement in the domain of power.
>
> (EIGE, 2015a: 88)

One can notice that in 2005 Estonia (index score for power of 23.3) and Poland (24) were in a comparable situation and both much below the EU average of 31.4. By 2012, the situation for the EU has improved and the index score for power has reached 39.7 points. (Figure 5.3). Poland has come close to this result (38.5), while Estonia has seen an increase in the index value but much lower (27.9). In terms of economic power considered separately, in 2005 the EU score was 25.4, with Estonia (22.3) and Poland (21.1) below its average. In 2012, the scores for all three have risen, for Estonia the change was modest with the result of 23.3 while Poland with the score of 33.7 has surpassed the EU average of 31.7.

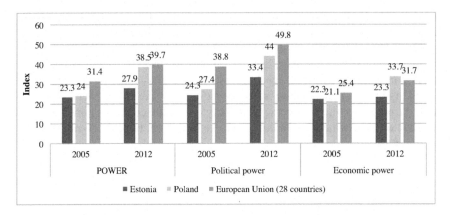

Figure 5.3 Scores for the domain "power" and its two sub-domains for Poland, Estonia, the EU (2005 and 2012)

Source: own elaboration based on: EIGE b (accessed on 27 August, 2017); EIGE (2015a: 89)

For the purposes of the Gender Equality Index, the score for the sub-domain of economic power is calculated on the basis of such indicators as: 1) share of members of boards in largest quoted companies (supervisory board or board of directors) (18+ population) and 2) share of members of central bank (18+ population). According to the indicators for 2012, the share of women among members of boards in the largest quoted companies was 8% in Estonia and 12% in Poland compared to 16% for the EU average. In the case of female representation among members of central banks the share for Poland (24%) was much higher and for Estonia (18%) marginally higher than the EU score (17%). In contrast, it is worth paying attention to the structure of the population by sex in studied EU countries: in 2012 women represented 51.6% of Poland's population of 38.54 million inhabitants and 53.4% of Estonia's population equaled 1.33 million people (EIGE b; EIGE, 2015a: 89). Despite the significant difference in the absolute numbers of the population, women accounted for more than half of the population in both countries. However, this fact was not reflected in their involvement in decision-making positions on corporate boards and central banks where they are greatly under-represented.

Conclusions

The advancement of gender balance on corporate boards in the EU has been achieved in part by political and regulatory pressure with the *Strategy for equality between women and men* introduced in 2010. Still, unfortunately, significant progress appeared in few member countries. The largest percentage point increase was recorded in Italy (+25.2%). In Poland, the improvement amounted to 8.3% and in Estonia only to 1.2% (EC DG JUST, 2016: 2–3).

The studies prove that the rise of percentage of women's representation on corporate boards is more easily achieved with gender equality instruments. In all Member States with the highest percentage of the share of women on corporate boards positive actions exemplified by quotas mechanisms (either obligatory or voluntary) are applied. It proves that the gender equality instruments (representing at least so-called soft law) are indispensable to accelerate the equality between men and women in decision-making. They should aim, among other things, at:

*   erosion of gender stereotypes,
*   increasing women's self-confidence through promotion of examples of women's success,
*   enhancing women's professional development through courses,
*   promoting work–life balance,
*   ensuring safe and healthy working environment and non-discriminatory treatment of men and women.

Only such intersectional and multidimensional actions enable the overcoming of obstacles encountered by women in decision-making such as sexism, glass ceiling, sticky floor, glass walls or sexual harassment. Tools for enhancement of gender equality on corporate boards can be adopted by individual companies or by groups of companies on their own initiative as part of their corporate governance (e.g. GE Poland has introduced a diversity policy under which several different programs enhancing women's career development were implemented) and can include clear and non-discriminatory application and selection criteria for board members, adoption of gender equality plan as a board's operational or strategic objective and adoption of networking programs for women or by third parties, and can by exemplified by databases of female board member candidates, networks of women occupying CEO and managerial posts, or development of programs promoting women's entrepreneurship (Słomka-Gołębiowska, 2016: 38–41). It is worth emphasizing that such actions seem to be more effective if they are pre-scribed by legally binding instruments.

In Poland, legal obligation to adopt gender equality measures refers only to parliamentary elections to Sejm (lower chamber of Polish Parliament) and to the European Parliament as well to local elections (municipal, county council and voivodeship council elections). The Election Code (Journal of Laws from 2011 No. 21 item 112 as amended) requires that the number of candidates of either gender on a constituency list must not be lower than 35% of total number of can-didates (Sejm, 2011). In addition, in elections at county level, for a list consisting of three candidates, there must be at least one candidate representing each sex. When it comes to women on corporate boards there is no universally binding legal instrument devoted to gender-balanced representation. Gender quotas are included either in internal law or soft law, e.g. Warsaw Stock Exchanges' Code of Good Practice that obliges WSE-listed companies to publish a description of their diversity policy for corporate governing bodies and its key managers on their website, although it does not prescribe any sanctions for non-compliance, and the

Ministry of the State Treasury's ordinance for partially state-owned companies to select qualified supervisory board members while considering gender balance (Deloitte, 2017: 63). In Estonia, there are no national measures nor quotas in place (EC DG JUST, 2016: 6–7).

The divergence or the absence of regulation on women's representation on corporate boards at national level in EU Member States, including Poland and Estonia, resulting, to some extent, from a lack of such legislation at EU level, has different and long-term consequences. It does not only lead to the discrepancies in the number of women among executive and non-executive directors and different rates of increase across Member States, but it also poses barriers to the EU internal market by imposing divergent corporate governance requirements on companies which is particularly burdensome in the case of those operating across borders. In this perspective, the issue of gender balance on corporate boards seems to be both a legal and a socio-economic matter affecting the functioning of companies and states alike.

Notes

1   This chapter was prepared on the basis of the results of the research conducted by Dr Marta Pachocka and Dr Aleksandra Szczerba-Zawada from September 2016 to September 2017 in the framework of the project: "CEWSE – Centre of Excellence at Warsaw School of Economics on European Union's Security and Stability in a new Economic, Social & Geopolitical Settlement" co-financed by the European Union under the Erasmus+ Programme (Decision No: 575418-EPP-1–2016–1-PL-EPPJMO-CoE).
2   More about the conceptual framework and methodology of the GEI: EIGE (2013: 14–54) and EIGE (2015a: 11–27).

References

Aluchna, M. 2017. Women on boards: The Polish experience within the context of EU recommendations in Caliyurt, K. (ed.), *Women and Sustainability in Business: A Global Perspective*, Oxon/New York: Routledge, 104–120.

Aluchna, M., Krejner-Nowecka, A., Tomczyk, E. 2016. Women on corporate boards in Poland: The current state of art, *Society and Economy*, 17(3), 227–248.

Bałandynowicz-Panfil, K., Opacka, U. 2005. *Gdańsk Gender Budget Initiative*, Gdańsk: The Network of East-West Women NEWW Polska, www.neww.org.pl/download/Gdansk_Gender_Budget_Initiative.pdf, accessed 27 August, 2017.

Bell, M. 2011. The principle of equal treatment: Widening and deepening in Craig, P., de Burca, G. (eds.), *The Evolution of EU Law*, Oxford: Oxford University Press, 611–639.

Bojarski, Ł. 2016. Poland – New Government Plenipotentiary for Equal Treatment with different mandate, problems with the budget of the Ombud – Polish Equality Body, European Commission, Directorate-General for Justice and Consumers (EC DG JUST) – European network of legal experts in gender equality and non-discrimination, News Report, February 17, 2016, www.equalitylaw.eu/country/poland, accessed 27 August, 2017.

Budżet Równych Szans, https://genderbudgeting.wordpress.com/, accessed 27 August, 2017.

Commissioner for Human Rights (in Poland), www.rpo.gov.pl/en, accessed 27 August, 2017.

Council of the European Union (CEU). 2011a. Council conclusions on the European Pact for gender equality for the period 2011–2020, 3073th Employment, Social Policy, Health and Consumer Affairs Council Meeting, Brussels, 7 March, 2011.

Council of the European Union (CEU). 2011b. Review of the implementation of the Beijing Platform for Action – Women and the Economy: Reconciliation of work and family life as a precondition for equal participation in the labour market – Council Conclusions, 17816/11, SOC 1050, Brussels, 2 December, 2011.

Council of the European Union (CEU). 2014. Council conclusions on Women and the economy: Economic independence from the perspective of part-time work and self-employment, Employment, Social Policy, Health and Consumer Affairs Council Meeting, Luxembourg, 19 June, 2014.

Council of the European Union (CEU). 2017. Proposal for a Directive of the European Parliament and of the Council on improving the gender balance among directors of companies listed on stock exchanges and related measures – Progress Report, 9496/17, Brussels, May 31, 2017, http://data.consilium.europa.eu/doc/document/ST-9496-2017-INIT/en/pdf, accessed 27 August, 2017.

Court of Justice of the European Union (CJEU). 1978. Judgment of the Court of 15 June 1978, Gabrielle Defrenne v Société anonyme belge de navigation aérienne Sabena, Reference for a preliminary ruling: Cour de cassation – Belgium, Equal conditions of employment for men and women, Case 149/77.

Deloitte Global Center for Corporate Governance (Deloitte). 2017. Women in the boardroom: A global perspective, 5th ed., www2.deloitte.com/global/en/pages/risk/articles/women-in-the-boardroom5th-edition.html, accessed 27 August, 2017.

European Commission (EC). 2011a. Commission staff working paper: The gender balance in business leadership, SEC (2011) 246 final, Brussels, March 1, 2011, http://ec.europa.eu/justice/gender-equality/files/gender_balance_decision_making/110301_gender_balance_business_leadership_en.pdf, accessed 27 August, 2017.

European Commission (EC). 2011b. *Strategy for Equality between Women and Men 2010–2015*, Luxembourg: Publications Office of the European Union.

European Commission (EC). 2012. Special eurobarometer 376: Women in decision-making positions – report, http://ec.europa.eu/commfrontoffice/publicopinion/archives/ebs/ebs_376_en.pdf, accessed 27 August, 2017.

European Commission (EC). 2013. Report from the Commission to the European Parliament and the Council on the application of Directive 2006/54/EC of the European Parliament and of the Council of 5 July 2006 on the implementation of the principle of equal opportunities and equal treatment of men and women in matters of employment and occupation (recast), {SWD(2013) 512 final}, COM(2013) 861 final, Brussels, 6, December, 2013.

European Commission (EC). 2014. Commission Recommendation of 7.3.2014 on strengthening the principle of equal pay between men and women through transparency (Text with EEA relevance), C(2014) 1405 final, Brussels, 7, March, 2014.

European Commission (EC). 2015a. Report from the Commission to the European Parliament, the Council and the European Economic and Social Committee on the application of Council Directive 2004/113/EC implementing the principle of equal treatment between men and women in the access to and supply of goods and services, COM(2015) 190 final, Brussels, 5, May, 2015.

European Commission (EC). 2015b. *Strategic Engagement for Gender Equality 2016–2019*, Luxembourg: Publications Office of the European Union.

European Commission, Directorate-General for Employment, Social Affairs and Equal Opportunities (EC DG ESAEO). 2007a. *Decision-Making: Exchange of Good Practices*, Luxembourg: Office for Official Publications of the European Communities.

European Commission, Directorate-General for Employment, Social Affairs and Equal Opportunities (EC DG ESAEO). 2007b. Opinion on EU Network of Women in Economic and Political Decision-Making Positions, ec.europa.eu/social/BlobServlet?docId=6235, accessed 27 August, 2017.

European Commission, Directorate-General for Employment, Social Affairs and Equal Opportunities (EC DG ESAEO). 2008. *Women and Men in Decision-Making 2007 – Analysis of the Situation and Trends*, Luxembourg: Office for Official Publications of the European Communities.

European Commission, Directorate-General for Employment, Social Affairs and Equal Opportunities (EC DG ESAEO). 2009. *Women in European Politics – Time for Action*, Luxembourg: Publications Office of the European Union.

European Commission, Directorate-General for Employment, Social Affairs and Equal Opportunities (EC DG ESAEO). 2010. *More Women in Senior Positions – Key to Economic Stability and Growth*, Luxembourg: Publications Office of the European Union.

European Commission, Directorate-General for Justice (EC DG JUST). 2012. *Women in Economic Decision-Making in the EU: Progress Report: A Europe 2020 Initiative*, Luxembourg: Publications Office of the European Union.

European Commission, Directorate-General for Justice (EC DG JUST). 2013. *Women and Men in Leadership Positions in the European Union 2013*, Luxembourg: Publications Office of the European Union.

European Commission, Directorate-General for Justice and Consumers (EC DG JUST). 2016. Gender balance on corporate boards: Europe is cracking the glass ceiling, Factsheet, July 2016, http://ec.europa.eu/justice/gender-equality/files/gender_balance_decision_making/1607_factsheet_final_wob_data_en.pdf, accessed 27 August, 2017.

European Commission, Directorate-General for Justice and Consumers (EC DG JUST a). Gender equality: Legislation, http://ec.europa.eu/justice/gender-equality/law/index_en.htm, accessed 27 August, 2017.

European Commission, Directorate-General for Justice and Consumers (EC DG JUST b). Gender equality: Documents, http://ec.europa.eu/newsroom/just/item-detail.cfm?item_id=52696#gender, accessed 27 August, 2017.

European Commission's Network to Promote Women in Decision-making in Politics and the Economy 2012. Working Paper: How to engage senior men to promote women to senior decision-making positions in their organizations, http://ec.europa.eu/newsroom/just/item-detail.cfm?item_id=52696#gender, accessed 27 August, 2017.

European Institute for Gender Equality (EIGE). 2013. Gender equality index report, Publications Office of the European Union–EIGE http://eige.europa.eu/rdc/eige-publications/gender-equality-index-report, accessed 27 August, 2017.

European Institute for Gender Equality (EIGE). 2015a. Gender equality index 2015 – measuring gender equality in the European Union 2005–2012, Publications Office of the European Union–EIGE, http://eige.europa.eu/rdc/eige-publications/gender-equality-index-2015-measuring-gender-equality-european-union-2005-2012-report, accessed 27 August, 2017.

European Institute for Gender Equality (EIGE). 2015b. Gender equality index 2015 – measuring gender equality in the European Union 2005–2012, Country profiles, Publications Office of the European Union–EIGE, http://eige.europa.eu/rdc/eige-publications/gender-equality-index-2015-measuring-gender-equality-european-union-2005-2012-report, accessed 27 August, 2017.

European Institute for Gender Equality (EIGE a). Country specific information: Poland and Estonia, http://eige.europa.eu/gender-mainstreaming/countries, accessed 27 August, 2017.

European Institute for Gender Equality (EIGE b). Gender statistics database, http://eige.europa.eu/gender-statistics/dgs, accessed 27 August, 2017.

European Institute for Gender Equality (EIGE c). What is gender mainstreaming, http://eige.europa.eu/gender-mainstreaming/what-is-gender-mainstreaming, accessed 27 August, 2017.

European Network of Equality Bodies (Equinet), www.equineteurope.org/Gender-Equality-and-Equal, accessed 27 August, 2017.

European Union (EU). 1957. Treaty establishing the European Economic Community, http://eur-lex.europa.eu/legal-content/EN/TXT/?uri=celex:11957E/TXT, accessed 27 August, 2017.

European Union (EU). 2012a. Consolidated version of the Treaty on the Functioning of the European Union, OJ C 326, 26.10.2012, http://eur-lex.europa.eu/legal-content/EN/TXT/?uri=celex%3A12012E%2FTXT, accessed 27 August, 2017.

European Union (EU). 2012b. Proposal for a Directive of the European Parliament and of the Council on improving the gender balance among non-executive directors of companies listed on stock exchanges and related measures, COM/2012/0614 final – 2012/0299 (COD), http://eur-lex.europa.eu/legal-content/EN/TXT/?uri=CELEX%3A52012PC0614, accessed 27 August, 2017.

European Union (EU). 2014. Directive 2014/95/EU of the European Parliament and of the Council of 22 October 2014 amending Directive 2013/34/EU as regards disclosure of non-financial and diversity information by certain large undertakings and groups (Text with EEA relevance), OJ L 330, 15 November, 2014, http://eur-lex.europa.eu/legal-content/EN/TXT/?uri=CELEX%3A32014L0095, accessed 27 August, 2017.

Gender Equality and Equal Treatment Commissioner (in Estonia), www.vordoigusvolinik.ee/?lang=en, accessed 27 August, 2017.

Hafner-Burton, E., Pollack, M.A. 2009. Mainstreaming gender in the European Union: Getting the incentives right, *Comparative European Politics*, 7(1), 114–138.

Human Rights Center (in Estonia), https://humanrights.ee/en/topics-main/vordne-kohtlemine/equal-treatment-network/, accessed 27 August, 2017.

Kupts, M., Rell, M. 2015. *Uuring mitmekesisusest Eesti ettevõtetes*. Tallinn: Poliitikauringute Keskus Praxis.

Laas, A. 2016a. *Estonia* – Country report on gender equality 2016: How are EU rules transposed into national law?, European Commission, Directorate-General for Justice and Consumers (EC DG JUST) – European network of legal experts in gender equality and non-discrimination, www.equalitylaw.eu/country/estonia, accessed 27 August, 2017.

Laas, A. 2016b. Estonia – office of the gender equality and equal treatment commissioner under-resourced, European Commission, Directorate-General for Justice and Consumers (EC DG JUST) – European network of legal experts in gender equality and non-discrimination, News Report, September 27, 2016, www.equalitylaw.eu/country/estonia, accessed 27 August, 2017.

Mazowiecki Urząd Wojewódzki w Warszawie (MUW). 2015. Konkurs "Budżet równych szans. Gender Budgeting dla samorządów", May 17, 2015, www.mazowieckie.pl/pl/urzad/aktualne-projekty/wspolpraca-z-samorzada/aktualnosci/10720,Konkurs-quotBudzet-rownych-szans-Gender-Budgeting-dla-samorzadowquot.html, accessed 27 August, 2017.

Ministerstwo Nauki i Szkolnictwa Wyższego (MNiSW). 2015. Rozporządzenie Ministra Nauki i Szkolnictwa Wyższego z dnia 27 października 2015 r. w sprawie sposobu i trybu wyłaniania kandydatów na członków Komitetu Polityki Naukowej oraz sposobu powoływania tych członków. Dz. U. 2015 poz. 1879. [Regulation of the Minister of Science and Higher Education of 27 October 2015 on the method and procedure for selecting candidates for members of the Scientific Policy Committee and the manner of appointing these members. Journal of Laws from 2015 item 1879].

Ministerstwo Pracy i Polityki Społecznej, Departament Analiz Ekonomicznych i Prognoz (MPiPS DAEP). Równość szans, http://analizy.mpips.gov.pl/index.php/rowno-szans.html, accessed 27 August, 2017.

Ministry of Social Affairs of the Republic of Estonia (MSA). Gender equality and equal treatment, www.sm.ee/en/gender-equality-and-equal-treatment, accessed 27 August, 2017.

More, G. 1999. The principle of equal treatment: From market unifier to fundamental right in Craig, P., de Burca, G. (eds.), *The Evolution of EU Law*, Oxford: Oxford University Press.

Pełnomocnik Rządu do Spraw Równego Traktowania (PRdsRT). 2017. *Raport z realizacji Krajowego Programu Działań na Rzecz Równego Traktowania za 2015 rok*. Warszawa, www.spoleczenstwoobywatelskie.gov.pl/sites/default/files/rraport_za_2015_przyjety_przez_rm.pdf, accessed 27 August, 2017.

Pełnomocnik Rządu do Spraw Społeczeństwa Obywatelskiego i Równego Traktowania (PRdsSOiRT), www.spoleczenstwoobywatelskie.gov.pl/, accessed 27 August, 2017.

Riigikogu 2004. Gender Equality Act. Passed 07.04.2004. RT I 2004, 27, 181.

Riigikogu 2008. Equal Treatment Act. Passed 11.12.2008. RT I 2008, 56, 315.

Sejm 2010. Ustawa z dnia 3 grudnia 2010 r. o wdrożeniu niektórych przepisów Unii Europejskiej w zakresie równego traktowania. Dz.U. 2010 nr 254 poz. 1700. [Act of 3rd December, 2010 on the Implementation of Certain Provisions of the European Union in the Field of Equal Treatment (Journal of Laws from 2010 No. 245 item 1700 as amended)].

Sejm 2011. Ustawa z dnia 5 stycznia 2011 r. Kodeks wyborczy. Dz.U. 2011 nr 34 poz. 172 ze zm. [Act of 5 January, 2011 Election Code (Journal of Laws from 2011 No. 34 item 172 as amended)].

Senden, L., Selanec, G. 2012. *Positive Action Measures to Ensure Full Equality in Practice between Men and Women, Including on Company Boards*, Luxembourg: Publications Office of the European Union. European Commission, Directorate-General for Justice (EC DG JUST).

Senden, L., Selanec, G. 2013. *Positive Action Measures to Ensure Full Equality in Practice between Men and Women, Including on Company Boards*, Luxembourg: Publications Office of the European Union. European Commission, Directorate-General for Justice (EC DG JUST).

Słomka-Gołębiowska, A. 2016. *Kobiety we władzach spółek giełdowych w Polsce. Czas na zmiany*, Warszawa: Fundacja Liderek Biznesu, www.fundacjaliderekbiznesu.pl/pliki/Raport_FLB_20-05_Final.pdf, accessed27 August, 2017.

Szczerba-Zawada, A. 2011. The principle of equal treatment for men and women as regards access to employment and working conditions in the light of the judicial decisions of the Court of Justice of the European Union, *Studia Iuridica Toruniensia*, 9, 230–149, http://dx.doi.org/10.12775/SIT.2011.019, accessed 27 August, 2017.

Zawidzka-Łojek, A., Szczerba-Zawada, A. (eds.). 2015. *Prawo antydyskryminacyjne Unii Europejskiej*, Warszawa: Instytut Wydawniczy EuroPrawo.

Zielińska, E. 2016. *Poland* – Country report on gender equality 2016: How are EU rules transposed into national law? European Commission, Directorate-General for Justice and Consumers (EC DG JUST) – European network of legal experts in gender equality and non-discrimination, www.equalitylaw.eu/country/Poland, accessed 27 August, 2017.

6 Socio-economic perspective on women on boards

An African perspective

Justina Mutale and Anna Masłoń-Oracz

Introduction

To facilitate development and foster opportunities for women entrepreneurs, not only in Africa, local institutions need to be strengthened in terms of gender and equality-focused practice. The equal society, regardless of methodological nuances, is encompassed with non-discrimination, equal treatment and equal opportunities (McCrudden and Prechal, 2009).

This chapter includes parallel and independent analysis carried out on two levels: companies level and regional level.

The examination applies a down-to-top model, in other words, the analysis is commenced from the studies on actions and strategies at the level of the companies and then at the level of the region.

The stated research problem, defined task and the objectives of this chapter determined the research methodology. The following methods are used:

1   Analysis of the literature, source materials as well as program documents; and
2   Comparative and descriptive analysis.

The completion of the defined research task and objectives was based on foreign literature, mainly including English-speaking economic literature devoted to women's empowerment, gender equality and corporate strategies.

Women on boards – African perspective

Recently McKinsey & Co. undertook research at over 200 companies and interviews with more than 30 women leaders across Africa. The finding were released in the report *Women Matter Africa* (McKinsey & Co., 2016) and highlights that the continent has taken big strides regarding women's representation in the private and public sectors. In general, one can observe that Africa has more women in executive committee, CEO and board roles in companies than the average worldwide (McKinsey & Co., 2016). Yet women are still under-represented at every level of the corporate ladder – non-management and middle and senior management – and fall in number the higher they climb. The outcomes are confirmed in the other research made by Women Board Directors in the Fortune Global 200 and beyond, presenting Africa on the fifth position in the regional comparison of women on boards, which proves that outside of the three largest economies, more and more countries are taking steps to improve women's board representation through legislative mandates or private sector efforts.

In 2015, the African Development Bank carried out a survey on board diversity in Africa. The survey found that women make up 14.4% of boards of blue-chip companies in Africa, making Africa a region with the third highest proportion of women on boards globally, superseded only by Europe and North America (ADB, 2015). The survey also revealed that even with the least per capita income, the percentage of African women directors surpassed the percentages in other regions of the world. The report therefore concluded that the level of women's economic participation in Africa is much closer to their male counterparts than those in South Asia and other parts of the world (ADB, 2015).

The Report from the African Development Bank indicates that some companies in Africa – such as Safaricom (mobile phone giant) of Kenya, East African Breweries (beer makers) and Sasko (food manufacturers) of South Africa – have more than 30% women representation on their respective boards (ADB, 2015). While this indicates a relatively strong representation, it falls far short of reflecting the contributions of women to Africa's economy in general. Women in Africa comprise over half of Africa's growing population, and yet they make up 70% of the informal sector, where work is poorly paid and not stable. The UN Food and Agricultural Organization states that the African food chain depends on women, who contribute up to 70% of the crop production, 50% of animal husbandry and 60% of marketing stall traders (UNFAO, 2011). Despite the sincere efforts of

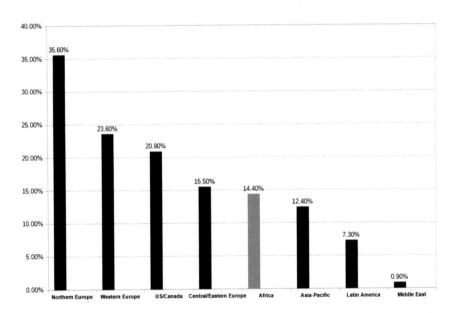

Figure 6.1 Region comparison of women on boards

Source: 2015, CWDI Report on Women Directors of Fortune Global 200: 2004–2014 major corporations, the proportion of women quickly drops as one looks higher up the corporate hierarchy (ADB, 2015).

African women have demonstrated and continue to demonstrate their ability and willingness to contribute to the development of their continent through their participation in employment, business, politics, women's movements and affirmative action. To accelerate the process, the African Union declared 2015 as the *Year of the Empowerment of Women in Africa* (AU, 2015). Following that, 2016 was declared as the *Year of Human Rights in Africa, with a special focus on the Rights of Women and Girls* (AU, 2016). This year, 2017 marks seven years since the launch of the African Women's Decade by the African Union, 14 years since the adoption of the Maputo Protocol (African Charter on Human and People's Rights and the Rights of Women) and 24 years since the Pre-Congress of the 7th Pan-African Congress (PAC) held in Kampala in Uganda (AU, 2017). In 2013, the African Union adopted Africa's Agenda 2063 as the continent's development roadmap, with a special focus on the achievement of gender quality and women's empowerment (AU, 2017). All the above instruments, affirmative actions and initiatives seek to promote and place great emphasis on the rights of women to equality of opportunity and equality of participation in the workplace and the economy (MEWC, 2016).

In addition, African women have been an integral part of the various global initiatives and affirmative actions aimed at achieving women's empowerment and gender equality (UN, 2013). From the women's suffrage movement in the 19th century, moving on to the Convention on the Elimination of All Forms of Discrimination Against Women (CEDAW), adopted by the UN in 1979 (UN, 2000–2009), followed by the Beijing Platform for Action declared at the 1995 UN Fourth World Conference in China (UN, 1995), gender equality and women's empowerment have been included as a priority in the UN Millennium Development Goals (MDGs) (UN, 2013) and have once again been highlighted as a priority in the Post-2015 UN Sustainable Development Goals (SDGs) (UN, 2017).

Among other targets to achieve gender equality and women's empowerment, Goal No. 5 of the SDGs strives to "ensure women's full and effective participation and equal opportunities for leadership at all levels of decision-making in political, economic and public life" (UN, 2017).

Consequently, the theme for the 61st Session of the UN Commission on the Status of Women (CSW61) held in March 2017 was focused on the "Economic Empowerment of Women in a Changing World of Work". The UN has also instituted a high-level panel on women's economic empowerment. Both initiatives apply to women in Africa and the rest of the world (UN, 2017).

African economies have been growing, and at the center of this growing continent are women ready to make a difference. While many African women have become involved in the development of the continent, millions more are left behind. In 2013, the *Economist* reported that over the past decade six out ten of the world's fastest growing economies have been in Africa. In just a few years, Africa's economy has grown faster than that of East Asia and other parts of the world (Economist, 2013). In addition, African women have attained the requisite higher levels of education and are adequately qualified to participate on equal footing with their male counterparts in the corporate boardrooms and elsewhere (Fraser-Moleketi, 2015).

As stated by the 2015 African Development Bank Report, there are many competent women working in private companies in Africa and there is no shortage of qualified candidates for roles in senior management or to serve on boards. However, only a privileged group of women manage to find work in the corporate world. This leaves the majority of women in Africa at the periphery of leadership and decision-making, thereby giving men top positions and dominance of corporations (ADB, 2015).

Women in Africa are still fighting an uphill battle to get equal representation on corporate boards. However, the advent of globalization has seen women on the African continent moving with the rest of the world towards an era where attitudes and behavior towards women are changing (IFC, 2011). In recent years, gender dynamics have evolved in Africa with the role and perception of women in society evolving as a result. While it is inspiring to see that over the years positive gains have been made towards gender equality and women's empowerment, it is evident that these gains are too few and far between. A huge gender gap still exists in Africa and the rest of the world, with only a few women, who have so far had the privilege to hold very prominent and visible high-ranking positions of real power, real influence and real authority in politics, business, society and all other walks of life (OECD, 2013).

The most significant barrier to female leadership in Africa as in other parts of the world is that, despite the women's suffrage movement and various initiatives and affirmative actions for gender equality, there still exists a huge gender gap in the leadership system around the world. This has been created by an institutionalized form of gender discrimination that is embedded in the failure to adjust the male work model to fit the needs of women (OECD, 2013). Even in the 21st century, the world still lives in a patriarchal society where the majority of women continue to be discriminated against, and women's potential contributions to politics, economic advancement and social progress have been marginalized by a system that discriminates against women and puts limits on women's full potential (OECD, 2013). While these initiatives and affirmative actions have made some visible strides, women to date are still lagging far behind their male counterparts in all areas and in nearly all parts of the world, because leadership roles in the economic, social and political systems of the world are still modelled on the ambitions and perspectives of men (OECD, 2013).

Graca Machel, former first lady of Mozambique and South Africa as well as international advocate for women's and children's rights, states that:

> the exclusion of women from boardrooms starts right from school. Making significant advancements in this area would require understanding the problem from a complete dimension of a woman's life span, starting by looking at the educational differences right from primary school, which contributes to gender disparity in the Boardroom.
>
> (Machel, World Economic Forum, 2015)

The reasons women in Africa are lagging behind in the boardroom are many. As stated previously, only a privileged group of women manage to find work in the corporate world, because the majority of board appointments continue to be made in a largely informal process, based on the proverbial 'old boys' ' networks, fed by family, clan, school, and business relations and connections. Just like other women around the world, female board members in Africa consider negative stereotypes and an 'old boys' club' culture as the most imposing barriers to their presence on corporate boards (ADB, 2015).

The existing design of leadership roles, which are based on patriarchal values, coupled with institutional discrimination against women form a huge hindrance to African women's ability to realize their full potential on corporate boards and other areas. In Africa and many parts of the world, cultures and social conditioning prevent women from unleashing their full potential in leadership roles. Women are not provided with an enabling environment in a globally patriarchal society that does not give women enough opportunities. As a result, women in Africa still experience lack of access to key services and economic opportunities. The level of gender inequality mirrors the stage of economic development, demonstrating a link between social inequality and work inequality. Opening economic potential by increasing women's economic participation would change the fortunes of the continent (World Bank, 2009).

A good example of African women's political and economic efficacy is Rwandan women. After the devastating genocide, Rwandan women have risen from the conflict stronger than any other woman in the world, taking up positions of power in politics, business and other walks of life. With approximately 64% women in Parliament, Rwanda remains the only country in the world with a female-dominated parliament. Observers attribute Rwandan women's impressive performance in the elections to a decision by political parties to give both genders equal chances of making it to parliament, as opposed to past tendencies when men would largely occupy more strategic positions on party electoral lists (USAID, 2009).

The centrality of gender equality in national development is underpinned by President Paul Kagame who reaffirmed his conviction that "gender equality is not just women's business, it is everybody's business and that gender equality and women's empowerment are critical to sustainable socioeconomic development" (Republic of Rwanda, 2010).

In Rwanda, success in economics mirrors the rise of women in politics. Approximately 45% of Rwandan businesses are owned by women. In the aftermath of the genocide, Rwandan women who lost their husbands found themselves thrust into the role of bread-earners without requiring permission from their men to lead (UNDP, 2013). Without men from whom to seek permission, Rwandan women found themselves involved in agriculture, having to take over their deceased husband's, father's, brother's or uncle's farms. Consequently, the economy of Rwanda has since tripled in size and has grown at an average of over 6% since 2004 (Mbabazi, 2013)

Research by the Commonwealth Secretariat found that in Africa state-owned enterprise boards were made up of at least 30% women; this is more than the number of Commonwealth countries from all other regions combined (The

Commonwealth, 2017). The report states that this success is not, however, true across the region, with a regional average of 25.1% with some individual countries having levels of 0%. Seychelles is highlighted as having the highest percentage in the region at 45% and the highest throughout the 44 Commonwealth countries for which data was available. When it comes to Private Sector Boards in Africa, the research shows that the number of women on boards in the private sector were far lower than that of women on state-owned enterprise boards, with Rwanda being the only country achieving over 30% women on boards. The report concluded that a third of African Commonwealth countries researched had less than 10% women on private sector boards (The Commonwealth, 2017).

The Rwandan Minister of State in charge of agriculture proudly asserts that: "Bringing women out of the home and field has been essential to our rebuilding. We are becoming a nation that understands that there are huge financial benefits to equality" (Mbabazi, 2013)

The 2015 McKinsey Global Institute Report states that Africa could see its economy grow by $300 billion by the year 2025 if the continent can achieve gender equality in the place of work by creating space for women to participate in the labor markets on equal footing with their male counterparts (McKinsey, 2015). By so doing, the economic gains of the continent could reach as high as $700 billion or just under its overall Gross Domestic Product of $1.7 trillion. The report further points out that increasing the number of women's participation in the labor force and moving them to productive areas of the economy, in addition to giving women an equal number of working hours as their male counterparts, could yield further billions for the continent's economy (McKinsey, 2015).

The 2015 African Development Bank Report focusing on board diversity in Africa made a list of recommendations to boost female participation on corporate boards, which included furthering research on the situation of women on corporate boards, keeping track of obstacles and progress, mandated public reporting of board composition by listed companies and making board diversity as a listing requirement (ADB, 2015).

According to the Report, the 307 top listed companies from 12 African stock exchanges covered in the study have a total of 2,865 seats on their boards of directors, of which 364 (an average of 12.7%) are held by women, with large-cap companies having a higher proportion at 14.4% (ADB, 2015).

This indicates that for every eight board seats, seven are occupied by men and only one by a woman. Out of the 307 African companies included in the survey, 101 or 32.9% have absolute male boards (ADB, 2015).

Kenya ranks highest in Africa on the proportion of women on boards of blue-chip companies at 19.5%; South Africa is second at 7.4%; while Botswana and Zambia tie at 16.9%. Tanzania is at 14.3%, Uganda at 12.9% and Nigeria at 11.5% while Egypt is at 8.2%. Tunisia (7.9%) and Cote-d'Ivoire (5.1%) have an average of less than one in ten board members as women (ADB, 2015).

Safaricom in Kenya has five women out of its 11 board members at 45.5%. Safaricom is ranked as Africa's most admired brand according to Brand Africa 100 rankings (ADB, 2015).

The three other companies ranked on Brand Africa top ten with significant representation of women directors are Sasko (South African food manufacturers) at 33%, East African Breweries of Kenya at 27% and MTN mobile phone operators at 21%. MTN is ranked first in the Brand Africa 100 ranking (ADB, 2015).

Nigerian Star Beer, which is ranked tenth in Brand Africa 100 ranking, only has two women out of 15 directors at 13.3%. The rest of the top ten most admired brands ranked in Brand Africa 100, which include Globacom (mobile phones), Dangote (cement), Mukwano, Simu TV (television), Zenith Bank (Banking) and Peak Milk (milk manufacturers) appear not to have any women on their boards, with Dangote Cement having an entire board comprised of men (ADB, 2015).

Three South African companies hold the next highest percentages in the ADB rankings: Impala Platinum (38.5%), Kumba Iron Ore (36.4%) and Woolworths Holdings (30.8%).

Among mid-cap companies, Stanbic Bank of Uganda and Barclays Bank of Botswana both have 33.3% women directors. Kenya Power & Lighting and Lafarge of Zambia lead the small-cap companies with 33.3% women board directors, while Camelot Ghana lead the micro-caps with three women directors out of six at 50% (ADB, 2015).

Although quotas are the most immediate way to generate a large increase in female representation on boards, many firms in Africa have voluntarily taken proactive steps towards gender parity on corporate boards, often with the assistance of advocacy groups. In addition, some African governments have taken necessary steps to institute women's representation in boardrooms. Kenya and South Africa have government mandates for women's representation on the boards of state-owned companies, while the private sector of Kenya, Morocco, Malawi, Nigeria and South Africa have integrated diversity into their principles of good corporate governance (ADB, 2015).

Women on boards in the mining industry with special focus on South Africa

According to the Pricewaterhouse Cooper (PwC) Report of 2013 on *Women in Mining*, South Africa holds the top position in gender diversity out of the top 100 mining companies in the world, with an average of 21.5% of women on boards (PwC, 2013). The report sought to establish facts around the representation of women on boards and other senior management positions in the mining industry. The report agrees with other studies regarding the strong correlation between improved financial performance and the increased participation of women on boards. It finally concluded that a growing body of evidence has shown a strong business case for increasing the representation of women on boards (PwC, 2013).

The report further asserts that profit margins are higher for mining companies that have women on their boards, which is consistent with the findings of a study by Catalyst, which found that companies with high female board representation tend to have higher return on sales, as well as higher return on invested capital and higher return on equity (Catalyst, 2007). Similarly, a study by the Credit Suisse

Research Institute also found that companies that have women on their boards demonstrate a higher return on equity, as well as lower gearing, higher price/book value with a better than average growth (Credit Suisse, 2012).

Many studies have demonstrated why it makes good business sense for any company or industry to have a diverse board. Some countries in Africa, such as South Africa, have put in place legislation which ensures that companies and industries adhere to having gender diversified boards. Studies have also shown that gender diversity yields a positive impact on the financial and social success of any company (PwC, 2013). Mining companies listed on the Johannesburg Stock Exchange in South Africa have been reported to have the best level of female board representation, while those listed on the London Stock Exchange are reported as having the worst levels of female representation. Globally, Stock Exchange Average percentages of women on the boards of the top 100 mining companies are indicated as follows: South Africa (JSE 21.05); Australia (ASX 11.97); US (NYSE 7.34); Hong Kong (SEHK 6.02); Canada (TSX/TSXv 5.24); UK (LSE/ AIM 4.27) (PwC, 2013).

South Africa has introduced policies aimed at gender equality that apply to companies incorporated in, or those that operate in and/or are publicly traded in the country. In South Africa, there are a number of laws, rules and regulations, which encourage or require companies to ensure and accelerate sustainable participation of women in the economy (PwC, 2013). For example, as part of South Africa's Broad-Based Black Economic Empowerment (B-BBEE) Codes of Good Practice, small South African enterprises and medium to large South African enterprises are all encouraged to ensure greater representation of their board and senior management positions are held by persons who are considered 'Historically Disadvantaged South Africans (HSDAs)' (PwC, 2013). This group includes women. The South African government has also put in place several other programs aimed at supporting or increasing female ownership of companies. These include, the Gender and Women Empowerment Unit, which aims to support women-owned enterprises; the 2010 South African Mining Charter, aims to transfer 26% ownership of the mining industry to HDSAs, which includes women. Although compliance with these corporate governance principles is not mandatory, companies are required to disclose noncompliance in their annual reports. As demonstrated by South Africa, gender equality regulation can lead to improved gender diversity (PwC, 2013).

Research has shown that a more gender-diverse board results in better financial performance. Out of the top 500 mining companies surveyed by PricewaterhouseCoopers, 18 mining companies with 25% or more women on their boards had an average net profit margin of 49% higher than the others in the 2011 financial year (PwC, 2013). The PwC research also shows that those mining companies who have women on their boards have a higher average profit margin overall of about 23% than the average net profit margin for the top 100 mining companies, who have only 20% (PwC, 2013). The report compared return on equity, price/ earnings ratio, shareholder yield, market capitalization and net profit margin to the percentage of women on boards for the top 500 mining companies and found a positive correlation between net profit margin and market capitalization. The findings of the PwC report are consistent with those of other studies on gender diversity and corporate performance, including the 2007 study by Catalyst, which found that over a six-year period, companies that had more women on their boards outperformed their rivals by 42% higher return on sales, 66% higher return on invested capital and 53% higher return on equity (Catalyst, 2007). The Credit Suisse Research Institute also found that companies with women on their boards have a higher return on equity, lower gearing, higher price/book value and better than average growth (Credit Suisse, 2012).

Anglo-American, which has a secondary listing on the Johannesburg Stock Exchange, is a multinational mining company based in Johannesburg, South Africa and London in the UK. Gender diversity is a key strategic priority for Anglo-American (PwC, 2013). To ensure gender diversity, Anglo-American have put in place a number of initiatives aimed at improving female representation in its workforce, which is aligned with the company's vision of being an employer of choice in the mining industry (PwC, 2013). To support this objective, the Anglo-American Group Executive Committee have endorsed the setting of formal targets to measure the proportion of women in the workforce as a whole, as well as within the management teams. Each business unit and discipline within Anglo-American is required to establish its own internal targets that contribute to the overall corporate level target (PwC, 2013). As part of the approach, gender statistics are periodically reviewed by each business unit in its Quarterly Performance Report in order to identify areas where good progress is being made, and to ascertain where additional intervention might be required (PwC, 2013). In order to promote and replicate internal best practice on gender diversity, Anglo-American publish a '*Gender Diversity Compendium*' regularly, which is circulated internally. The compendium highlights initiatives that have been successful around the world in improving the number of women represented in the Anglo-American workforce. These are categorized according to the following four strategic themes: (1) establishing a conducive working environment; (2) driving gender diversity through robust workforce planning and recruitment; (3) accelerating gender diversity through employee development; (4) improving communication and understanding of gender diversity objectives (PwC, 2013).

According to Pricewaterhouse Cooper, the mining industry lags behind all other industries, including the oil and gas industry, at just 4% of board seats occupied by women. The report states that the low proportion of women in the mining workforce is compounded at the board level. It is therefore apparent that the mining industry is faced with unprecedented challenges in the search for talent (PwC, 2013). The PwC report states that as demographics change and demand for natural resources grows, the ability by mining companies to find the right talents with the specialized skills to meet the demand is becoming severely stretched. Furthermore, the Conference Board of Canada found that boards with three or more women demonstrated different governance behaviors to those with all male boards (Conference Board of Canada, 2002). It stated that the more gender balanced boards were, the more likely they were to ensure better communication, adhere to a code of conduct, identify suitable criteria for measuring strategy and monitor its implementation. Such boards were also more likely to focus on gender diversity, employee satisfaction and corporate social responsibility. The conference report points out that a gender-diverse board is more effective and draws on a range of experiences and perspectives (Conference Board of Canada, 2002). Other publications, such as the Lord Davies Report and The Female FTSE Board Report titled *Milestone or Millstone* reported that companies perform better when they include people from a diverse range of perspectives and backgrounds, including a good gender balance (UK Department of Business, 2011). The Lord Davies Report concluded that: "Inclusive and diverse boards are more likely to be effective, better able to understand customers, and stakeholders and also companies benefit from fresh perspectives, new ideas, vigorous challenges and broad experience, which leads to better decision making" (Davies, 2012).

Furthermore, states the report, diverse boards are important to prevent '*groupthink*'. Boards that are formed of people with similar experiences and backgrounds tend not to question decisions. By having directors from a wider range of backgrounds, companies experience more rigorous questioning by the board. Therefore, increasing the number of female representation on boards could make a significant difference to the mining industry (Sealy and Vinnicombe, 2012).

External stakeholders continue to exert greater influence on mining companies in Africa, where communities influence governments and political parties to affect mining licenses and legislation. There is also frequent employee unrest with strikes over pay and working conditions. Having a board that can deal most effectively with such situations and issues can make a huge and positive impact in the performance of a company. Research has shown that mining companies that have an environmental policy also tend to have a higher percentage of women on their board and on the HSEC than those that do not have a stated environmental policy (PwC, 2013).

McKinsey & Co. conducted a large-scale research survey of more than a thousand managers from a wide range of companies and found that differences exist in the frequency with which men and women use different leadership behaviors (McKinsey, 2008, 2013). An academic research conducted at INSEAD indicated that women outperform men on seven out of the top ten leadership qualities, and most decidedly on team building and emotional intelligence. The global mining sector has more (and sometimes competing) stakeholders than most industries, including: governments, investors, lenders, employees, communities, NGOs, and the environment (INSEAD, 2017). Given the qualities identified in the INSEAD research, it would suggest that mining is a sector that could benefit from increased female participation. Having a higher gender balance within the mining industry would increase the likelihood of having more of these qualities in the industry's leaders. Organizational cultures also need to support a more gender-balanced approach to leadership (INSEAD, 2017).

Leeds University Business School found that having at least one female director on the board reduces a company's chances of going into liquidation by approximately 20%. Having two to three female directors, therefore, would further reduce the risk of bankruptcy. The report suggests that diversity of opinion is an advantage that women bring to the board (Leeds University Business School, 2017). Other possible explanations include the notion that women resist high debt while being better at cash-flow management and are better, on average, at people management (Leeds University Business School, 2011). Halla Tomasadottir, the Icelandic fund manager who predicted the 2008 credit meltdown, has been quoted as saying there was an extreme imbalance in the business world and that:

> [w]hile male values are about risk-taking, short-term gain and focus on the individual, female values attend towards risk awareness, the long term and team goals. What is needed for a successful future is a better balance between the two and a greater focus on longer-term sustainability.
>
> (Sundelrand, 2009)

The American Accounting Association Journal published a study in December 2012 that found that female presence on a company board reduced the chance of financial restatements by about 40%. It showed that: "The presence of at least one woman on an otherwise male board is associated with a likelihood of restatement that is 62% the likelihood without gender diversity" (American Accounting Association, 2012).

Other factors included requiring a board's audit committee to be comprised entirely of independent directors, one of them with financial expertise. Mandating the board to meet at least four times annually was found to have only half the effect of one female director. The authors of the study assert that the reason for this is the measure of independence that diversity confers upon corporate boards (American Accounting Association, 2012).

Conclusions

Despite accelerated progress in many spheres of society the presence of women on corporate boards in Africa has been relatively slow, with many firms still having all-male boards. Structural and individual factors contribute to the constrained progress in the appointment of women on corporate boards in Africa. In their quest for women's economic empowerment, some countries and firms in Africa have implemented various measures to accelerate and increase women's presence on boards. However, corporate governance in Africa is still in its infancy stage and measures to diversify are not followed or enforced sufficiently.

African women and their potential contributions to economic advancement and social progress have over the years been marginalized. In failing to utilize the full potential and talents of their female populations, African countries are under-investing in the human capital needed to assure sustainable development. Utilizing women's potential could increase economic growth, reduce poverty, enhance societal well-being and help ensure sustainable development for Africa. Despite the proven link between increased profitability and the presence of women in high-level positions in corporate boardrooms, progress in Africa remains somewhat slow. Barriers preventing women's full participation on corporate boards are well known and include a mix of cultural factors, an ingrained negative mind-set and stubborn forms of behavior conforming to 'old boys' club' mentality, with a tendency to tap into a much narrower band of women leaders than is possible from the available talent pool. Opening economic potential by increasing women's economic participation would change the fortunes of the continent. As demonstrated by Rwandan women, increasing the number of women on corporate boards and adequately harnessing and channeling women's full potential towards the corporate industry would help accelerate the development of Africa and alleviate some of the problems faced by the continent, including widespread poverty and its feminization.

References

ADB 2015. *Where Are the Women: Inclusive Boardroom in Africa's Top Listed Companies*, African Development Bank, www.afdb.org/fileadmin/uploads/afdb/Documents/Publications/Where_are_the_Women_Inclusive_Boardrooms_in_Africa%E2%80%99s_top-listed_companies.pdf, accessed 15 March, 2017.

American Accounting Association 2012. *Women on Corporate Boards Foster Better Financial Reporting*, American Accounting Association, December 2012, http://aaahq.org/newsroom/WomenCorpBoard11_16_12.htm, accessed 28 May, 2017.

AU 2010. *Gender Equality and Women's Empowerment: African Women Decade*, African Union, www.africa-union.org/root/AU/Conferences/2010/april/wgd/wgd.html, accessed 18 March, 2017.

AU 2015. Year of Women's Empowerment and Development Towards Africa's Agenda 2063, AU Echo, Newsletter of the AU Commission Issue 1 2015, https://au.int/sites/default/files/documents/31358-doc-au_echo_january_2015.pdf, accessed 17 March, 2017.

AU 2016. 2016: African Year of HumanRights, with a Special Focus on Women and Girls, African Union Press Release, January 27, 2016, https://au.int/en/pressreleases/19615/2016-african-year-human-rights-particular-focus-rights-women, accessed 17 March, 2017.

Catalyst 2004. *The Bottom Line: Connecting Corporate Performance and Gender Diversity*.

Catalyst 2007. The bottom line: Corporate performance and women's representation on boards, www.catalyst.org/knowledge/bottom-line-corporateperformance-and-womens-representation-boards, accessed 26 May, 2017.

Committee on Women's Rights and Gender Equality 2015. Working document on women's careers in Science and University and glass ceilings encountered, www.europarl.europa.eu/sides/getDoc.do?pubRef=-//EP//TEXT+REPORT+A8-2015-0235+0+DOC+XML+V0//EN, accessed 15 February, 2017.

The Commonwealth 2017. *Women on Boards across the Commonwealth: Commonwealth Secretariat*, London, http://thecommonwealth.org/sites/default/files/inline/P14766_SGO_Women%20on%20Boards_11WAMM-E-copy.pdf, accessed 15 March, 2017.

Concentrance Consulting Group 2006. Impact study of entrepreneurial development resources, prepared for the U.S. small business administration under contract SBAHQ04F0346, www.sba.gov/idc/groups/public/documents/sba_program_office/ed_impact_study_04.pdf, accessed 18 March, 2017.

Conference Board of Canada 2002. *Women on Boards Not Just the Right Thing . . . but the "Bright" Thing*, The Conference Board of Canada, 2002, www.europeanpwn.net/files/women_on_boards_canada.pdf, accessed 15 March, 2017.

Credit Suisse 2012. Gender diversity and corporate performance, *Credit Suisse Research Institute*, August 2012, https://infocus.credit-suisse.com/data/_product_documents/_shop/360145/, accessed 28 May, 2017.

Davies, E.M. 2012. Women on Boards, Lord Davies Report, March 2012, https://www.gov.uk/government/uploads/system/uploads/attachment_data/file/31714/12-p135-women-on-boards-2012.pdf, accesed 28 March, 2017.

The Economist 2013. Development in Africa: Growth and Other Good Things, *The Economist*, May 1st 2013, https://www.economist.com/blogs/baobab/2013/05/development-africa, accessed 28 March, 2017.

FAO 2011. *The Role of Women in Agriculture*, United Nations Food & Agricultural Organisation, www.fao.org/docrep/013/am307e/am307e00.pdf, accessed 15 March, 2017.

Fraser-Moleketi, G. 2015. *How Can We Increase the Number of Women in Africa's Board Rooms*, World Economic Forum, www.weforum.org/agenda/2015/06/how-can-we-increase-the-number-of-women-in-africas-boardrooms/, accessed 15 March, 2017.

Fredman, S. 2009. *Making Equality Effective: The Role of Proactive Measures*, European Network of Legal Experts in the Field of Gender Equality, Cheltenham, UK: Edgar Elgar Publishing Limited.

IFC 2011. *Women on Boards: A Conversation with Male Directors*, International Finance Corporation, www.ifc.org/wps/wcm/connect/b51198804b07d3b2acabad77fcc2938e/Focus9_Women_on_Boards.pdf?MOD=AJPERES, accessed 15 March, 2017.

INSEAD 2017. Gender Initiative, INSEAD The Business School for the World, https://www.insead.edu/centres/gender-initiative, accessed 11 March, 2017.

Leeds University Business School, 2011. More Women Needed in the Boardroom, Leeds Universty Business School, Tuesday 1 March 2011, https://business.leeds.ac.uk/about-us/article/more-women-needed-in-the-boardroom/, accessed 13 March, 2017.

Machel, G. World Economic Forum 2015, https://www.weforum.org/agenda/authors/graca-machel/, accessed 15 March, 2017.

Mbabazi 2013. Rwanda: Women's Post Genocide Success, Vision News, www.visionews.net/eijin-women%C2%B4s-post-genocide-success/, accessed 15 March, 2017.

McCrudden, C., Prechal, S. 2009. *The Concepts of Equality and Non-Discrimination in Europe:A Practical Approach*, European Network of Legal Experts in the Field of Gender Equality, file:///C:/Users/Justina/Downloads/ConceptsofEqualityDRAFT18 November2009%20(1).pdf, accessed 15 March, 2017.

McKinsey 2008. *Women Matter 2: Female Leadership, a Competitive Edge for the Future*, McKinsey & Co., www.mckinsey.com/client_service/eijingtion/latest_thinking/women_matter, accessed 15 March, 2017.

McKinsey 2013. Gender diversity in top management: Moving corporate culture, moving boundaries, McKinsey Report, November 2013, www.mckinsey.it/idee/gender-diversity-in-top-management-moving-corporate-culture-moving-boundaries, accessed 15 March, 2017.

McKinsey & Co. 2007. Women matter: Gender diversity, a corporate performance driver, https://www.mckinsey.com/business-functions/organization/our-insights/gender-diversity-a-corporate-performance-driver, accessed 15 March, 2017.

McKinsey & Co. 2015. Global Medial Report 2015: Global Industry Overview, https://www.mckinsey.com/~/media/McKinsey/dotcom/client_service/Media%20and%20Entertainment/PDFs/McKinsey%20Global%20Report%202015_UK_October_2015.ashx, accessed 16 March, 2017.

McKinsey & Co. 2016. Women matter: Reinventing the workplace to unlock the potential of gender diversity, https://www.mckinsey.com/~/media/mckinsey/global%20themes/

women%20matter/reinventing%20the%20workplace%20for%20greater%20
gender%20diversity/women-matter-2016-reinventing-the-workplace-to-unlock-the-
potential-of-gender-diversity.ashx, accessed 18 March, 2017.

McKinsey & Co. 2016. Women matter Africa, Report, August 2016, https://www.mckinsey.
com/global-themes/gender-equality/women-matter-africa, accessed 15 March, 2017.

MEWC 2016. African women's decade 2010–2020: Mid-term review, Make Every Woman
Count, http://makeeverywomancount.org/index.php?option=com_content&view=categ
ory&id=40&Itemid=62, accessed 15 March, 2017.

OECD 2013. *Gender and Sustainable Development: Maximising the Economic, Social and
Environmental Role of Women*, Paris: OECD, www.oecd.org/social/40881538.pdf,
accessed 15 March, 2017.

PwC 2013. *Mining for Talent: A Study of Women on Boards in the Mining Industry*, WIM
(UK) & Pricewaterhouse Coopers, www.pwc.com/gr/en/publications/assets/mining-for-
talent.pdf, accessed 15 March, 2017.

Republic of Rwanda, 2010. National Gender Policy, Final Version, July 2010, Ministry of
Gender and Family Planning, Republic of Rwanda, menengage.org/wp-content/
uploads/2014/06/Rwanda-Gender-Policy.doc, accessed 13 March, 2017.

Sealy, R., Vinnicombe, S. 2012. The female FTSE board report 2012 – Milestone or millstone cranfield university school of management, 2012, www.som.cranfield.ac.uk/som/
eijing-content/research/documents/2012femalftse.pdf, accessed 15 March, 2017.

Sundelrand, R. 2009. After the Crash, Iceland's Women Lead the Rescue, *The Guardian*,
22 February 2009, www.theguardian.com/world/2009/feb/22/iceland-women, accessed
17 March, 2017.

UK Department of Business, Innovation and Skills, Women on Boards UK Department of
Business, Innovation & Skills, February 2011, www.gov.uk/government/uploads/system/
uploads/attachment_data/file/31710/11-745-women-on-boards.pdf, accessed 15 March,
2017.

UNDP 2013. Rwanda country context, United Nations development programme, http://
web.undp.org/evaluation/documents/ADR/ADR_Reports/Rwanda/ch2-ADR_Rwanda.
pdf, accessed 15 March, 2017.

UNFAO, 2011. The Role of Women in Agricualture, ESA Working Paper No. 11-02, March
2011, accessed 18 March, 2017.

United Nations 1995. The United Nations fourth world conference on women: Platform for
action, www.un.org/womenwatch/daw/eijing/platform/plat1.htm, accessed 15 March,
2017.

United Nations 2000–2009. Convention on the eliminations of all forms of discrimination
against women, www.un.org/womenwatch/daw/cedaw/cedaw.htm, accessed 15 March,
2017.

United Nations 2013. Millennium development goals and beyond 2015, www.un.org/
millenniumgoals/beyond2015.html, accessed 15 March, 2017.

United Nations 2017. *Transforming the World: The 2030 Agenda for Sustainable Development*, United Nations Knowledge Platform, https://sustainabledevelopment.un.org/
post2015/transformingourworld, accessed 15 March, 2017.

USAID 2009. Rwanda Investing in the Empowerment of Women in Business, Report
USAID September 2009. www.womenable.com/content/userfiles/BAH_Rwanda_
finalrpt.pdf, accessed 14 March, 2017.

Wittenberg-Cox, A., Maitland, A. 2007. *Why Women Mean Business*, Hoboken, NJ: John
Wiley & Sons, Ltd.

World Bank 2009. *Gender Equality as Smart Economics*, Washington, DC, www.
worldbank.org/en/topic/gender, accessed 15 March, 2017.

7 Women's experiences in top management teams (TMTs)

The case of Israeli national majority and national minority women

*Helena Desivilya Syna, Michal Palgi
and Maha Karkabi-Sabbah*

Introduction

Mainstreaming of women into top management teams (TMTs) is still slow-paced in most parts of the world. Stereotypical gender attitudes, values and behaviors towards women and institutional construction of gender relations persist in organizations. Consequently, the organizational culture tends to ignore women's voices, reflected in gender inequality at the organizational arena especially at the upper echelons (Desivilya Syna and Costea, 2015). At the same time there is some evidence suggesting that organizations are more open to leadership based on qualities traditionally viewed as feminine such as solidarity, capability of emotional expression, empathy towards others and actual assistance to others (Lewis, 2014). What mechanisms account for the difficulties to realize the benevolent women's potential at top strategic forums?

Extant research clearly points that some of the intricacies constitute an explicit exclusion, as women's slow pace of advancement into TMT is disproportionate to women's educational level, achievements and managerial competence (Seo et al., 2017). Once women attain such positions, inclusion barriers appear largely hidden. Yet, research lacunas loom large concerning women's experiences in TMTs once they attain such positions. What roles do women actually play? What are the relationships between women and their male peers at the top forums?

Prior research on Jewish women in Israel suggests that they experience difficulty in meaningfully expressing their voices and exerting influence in top management teams (Desivilya Syna and Palgi, 2014; Yassour-Borochowitz et al., 2015). However, there is a dearth of research relating to minority groups in Israel.

The study presented in the current chapter aims to diminish the research gaps noted previously, shedding light and comparing Jewish and Arab women's experiences at upper echelon forums.

Women's voices in TMTs in the era of diversity and complexity

Responding to the challenges of the complex era – featuring mounting diversity and social divisions – necessitates fostering equality among social groups, including promotion of gender equality. Attaining the latter goal entails women's meaningful participation in top leadership and management positions and their full-fledged involvement in strategic decision-making. Moreover, as suggested by several scholars, competition over talent will grow due to projected labor scarcity in developed countries that makes the advancement of women and their integration in upper echelon position a necessary strategic move (Burke and Major, 2014; Seo et al., 2017). There is evidence to suggest that women's involvement in top management teams improves the odds for business development, including growth in periodical stock prices and rise in earnings per share (Torchia et al., 2011). Beyond these concrete economic gains, women who actively participate in upper echelons of organizations serve as a role model for other talented women, motivating them to apply to senior management positions and promoting actual recruitment of qualified women to upper echelon positions (Seo et al., 2017).

Recent studies on women in top leadership positions show that diversity of decision-makers increases the odds of women's promotion to upper echelon positions and female leaders' tenure at the top (Cook and Glass, 2014; Glass and Cook, 2016). However, hitherto actual women's participation in corporate decision-making bodies is marked by significant challenges (Araújo-Pinzón, 2017; Seo et al., 2017).

Indeed, research on the intersection of gender, leadership and management show that notwithstanding some progress in women's entry and involvement at upper echelons, they still encounter considerable barriers on their path to full-fledged participation in top management forums (Debusscher, 2016; Nicolson, 2015; Silva et al., 2016). The crucial questions subsume the nature of the barriers and what mechanisms underlie their persistence. Extant theorizing has not yet fully captured the underpinnings of women's exclusion from top management, particularly its implicit aspects.

Thus, our study attempted to explicate in depth what actually happens in top forums. Prior research focused by and large on the representation rates as an indicator of women's involvement in TMTs and their influence on financial performance (Adams and Ferreira, 2009). Studies capturing the dynamics in the 'black box' have been scarce (Nielsen, 2010; Glass and Cook, 2016). Moreover, the gender perspective has rarely been employed in such research (Sheridan et al., 2010). The low ratio of women in top decision-making bodies is only part of the problem; the main issue focuses on the roles actually played by women in these forums. Hence, a thorough explication of women's 'place' in TMTs discerning phenomena such as gendered construction of power relations, gender stereotyping in decision-making processes and networking patterns is deemed important (Nicolson, 2015). We focus on the mechanisms underlying women's limited involvement in strategic decision-making.

One component of such a mechanism revolves around gender as an important factor of social categorization, enhancing its prominence and adverse influence, reflected in women's covert exclusion from group decision-making processes and full-fledged participation. The main explanation for this phenomenon draws on theories of *social categorization* and *social identity* (Tajfel and Turner, 1986) and the notion of *faultline* (van Knippenberg et al., 2011). According to these models people define their social identity through distinction from others that is embedded in their group membership. Coming across individuals from other groups triggers the categorization process and stimulates an inclination to view one's group in more positive terms than other dissimilar groups (*in-group favoritism*). The latter phenomenon may influence the initial features of TMTs composition; namely, attracting 'in-group' members at the expense of discouraging 'out-group' members. Moreover, *in-group favoritism* presumably influences the organizational culture and actual interactions within TMTs, mitigating the 'out-group' members' attempts to voice their concerns and affect change (Mooney and Amason, 2011).

Consequently, women appear to be performing mainly communal functions: facilitating TMTs development, encouraging open debate, enhancing monitoring mechanisms, but have limited impact on operational control. Women's contribution to decision-making and their strategic involvement tends to be mitigated by perceptions of women as still underqualified therefore unequal partners (Desivilya Syna and Palgi, 2014; Nielsen, 2010; Sheridan et al., 2010).

Social construction of women's status constitutes another component of the mechanism implicitly excluding women from meaningful involvement in strategic top forums. Their inferior gendered social status contributes to tenacity and reinstatement of the glass ceiling (Calas et al., 2014). Extant findings corroborate this tenet showing that TMTs are not gender neutral, but the manifestations of gender construction are subtle (Casey et al., 2011; Glass and Cook, 2016; Silva et al., 2016). Thus, male elites persist and women keep fulfilling their *token* roles (Desivilya Syna and Costea, 2015; Desivilya Syna and Palgi, 2014; Lewis and Simpson, 2012). The token women encounter three challenges: performance-directed demands that decide whether to overachieve or diminish exposure; isolation, reflected in the salience of their differences in contrast with men's commonalities; and distortion of the corporate woman image, manifested in the perpetuation of entrapment and restricted advancement opportunities.

Findings on the relationship between women's involvement in TMTs and performance of these forums are inconsistent (Adams and Ferreira, 2009; Glass and Cook, 2016; Noland et al., 2016; Terjesen et al., 2009). Some evidence points to the positive impact of women's presence in TMTs on organizational innovation and performance. Albeit, these positive effects seem to depend on other factors: the nature of women's involvement, women constituting a critical mass in TMTs, the type of economy and the sociopolitical context, the organizational sector, the circumstances upon women's assuming leadership position and the strength of corporate governance. A recent study on Norwegian boards of directors shows that women's active involvement in TMTs also depends on the board leader's assertive management encouraging the board's culture of openness to diversity. Such a firm management pattern enhances female directors' contribution to decision-making despite constituting a minority (Boğaç Kanadlın et al., 2017).

Notwithstanding the barriers, women entrepreneurs display agency, paving their way to the top while resisting gender-stereotypic business orientations (Lewis, 2014). They seem to crystallize novel business leaders' multifaceted identities, merging seemingly discordant elements: on the one hand displaying femininity-based management, accentuating relationships, exchange and cooperation; on the other hand, emphasizing professionalism, manifested in strong task orientation. This unique, non-ostracized women's entrepreneurial identity points at the complexity of women's voices at upper echelons that evolve in a dynamic fashion and begin to challenge male voices in the business arena.

Recent research shows that in-group favoritism, faultlines and gendering in organizations are exacerbated for minority women accentuating their 'stranger' and 'outsider' positions. The construction of the inferior power status is pronounced as gender interconnects with minority status, reflected in the phenomenon of intersectionality (Arar and Abu-Rabia-Queder, 2011; Kohlman and Krieg, 2013; Knights and Omanović, 2016). The patriarchal norms are highly prevalent in the Arab society, restricting occupational opportunities of women by preventing them from work or relegating them to jobs that prioritize domestic work and childrearing (Abu-Baker, 2016). Thus, the number of Palestinian women holding senior positions in the labor market is low and stood at 2.9% in 2015 (Mizrachi-Simon, 2016). Although this rate increased over time it is still low relative to Jewish women and Palestinian men (8.7% and 6.0%, respectively).

In sum, drawing on extant literature on gender in organizations and our prior empirical studies, this chapter explicates Israeli Jewish and Arab women's experiences in TMTs. How do the barriers and coping patterns designed to resist and overcome them play out in the Israeli scene of TMTs and especially in the boards of directors (BODs)? What similarities and differences emerge between Jewish and Arab women at upper echelons? What roles do they actually play? How do they express their voices and exert influence?

We examine and discuss phenomena such as in-group favoritism, faultlines and intersectionality. Specifically, the focus is on factors promoting versus impeding women's influence and voices in TMTs and elucidating the mechanisms underlying the encouraging in contrast with the interfering forces.

The chapter focuses on the perspectives of women in upper echelon positions (mainly BOD members) on their involvement in strategic decision-making. The main queries comprise:

a   What is the nature of their involvement?
b   What is their perceived impact?
c   What are their strengths (successes)? Why – what factors make it possible?
d   What are their difficulties, barriers, challenges? Why – what factors impede their progress? How – how do they cope with difficulties and challenges?
e   What are the consequences of their involvement in TMTs on decision-making and performance of TMTs and the organization as whole?

Figure 7.1 Research model

In accordance with these queries our research model concentrated mainly on the processes characterizing the TMT meetings:

- Input: contextual elements: background culture and policies.
- Throughput: TMT processes – in-group favoritism, faultlines and intersectionality.
- Output: consequences of women's involvement in TMTs on decision-making.

The Israeli scene of top management teams

Israel's standing according to the most recent (2016) Global Gender Gap Index (GGGI) of the World Economic Forum, an indication of national commitment to gender equality, is 49 out of 145, showing substantial gaps. While Israel displays gender equality in educational attainment, gender gaps loom particularly large in economic participation and opportunities (rank 62), especially in wage inequality and the number of senior officials, legislators and managers. Political empowerment also evinces gender disparities (rank 48) particularly with regard to representation in the parliament and ministerial positions.

Conceivably, tight patriarchal cultures proliferated by the Israeli institutions along with strong traditional and conservative emphasis in the Arab communities impede the possibility of challenging organizational gendering by Israeli women in TMTs (Desivilya Syna and Yassour-Borochowitz, 2008). Presumably, this trend is prominent in TMTs dominated by Arab male members, characterized by tight traditional, masculine cultures propagated by the local communities, compounding the influence of the central social institutions and coloring the organizational culture, political representation and practices of these top forums (Lee and Kramer, 2016).

The legal and socio-economic context of the study

In 1993 a new clause in the Law of Governmental Companies was enacted referring to women's representation. The law stated that there should be suitable gender representation in the boards of directors of governmental companies. In 2007 this law was amended stating that a suitable representation is 50% of boards of directors. This amendment has increased the number of women directors in governmental companies from 7% in 1993 to 44% in 2010. Another clause applies to all public companies. It states that if a board is composed of one gender only, any new appointment must be of the other gender (http://women.gov.il/WomenInIsrael/ ConferencesAndEvents/Pages/Representation.asp).

The Catalyst survey (Desheh, 2014) of the 100 most capitalized Israeli public companies, the TA-100 stock exchange market index, shows unequal representation of women in their TMTs. According to this survey, 19.0% of the managers, 7.5% of the CEOs, 17.2% of the members of BODs and 2.0% of the chairs of BODs in these companies are women.

Methodology

Research process and tools

The study is based on a qualitative approach. Semi-structured interviews were conducted with six Jewish and five Arab women members of BODs to capture their experiences at TMTs. We located their names through personal contacts and women's organizations. The age range of the participants is 38–70, and all have an extensive experience in boards of directors and in management of economic and social enterprises.

The interview guide consisted of five questions that included a description of the interviewee's career; the reason she sought or accepted the appointment in the BOD; her description of what happens in the BOD meetings, of a successful BOD meeting and a less successful one – what role she played in each of them; and some general questions regarding the role of women in BODs.

The interviews were conducted by the three principal researchers separately and lasted from 45 to 90 minutes. They were recorded and transcribed.

Data analysis

The interview data was content-analyzed following the principles of qualitative research. Accordingly, we analyzed the data in three phases: (1) 'open coding' – we read through each interview in order to get first ideas of the central topics emerging from the interview; (2) next we performed a mapping analysis that crosswise accumulated the data; and (3) we reverted to the interviews attempting to focus the analysis by tracing the interviewees' stance with regard to topics or notions stemming from the literature such as significant turning points and contextual influences (Shkedi, 2003; Strauss and Corbin, 1998).

We embraced the feminist tradition of highlighting women's own voices in forming the narrative of their experiences (Marshall, 1995; Parsons and Priola, 2012).

Findings and discussion

From a wide variety of topics which emerged in the data analysis, we attempted to identify shared themes and illuminate the main ones, characteristic of women involved in top management teams, notably boards of directors in different organizations. We selected from the themes repeated in the interviews three which are portrayed in this chapter: (a) negotiating authority: a champion – embracing a critical stance and taking risks, (b) negotiating value and commitment – over-performing: preparation, creativity, learning and monitoring; and (c) negotiating support – alleviating solitude at the top.

Several characteristic examples were chosen, conforming with each of the three themes and reflecting the interviewees' voice in the appropriate context. All the interviewees are indicated by the initials of their first names and by either A (an Arab woman) or J (a Jewish woman).

Negotiating authority: a champion – embracing a critical stance and taking risks

The findings show the hindrance of gendering on women's odds of breaking through the glass ceiling. Hence, they face the challenge of negotiating their status; namely, improving their position and establishing their legitimacy while interacting with men at upper echelons (Kolb and McGinn, 2009). Negotiating authority appears a critical pre-condition to exerting influence on strategic decision-making in top forums.

Most of the women we interviewed portrayed themselves as champions paving their way to the top in male-dominated organizational settings. This trend was especially salient among the Arab women, who encountered a compounded gender bias, as succinctly expressed by **HA**, a veteran Arab PhD, manager, consultant and member of numerous TMTs:

> *Yes, I did have an influence, set an example for many women that it's possible to be at powerful positions. There was a strong influence if not directly then indirectly. I and a few other women started from scratch (zero point). It was not a standard for women to get higher education. I was the first one who gained PhD at Israeli University. It was very difficult, looking back at the path that I and a few other women have gone through, we have had many barriers on our way, but we paved the way for other women.*

G, an experienced Arab woman in public and non-governmental TMTs, emphasized the intricacies and risks involved in the champion's role:

> *After the uprisings thought that I have to build institutions within the Arab society. Thus, I started as part-time at XXX at low wage, but took the risk to develop something new.*
>
> *Initially did not have doubts but was concerned how to build the Center, deliver the goods so it can have an impact. . . . In 2007 it was different,*

> *I remember I was the only woman with 50 men in the room . . . and the men came they shook hands with other men and I was asked where is the coffee. . . . My response was the coffee is there go ahead and make yourself. . . .The local government officials turned to the Arab Monitoring Committee with doubts how they can appoint women who don't have an idea in local politics/government. Thus, the first thing was to appoint me – a woman who was charged with research – mapping the field of local government. and I also made field trips to all of the local governments. . . . The Israeli politics is highly chauvinistic, hardly any women in local governments.*

Similar narratives emerged from the interviews with the other three Arab research participants: **B** – a Druze, 50 years old, married MA graduate in public administration, consultant of women's status for local governments; **S** – a Christian accountant, in early forties, married with three children, a BOD member of a financial company; and **RO** – a Christian Arab lawyer in early forties, married with three children, employed in a large law firm in the Jewish sector, a veteran of a BOD.

They emphasized the strategy of making their voices heard in the meetings rather than being silent in order to counteract their implicit exclusion and establish their legitimacy.

All of the Arab interviewees highlighted their role as the "front runner" setting the stage for upper echelon women in the Arab society, as put by **G**:

> *It will be easier for the young generation to influence decision-making.*

The necessity to negotiate authority and legitimacy by embracing a critical stance was also evident in the experiences of the Jewish study participants.

M, a married woman in her sixties and a veteran of numerous BODs in business and public sector contends that expressing an authentic voice, albeit unpopular and nonconsensual, is highly important:

> *Very active; director's duty to oversee as an external party: to think how to improve the job performance. Need the capability to say things when it is unpopular. . . . Usually very few positive things . . .*
>
> *Even if there is no immediate impact, it stirs discussion. . . . My definition of successful meeting is not necessarily reaching consensus but rather having a plurality of opinions and having discussion. . . . Women who speak their voice are seen as witches.*

Akin to the Arab women, **M** also notes her function as a champion:

> *At first people pitied my husband as I was not around, did not attend parents' days, but then became a role model.*

HE, a faculty member in Political Science at an academic institution and an expert in public policy who serves as a representative of the public in BOD of a municipal council, also stresses the need of embracing a critical stance and sounding a clear voice in order to establish legitimacy:

> *Very active, pushing for change/reforms try to persuade residents to take responsibility and participate, including youth. . . . We ask for explanation and are resolute in this regard. Men see it as a hormonal disturbance. . . .*
>
> *Voicing concerns (asking questions, raising issues) due to civic responsibility I need to be there to make sure that the procedure and processes are such that protect the public interests in light of personal interests of the BOD members.*

MO, an economist and MA graduate in organizational development and consulting, in late thirties, a BOD member of public holdings companies, corroborates the need for a critical stance in negotiating authority:

> *Ask lots of questions, mainly re: numbers in the financial reports. Others do not ask so much. They know each other for many years. When I ask questions, there is no way I won't get answers; if I am to approve the budget/financial report or make decision, need to understand everything thoroughly.*

In sum, both the Arab and Jewish study participants evinced the prominence of a resolute, frequently non-conformist, active stance as the strategy to establish their legitimacy and authority (Desivilya Syna and Costea, 2015). They also pointed at their champion role, encountering significant barriers on their path of exerting influence in TMTs. The second theme depicts the evolutionary, arduous process of senior women's journey to meaningful participation at the top.

Negotiating value and commitment: over-performing, preparation, creativity, learning and monitoring TMT processes

The interviews point at the persistence of male elites and women continuing to play their token roles at upper echelons (Desivilya Syna and Costea, 2015; Desivilya Syna and Palgi, 2014; Lewis and Simpson, 2012). This trend is particularly salient (but by no means exclusive) in the narratives of the national minority women, reflecting the phenomenon of intersectionality (Arar and Abu-Rabia-Queder, 2011; Kohlman and Krieg, 2013; Knights and Omanović, 2016). These women face not only organizational gendering directed at all women, but also operate within a conservative society, saturated with strong patriarchal norms, stressing women's place at the domestic sphere (Abu-Baker, 2016).

The Arab and Jewish women's experiences reveal a clear tendency of dealing with performance-directed demands through attempts to overachieve (Lewis and Simpson, 2012). They stress preparation to meetings, collecting information and learning about the subject matter so that they can exhibit competence and match the implicit demands of their male counterparts at TMTs.

B and **S**, the Arab interviewees, described their extensive efforts to prove that they have the capacity to hold and fulfill the demands of senior positions. They feel that men do not take them seriously and consider their presence as an affirmative action, as put by **B**: *The Mayor used my position during the election to show that he is concerned about women's affairs, nothing more than that.*

S adds: *At the beginning, the men took me no more than rubber stamp, but soon, they understand that I am not.*

All of the study participants reported that stepping into the top management position carries substantial responsibility; therefore, they invest vast energies and time in preparing prior to any meeting by studying the relevant materials. By contrast, they described the men as investing much less efforts in work-related actions.

For instance, **G** (A) claimed:

> *At the current phase my influence is changing the setting. I am doing the ground work and setting the stage for organizational, cultural change. But, need to constantly struggle to be a part of the mainstream especially at the governmental committees where an Arab woman is a stranger.*

HE (J) corroborates the perceived necessity of preparation and exhibiting competence as a pre-condition to potential meaningful involvement at a BOD:

> *At first I was a 'silent channel' in order to learn, have not had enough experience. Nowadays I am trying to make the BOD operating in an orderly fashion and especially as far as decision-making is concerned. Usually the members are supposed to get the materials ahead of the meeting, they should come prepared and participate and not be stuck in their mobiles. A year ago I deliberately asked to videotape the meeting; they laughed at me.*

MO (J) reveals a similar belief:

> *I like to learn about the subject matter of the company/organization where I serve as a director. I asked to make a field trip. If they want to increase investment, I need to understand why?*

HA (A) stresses the need to exhibit effective performance in order to gain credit and influence:

> *Being a woman in a male context had a positive impact, as those before me have not succeeded to have an impact or do a good job. I did a good job and changed the situation for the better so the reactions were positive.*

Most of the interviews posited that they have been still performing the communal functions at BODs, ensuring adherence to the procedural rules of decision-making and monitoring performance and relayed 'feminine patterns' in their attempts to exert influence, as manifested in the following quotes:

> *My actions and women's actions mostly revolve around procedural control . . .*
>
> *Women influence more in more 'feminine' issues, e.g., education. Less influence on actual decisions/outcomes: over the four years have not succeeded to convince the BOD for videotaping the BOD meetings. My influence is rather low as I am not politically involved in the municipal council. In order to influence you need to devote a lot of time, be there frequently. I can have more impact in the education domain and the future generation. . . . We are highly responsible, more orderly in decision-making, I just hope that when we get to the top we won't behave as men do . . . We were not there for a long time, hence we have to close the gap and therefore are not ashamed to ask questions. . . . We women are persistent, more profound (we 'dig', are stubborn, keep asking questions), men make quick decisions, seek quick solutions, cut it short.*
>
> *. . . Often, there is no strategic planning for the long run. The meetings are convened in crisis situations rather than prioritizing different projects, e.g., play-ground. I feel like a kindergarten teacher.* (**HE**, J)

M (J) adds:

> *Women are more sophisticated than men. They think differently; their solutions are much better; their perception is better, they can see multitude of aspects and they also take into account time, the dividends, compare to alternatives; they are better in economic decisions; they can look at three things simultaneously; they are often not appreciated as males' thinking is very focused; men look at the short-term outcomes; what will influence the nearest quarter and when a woman says one needs to look at the second and third as well it's less interesting for them.*

G (A) indicates her dream or fantasy of reaching an equal status at TMTs: *Arab men accepting a woman as their* **boss** .

R (J), a professor of OB and gender studies and the University president's adviser on women's affairs (in early fifties), points at *subtle exclusion of a female professional – a stranger*.

R (J) relays an experience of lack of influence on strategic decision-making, especially on financial matters, despite expertise in OB and gender studies:

> *When I raised the issue of insufficient representation of women at BOD, the CEO (a high tech, wealthy man) commented that it's not a feminist organization, it has a different agenda.*
>
> *Women are not expected to have interest in financial matters. Money does matter. In fact, it's a kind of a norm for members of the BOD to make financial contribution to the cause of the organization and I cannot do it, I am not in business.*

Presumably a male-dominated organizational culture of most BODs impinges on women's capacity to play at equal ground. Indeed, **R** (J) describes different experiences at women's boards (those composed exclusively of women):

> *By contrast, in women's board, in a new social venture where I served at the advisory committee, there was a different organizational culture and different management style: it is participatory and decisions are made based on consensus; were able to identify mutual goals. The CEO was a woman volunteer.*

Importantly, as pointed by **G** (A), perpetuating male dominance at BODs stems from women's proclivities of following the mainstream – the male role model.

> *Some Arab women succumb to the pressure, they behave like men to gain influence or yield to their power, especially in the older generation. The restraining forces are Arab men and older Arab women. For example, Arab men socialize after "work"/business. I cannot do it. . . . I use a cooperative/ participatory management, older women and men view it weird.*

In sum, the main narrative of the interviewees, still to a large extent 'token women', points at the challenge to prove their competence and the capability to act as equal partners at TMTs. Their self-praised and managerial qualities supposedly fitting the complex era of diversity, remain still marginal and underrated by their male counterparts (Burke and Major, 2014; Desivilya Syna and Costea, 2015; Seo et al., 2017). They do not constitute a critical mass, allowing them to change the rules of the game and institute different management cultures and team processes at the top forums. The findings show that the atmosphere at the top gradually changes, especially for the younger generation, but this trend is rather slow (Araújo-Pinzón, 2017; Boğaç Kanadlın et al., 2017; Lewis, 2014).

Akin to the prior theme of negotiating authority, the interviews point at considerable similarities, even overlap, in Arab and Jewish women's experiences as token women. In both cases senior women need to work hard in order to ascertain their entitlement of upper echelon positions. However, the burden of proof appears heavier for the Arab women.

Meanwhile women in TMTs keep facing another challenge of token women: engaging the solitude at the top by building their support networks (Kolb and McGinn, 2009; Lewis and Simpson, 2012). These experiences are manifested in the interviewees' experiences underlying the third theme.

Negotiating support: alleviating solitude at the top

Most of the research participants conveyed a sense of isolation and solitude in the top forums. They felt "different", standing out in light of men's commonalities. The interviewees reported loneliness, describing the immediate context of the TMT as a patriarchal setting, especially in cases where they were the only woman in the top forum. As put by **S** (A): *the fact that you are alone is not comfortable at all.*

G (A) underscores the sense of being an "alien" who does not get respect at the male top forum:

> *When a man talks, everybody listens, when a woman speaks, the men look at their mobiles or talk amongst themselves.*

S's (A) experiences point at implicit exclusion, especially of Arab women, and isolation through concrete actions, such as the timing of important meetings:

> *The difficult timing of meetings; usually the meetings take place either after workday or are held for long hours during the day. They never take into consideration that you have a family. Every one of them wants to set a meeting after his workday, even after the meeting, they are going to a restaurant and I am going to my children.*

The strategies for engaging solitude, exclusion and isolation include women's solidarity, cooperation and forming coalitions; namely, building support networks. It is worth noting that the Arab participants, experiencing a compounded gender bias, were very explicit, even adamant about the need to enhance women's support networks, as reflected in their narratives:

G (A) claims:

> *Women's solidarity can counteract to some extent this asymmetry in power between women and men. They gain confidence, expertise and sensitivity/ awareness to power games; they can select the appropriate response more effectively, they gain better capability as to how to use power.*

She also suggests *building coalition with Jewish women who are also a minority* and provides concrete practical suggestions based on her own experience

> *When I speak and they do that I use a power trick, I become silent and wait until they stop talking . . . I use my body language to signal equal stance and wear appropriate clothing.*

B (A) stresses the need for building women's coalitions and especially women's teams:

> *Recruit more women to work together as a source of power; working as a team is helpful, since men don't cooperate with women, I sought the support of others and set up women's committees for cooperation.*

In a similar vein, **R** (A) maintained that *the fact that she cooperates with another woman makes it easier for her to speak without hesitation.*

The Jewish study participants also emphasized the need to rectify the persistent exclusion and isolation of women at top forums and allowing their unique voices to be sounded by the expansion of women's representation in TMTs and enhancement of their meaningful involvement, as stated by **M** (J):

> *Women like less voicing criticism they tend to apologize for that, they don't like to hurt anybody. Men mix business and social in tandem; women separate these domains; take refusal more personally . . . Studied agricultural economics, was the only woman among 35 men, was considered an exception, but then became a role model . . . It's disappointing that there are not enough women at the top. My daughter once said: Do you think I will be a career woman like you?*

and provides a specific example how she attempted to materialize such a goal:

> *The CEO declared she wants to end her term (was 69). She sent 8–9 candidates and I saw a woman who managed a steel company with a photo of a young beauty who the men did not even consider because of her look and I said I want to interview her as well. They asked why I want her? After I met her and had a great interview they asked how did I know? I said a woman who leads a steel company ought to be special. Out of eight in this BOD, two are women (one due to her job/role). In another, 2 out of 9. Things do not change. It's men's as well as women's fault; the latter don't always want it. They have difficulty with rejections.*

To recap, women still feel and are viewed by their male counterparts as strangers at upper echelons rather than equal partners. This sense is particularly salient in Arab women experiences, presumably due to the phenomenon of intersectionality (Arar and Abu-Rabia-Queder, 2011; Kohlman and Krieg, 2013; Knights and Omanović, 2016). To counteract the endurance of a glass ceiling, reflected in isolation and exclusion, women reckon the need and make actual attempts to engage this toil through improvement of their capacities to negotiate support that is expanding their networks and enhancing their effectiveness (Kolb and McGinn, 2009; Lewis, 2014; Seo et al., 2017).

Conclusions

Extant research on the intersection of gender, leadership and management pointed at some progress in women's involvement at upper echelons; however they still face significant challenges while attempting to meaningfully participate in top forums (Debusscher, 2016; Nicolson, 2015; Silva et al., 2016). The current study endeavored to examine the nature of the barriers and the mechanisms underlying their persistence.

Specifically, we explicated in depth what actually happens in top forums, attempting to capture the dynamics in the 'black box' (Nielsen, 2010; Glass and Cook, 2016). We focused on the roles actually played by women in these forums, their perceived influence on the performance of the TMTs, the factors encouraging and forces impeding their impact.

We also aimed to enrich the knowledge base on national minority women at TMTs, previously barely studied. Hence, this research was designed to shed light and compare Jewish and Arab women's experiences at upper echelon forums.

The findings pointed at three considerable challenges encountered by women in top forums: the need to establish their legitimacy and authority, proving their competence and capacity to fulfill top management roles and forming support network to counteract exclusion and isolation.

These emerging experiences in the study participants' narratives corroborate the hindrance of gendering and the effects of faultlines on women's odds of breaking through the glass ceiling (Calas et al., 2014; Kolb and McGinn, 2009).

Negotiating authority appears a critical pre-condition to exerting influence on strategic decision-making in top forums. Most of the women we interviewed portrayed themselves as champions at upper echelons in male-dominated organizational settings.

Both the Arab and Jewish women manifested the salience of a resolute, non-conformist, active stance as the strategy to establish their legitimacy and authority (Desivilya Syna and Costea, 2015).

The second main theme portrayed the evolutionary, laborious climbing path of women to the top teams. The findings evince the tenacity of male dominance while women sustaining their token roles at the top (Desivilya Syna and Costea, 2015; Desivilya Syna and Palgi, 2014; Lewis and Simpson, 2012). This perception is especially prominent (by no means exclusive) in the experiences of the minority women, pointing at the phenomenon of intersectionality (Arar and Abu-Rabia-Queder, 2011; Kohlman and Krieg, 2013; Knights and Omanović, 2016). The Arab women encounter the overall exclusion faced by all women, but their glass ceiling is especially thick and even less penetrable due to strong patriarchal norms, relegating women to the domestic sphere (Abu-Baker, 2016).

The Arab and Jewish women's narratives point at their inclination to manage performance-directed demands by exerting extra efforts: preparation to meetings and extensive learning in order to evince competence in accordance with male standards (Lewis and Simpson, 2012). The women are not gender blind, rather are fully aware of the implicit exclusion. Although they stress their strong qualities, they still to a large extent maintain the 'token women' mentality. Their self-esteemed managerial capabilities, presumably desirable and pertinent in the complex era, do not yet penetrate the mainstream dominated by men (Burke and Major, 2014; Calas et al., 2014; Desivilya Syna and Costea, 2015; Seo et al., 2017). Women fall short of a critical mass, incapable of modifying the rules of the game and transforming the management culture at the top forums.

In the meantime, they experience solitude at the top, seeking and materializing ways to mitigate such isolation, through building their support networks (Kolb and McGinn, 2009; Lewis and Simpson, 2012; Seo et al., 2017). The sense of being a stranger is particularly salient among Arabs, pointing again at the phenomenon of intersectionality.

In sum, women's exclusion at top teams is perpetuated largely through implicit mechanisms such as institutional construction of gender power relations and faultlines. Albeit, an evolutionary, slow-paced process of change is under way, encouraged by women's own awareness of the impeding forces and their attempts of acting upon them (Boğaç et al., 2017; Lewis, 2014).

The findings point at marked similarities in the narratives relayed by the Arab and Jewish women. Nevertheless, the challenge for Arab women appears markedly greater in comparison to their Jewish counterparts due to compounded gender bias in the traditional, highly conservative society.

Where do we go next? One important future research direction would be to examine the perceptions and actual experiences of younger women at upper echelon forums to elucidate the facilitating mechanism of championship by older women who have allegedly paved the way to other women. Were they indeed effective forerunners? Is the temperature indeed warmer for younger women at the top, perhaps encouraged by younger men?

Another direction for future research would be to examine men's experiences as a minority versus a majority in TMTs.

References

Abu-Baker, K. 2016. Gender policy in family and society among Palestinian citizens of Israel: Outside and inside influences in Ben-Rafael, E., Schoeps, J., Sternberg, Y., Glöckner, O. (eds.), *Handbook of Israel: Major Debates*, Berlin, Boston: De Gruyter Oldenbourg, 453–473.

Adams, B.R., Ferreira, D. 2009. Women in the boardroom and their impact on governance and performance, *Journal of Financial Economics*, 94, 291–309.

Arar, K.H., Abu-Rabia-Queder, S. 2011. Turning points in the lives of two pioneer Arab women principals in Israel, *Gender and Education*, 23(4), 415–429.

Araújo-Pinzón, P., Concha Álvarez-Dardet, C., Ramón-Jerónimo, J.M., Flórez-López, R. 2017. Women and inter-organizational boundary spanning: A way into upper management?, *European Research on Management and Business Economics*, 23(2), 70–81.

Boğaç Kanadlın, S., Torchia, M., Gabaldon, P. 2017. Increasing women's contribution on board decision making: The importance of chairperson leadership efficacy and board openness, *European Management Journal*, http://dx.doi.org/10.1016/j.emj.2017.03.006

Burke, R.J., Major, D.A. 2014. *Gender in Organizations: Are Men Allies or Adversaries to Women's Career Advancement?* Northampton, MA: Edward Elgar.

Calas, M.B., Smircich, L., Holvino, E. 2014. Theorizing gender – and – organization: Changing times . . . changing theories? in Kumra, S., Simpson, R., Burke, R.J. (eds.), *The Oxford Handbook of Gender in Organizations*, New York, NY: Oxford University Press, 17–52.

Casey, C., Skibnes, R., Pringle, J. 2011. Gender equality and corporate governance: Policy strategies in Norway and New Zealand, *Gender, Work and Organization*, 18(6), 613–630.

Cook, A., Glass, C. 2014. Women and top leadership positions: Towards an institutional analysis, *Gender, Work and Organization*, 21(1), 91–103.

Debusscher, P. 2016. Analysing European gender equality policies abroad: A reflection on methodology, *European Journal of Women's Studies*, 23(3), 265–280.

Desheh, G. (ed.) 2014. *The Israeli Catalyst Report: Women Leading Business*. The Fourth Israeli Census Report 2013 Women's Representation in the TA-100 Companies Index, March.

Desivilya Syna, H., Costea, C.E. 2015. Gender effects in top management in Desivilya Syna, H., Costea, C.E. (eds.), *Women's Voices in Management: Identifying Innovative and Responsible Solutions*, London, UK and New York, US: Palgrave Macmillan, 3–15.

Desivilya Syna, H., Palgi, M. 2014. Gender outlook on top management: The Israeli case of decision-making dynamics at upper echelons in organizations, *International Business and Entrepreneurship Development*, 7(3), 199–215.

Desivilya Syna, H., Yassour-Borochowitz, D. 2008. The case of CheckpointWatch: A study of organizational practices in a women's human rights organization, *Organization Studies*, 29, 887–908.

Glass, C., Cook, A. 2016. Leading at the top: Understanding women's challenges above the glass ceiling, *The Leadership Quarterly*, 27, 51–63.

Knights, D., Omanović, V. 2016. (Mis)managing diversity: Exploring the dangers of diversity management orthodoxy, *Equality, Diversity and Inclusion: An International Journal*, 35(1), 5–16.

Kohlman, M.H., Krieg, D.B. 2013. Introduction: Intersectional dynamics of gender, family, and work inKohlman, M.H., Krieg, D.B., Dickerson, B.J.(eds.),*Notions of Family: Intersectional Perspectives, Advances in Gender Research, Volume 17*, Bingley, West Yorkshire, UK: Emerald Group Publishing Limited, ix–xxv.

Kolb, D., McGinn, K. 2009. Beyond gender and negotiation to gendered negotiations, *Negotiation and Conflict Management Research*, 2(1), 1–16.

Lee, Y., Kramer, A. 2016. The role of purposeful diversity and inclusion strategy (pdis) and cultural tightness – looseness in the relationship between national culture and organizational culture, *Human Resource Management Review*, 26(3), 198–208.

Lewis, P. 2014. Postmodernism, femininities and organization studies: Exploring a new agenda, *Organization Studies*, 35(12), 1845–1866.

Lewis, P., Simpson, R. 2012. Kanter revisited: Gender, power and (in)visibility, *International Journal of Management Reviews*, 14, 141–158.

Marshall, J. 1995. *Women Managers Moving on: ExploringCareer and Life Choices*, London, UK: Routledge.

Mizrachi-Simon, S. 2016. *Employment among Arab Women*, www.knesset.gov.il/mmm, (Hebrew), accessed 12 April, 2017.

Mooney, A.C., Amason, A.C. 2011. In search of the CEO's inner circle and how it is formed in Carpenter, M.A. (ed.), *The Handbook of Research on Top Management Teams*, Massachusetts, US: Edward Elgar, 35–48.

Nicolson, P. 2015. *Gender, Power and Organization: A Psychological Perspective on Life at Work*, London: Routledge.

Nielsen, S. 2010. Top Management Team Diversity: A Review of Theories and Methodologies, *International Journal of Management Reviews*, 12, 301–316.

Noland, M., Moran, T., Kotschwar, B.R. 2016. Is gender diversity profitable? Evidence from a global survey, Peterson Institute for International Economics Working Paper, 16–3.

Parsons, E., Priola, V. 2012. Agents for change and changed agents: The micro- politics of change and feminism in the academy, *Gender, Work & Organization*, 20(5), 580–598.

Seo, G., Huang, W., Caleb Han, S. 2017. Conceptual review of underrepresentation of women in senior leadership positions from a perspective of gendered social status in the workplace: Implication for HRD research and practice, *Human Research Development Review*, 16(1), 35–59.

Sheridan, A., Haslam Mckenzie, F., Still, L. 2010. Complex and contradictory: The doing of gender on regional development boards, *Gender, Work and Organization*, 53, 432–468.

Shkedi, A. 2003. *Words That Try to Reach: Qualitative Research – Theory and Practice*, Tel Aviv: Ramot.

Silva, A.K., Preminger, A., Slezak, S., Phillips, L.G., Johnson, D.J. 2016. Melting the plastic ceiling: Overcoming obstacles to foster leadership in women plastic surgeons, *Plastic and Reconstructive Surgery*, 138(3), 721–729.

Strauss, A., Corbin, J. 1998. *Basics of Qualitative Research: Techniques and Procedures for Developing Grounded Theory*, 2nd ed., Thousand Oaks, CA: Sage.

Tajfel, H., Turner, J.C. 1986. The social identity theory of inter-group behavior in Worchel, S., Austin, W.G. (eds.), *The Psychology of Inter-Group Relations*, Chicago: Nelson-Hall, 7–24.

Terjesen, S., Sealy, R., Singh, V. 2009. Women directors on corporate boards: A review and research agenda, *Corporate Governance: An International Review*, 17(3), 320–337.

Torchia, M., Calabrò, A., Huse, M. 2011. Women directors on corporate boards: From tokenism to critical mass, *Journal of Business Ethics*, 102(2), 299–317.

van Knippenberg, D., Dawson, J.F., West, M.A., Homan, A.C. 2011. Diversity, faultlines, shared objectives, and top management team performance, *Human Relations*, 64, 307–336.

WomenInIsreal. women.gov.il/WomenInIsrael/ConferencesAndEvents/Pages/Representation. asp (Hebrew), accessed 12 April, 2017.

Yassour-Borochowitz, D., Desivilya Syna, H., Palgi, M. 2015. In a different voice? The stories of women heads of departments in Desivilya Syna, H., Costea, C.E. (eds.), *Women's Voices in Management: Identifying Innovative and Responsible Solutions*, London, UK and New York, US: Palgrave Macmillan, 65–85.

Part IV
Business practice

8 Female entrepreneurship and boardroom diversity

The case of Russia

Irina Tkachenko and Irina Pervukhina

Introduction

In 1984 R. Edward Freeman published his classic book *Strategic Management: A Stakeholder Approach*, building on the process work of Russell Ackoff, Eric Trist, Ian Mitroff, Richard Mason and James Emshoff. The impetus behind stakeholder management was to build a framework that was responsive to the changes in the business environment in the 1980s and the resulting concerns of managers. Freeman understood stakeholders as any group or individual (e.g. customers, suppliers, communities, employees) who is affected by or can affect the achievement of an organization's objectives (Freeman, 1984: 5). For the next 20 years Freeman continued to develop the ideas of corporate social responsibility (CSR) and in the beginning of this century proposed a new approach to CSR – company stakeholder responsibility – as a new capability for organizations to develop (Freeman and Velamuri, 2008). Freeman and Velamuri outlined four levels of commitment to this new CSR:

* The basic value proposition
* Principles for sustained stakeholder cooperation
* Broader societal issues
* Ethical leadership

Freeman's model contributes to building up an image of a socially responsible company, performing locally or/and internationally. It also enhances monitoring and management of reputational risks in terms of the issues pertaining to CSR. The stakeholder approach helps the company act as the market maker for new environmentally and socially targeting products and services. Interaction with internal stakeholders results in higher employee loyalty due to their greater involvement in solving socially significant issues.

The relevance of the stakeholder model for corporate governance is explained by the growing crisis of confidence and trust in the business community, and in society in general. In order to regain the trust of a wide range of corporate players, companies are forced to start a dialogue with individuals, groups, organizations, communities and other interested parties which are subject to a certain influence from the company or which may affect the company's business activities. The stakeholder approach to running a firm seems to be the only acceptable business model that allows the company to consider interests of a variety of interacting groups.

The revival of trust in business is impossible without rethinking the role of gender diversity. Gender diversity on corporate boards is a growing necessity for companies to thrive and grow in today's environment. Diversity is considered an important driver of a board's effectiveness, creating a breadth of perspective among directors and breaking down a tendency towards group thinking.

Gender parity (or a desire for it) in the top management of the company is extremely significant as it offers opportunities for a non-traditional approach to the assigned task solution. There are different mechanisms for achieving such parity: from setting internal corporate voluntary targets to imposing quotas for gender diversity in the boardroom.

We describe how the challenge of board diversity is addressed internationally and examine how female representation on Russian boards is affected by gender inequality within the country. We look at what opportunities are open up to those women who would like to start and run their own business in Russia. We provide evidence of board composition in a sample of large Russian public companies and local (regional) companies and evaluate this evidence in terms of the effectiveness of more diversifying boardroom in the Russian corporate governance.

Challenges of gender diversity

Gender diversity in corporate leadership concerns efficient allocation of human talents as an economic resource. Following targets for diversifying corporate boards set by the European Commission (2012, 2014), many European countries have legislated an enforcing system for gender diversity. Some countries adopted the mandatory quota approach, with Norway taking the lead. Other EU Member States have followed Norway's example and have already begun introducing laws for company boards, including Belgium, France, Italy, the Netherlands, Spain, Portugal, Denmark, Finland, Greece, Austria and Slovenia (MSCI, 2014).

An alternate – voluntary – approach to legislated quotas was chosen by other countries, for example by the UK. This approach implies the setting of voluntary targets by companies to increase the number of board seats taken by women. The latest Davies Report (2015) reviewing board gender diversity observes that the UK voluntary approach is working. This voluntary approach has yielded positive results: since 2010 the percentage of women on boards has almost doubled and accounted for 23.5% (Hope, 2015).

In Asia and the Pacific boardrooms, gender diversity is significantly lower, compared with North America and Europe. Australia has the highest diversity in the region (18.2%), and the Republic of Korea the lowest (1.9%). India and Malaysia are the only Asian countries that impose mandatory quotas for gender diversity. In India, a new Companies Act was enacted in 2013 requiring all stock exchange listed companies to have at least one female on its board (Qian, 2016).

In developed countries research on corporate governance, including on the impact of women on boards, has been conducted in settings characterized by institutional environments, corporate governance and cultures that vary a great deal from those typical of emerging markets.

Russia, the largest country, expanding over the Eurasian continent, combines the European and Asian characteristics, which makes it quite difficult to position the country in the relevant group. That might be one of the reasons for Russia's discrimination in terms of the international research on corporate governance and board gender diversity in particular. Though the board composition and gender issues are on the agenda of numerous public and professional associations, the Moscow Exchange, the Bank of Russia, and the Organization for Economic Co-operation and Development (OECD), the Federal Agency for State Property Management (Rosimushchestvo)[1] has never addressed the challenge of gender diversity in the boardrooms for the last few years. The issue was considered a possible constituent in the analysis of statistical data on the board composition. When making decisions on the selection of executive candidates, the gender criterion is not a priority. Principle VI of the OECD Principles states that

> where board decisions may affect different shareholder groups differently, the board should treat all shareholders fairly. In carrying out its duties, the board should not be viewed or act as an assembly of individual representatives for various constituencies. While specific board members may indeed be nominated or elected by certain shareholders (and sometimes contested by others) it is an important feature of the board's work that board members, when they assume their responsibilities, carry out their duties in an even-handed manner with respect to all shareholders.
>
> (OECD, 2004)

By the Federal Law No. 208-FZ of 26 December 1995 'On Joint Stock Companies', firms with state ownership are required to have boards of directors as a factor of strategic corporate governance. In the commercial sector, the supervisory board and the board of directors are not very developed. The owners are trying their best to wriggle out of the boards, fearing the loss of control over the company. However, the issue of corporate governance has recently become urgent for business owners. It has evolved along with the growth of businesses, and owners taking back seats in operational management of the companies. The owners need the mechanism of regular control over the implementation of business objectives and work of the CEO. In addition, they need a mechanism for concerted owners' decisions on key issues of business development.

Numerous surveys show that diversity is still high on a board's agenda. According to Catalyst census in 2015, 80.1% of board seats at S&P 500 companies were taken by men, leaving a significantly lower 19.9% to female members. The ratio of new directorships at S&P 500 companies was also in favour of men: 73.1% versus 26.9%.

In Russia, promoting gender diversity is not yet a trend. There are still not many Russian companies demonstrating the intention to promote gender diversity in practice. There is no legislation in Russia pertaining to gender diversity on boards. In 2013, across all board member roles of the top 50 Russian public companies, only 7% were held by females with a maximum of three females on board. None of these companies had a female as a board chairperson. However, 44% of respondents considered that broadening the diversity of the board would have a positive impact on its effectiveness (PWC, 2013). One positive development is the slow but steady increase in the number of women serving on executive committees which in 2016 stood at just under 12% (Spencer Stuart, 2017). If this number continues to rise, it may broaden the traditional candidate pool from which non-executive directors are drawn.

Female entrepreneurship

The analysis of gender diversity of Russian corporate boards will be incomplete without the general overview of Russian women's participation in business activities. More and more Russian women are becoming business leaders. Russia has the world's fourth highest percentage of women business owners (32.6%) (Mastercard, 2017).

In March 2017, "Opora Russiyi", an all-Russia non-government organization of small- and medium-sized entrepreneurship, together with the Agency for Strategic Initiatives (ASI), presented the results of the third issue of the Women's Business Index (WBI) (Alekseeva, 2017). The WBI was first introduced in March 2016. It is a diagnostic tool for analyzing female entrepreneurship development in Russia. The WBI seeks to identify the level of favourable business conditions, social environment and individual female aspirations. It measures the quantity of female entrepreneurship development in Russia and considers such factors as the attitude of the society towards entrepreneurship, business climate, infrastructure for business start-ups and personal qualities of women.

The WBI analyzed the survey of 1,000 females residing in large cities from 18 to 55 years old, employed or temporarily unemployed, and 500 female executives and business owners. Key findings from the 2017 WBI are as follows. Russian women have a high potential of entrepreneurship; 13% of women, who are currently employed, are simultaneously developing their own businesses. The same percentage (13%) is determined to start a business. Further, 37% report that they can see themselves as business owners, but are not ready yet to make this move. Further, 24% say they consider a possibility of starting their own business but not in the coming years. Only 10% of the respondents comment that establishing and running a business is not for them.

According to the survey, 42% of Russian women see positive changes in how society perceives female entrepreneurship. The study found that while in 1990 women accounted for about 15% of the total number of entrepreneurs, up to now their share has almost doubled and equals 34%. Further, 33% of the surveyed women say that they are driven by financial rewards. The second most popular incentive is self-realization, an opportunity to implement their ideas – this factor is relevant for 27% of women. The availability of the start-up capital ranks the third (12%), while a year ago that factor was the need for more free time. Over the past few years, the proportion of women willing to start their own business has increased from 1% to 8%, due to a higher social status of the entrepreneur.

The survey also reported that every third women's project is socially aimed, therefore a distinguished characteristic of the Russian female entrepreneurship is its social orientation. The perspectives for female entrepreneurship in Russia are vast: currently women make up 54% of the country's population, while the proportion of women owning and operating business is 27%. This imbalance may be one of the main drivers of economic development for the country.

However, the global outlook on female entrepreneurship in Russia is less optimistic. Currently men's participation in the Russian labour force outsizes women's participation by 14% (Schwab and Sala-i-Martín, 2016–2017). The Female Entrepreneurship Index (FEI) ranks Russia 51st (score = 35.6, compared with number 1, the US, score = 82.9). The highest individual country's indicator is the proportion of highly educated business owners, the lowest is the export focus (Terjesen and Lloyd, 2015).

Russian companies, as before, do not favour women. The executive management is dominated by men. Prevalence of age-old stereotypes and male-dominated corporate cultures have kept the 'glass ceiling' intact. Most women are stuck to specific, usually low middle-level managerial functions such as human resources, public relations and communication, and finance and administration, rather than to top management positions (International Labour Organization, n.d.). The findings of the 2013 study, launched by the 'Committee of 20's'[2] in the collaboration with ExxonMobil, showed that the barriers for women's career advancement still exist today. These are the lack of support from other people, including family (54% of respondents) and a negative perception of women as leaders in the society (53% of respondents). In addition to the 'glass ceiling' concept, the 'sticky floor' issue has come into existence. It turned out that many barriers are more than just objective factors – they exist on the consciousness level. These factors are holding women back and do not allow them to climb the corporate ladder (Женщины в современной экономике: вызовы и решения, n.d.).

The Russian boardroom composition

The business case for gender diversity in the Russian boardroom has not been treated in much detail in empirical literature. One of the first studies of the role of women in the boardroom was conducted over a decade ago by the Research Center of the National Association of Independent Directors in 2004 and 2005 (Cherkaev, n.d.). Their analysis of Russian companies listed on Russian stock exchanges showed that female board representation was looked upon as a positive trend. At the same time respondents stated that women were strongly underrepresented in the boards of directors. In spite of the fact that Russian social reports followed the General Reporting Initiative Standards, they did not include such indicators as LA 11 (The percentage of total employees by gender and by employee category who received a regular performance and career development review during the reporting period), and LA 12 (Composition of governance bodies and breakdown of employees per employee category according to gender, age group, minority group membership and other indicators of diversity).

Back in 2004, women led only 3% of the Russian public companies, 53% of boards were all male; 32% of Russian companies had boards with one woman. The average female representation in boards of directors was 6.9%.

Over a decade has passed but there has been little progress. Legislative authorities have made no attempt to combat discrimination in the boardroom gender and to increase the number of women on corporate boards. In 2017, Spencer Stuart published the third edition of The Board Index, an annual study which analyses aspects of board governance, including composition, committees and remuneration among major listed companies. This survey analyzed the boards of 45 largest Russian companies from the 'Expert-400' ranking list and compared their performance with leading European countries as well as with S&P 500 companies in the US.

At the end of 2016, the proportion of female directors on Russian boards was only 7.2%, a decrease for the second successive year from 7.6% in 2015 and 8% in 2014, which is not in line with global heterogeneous trends in female board representation. Russian boards are the least diverse in terms of gender out of all the surveyed European countries, far behind the next lowest country which is Spain (16%). Norway continues to lead Europe in gender diversity (44.1% of all board seats are held by women), followed for the first time by France which, thanks to legislation, increased the percentage of women on boards from 11.5% in 2009 to 38.8% in 2016. Of the 72 executive directors who sit on Russian boards, only two are women. However, women account for 12.3% of 81 newly appointed directors, an increase over 9% the year before.

The number of women sitting on the executive committee of Russian companies has increased slightly from 11.3% to 11.9%. Experts view it as an evidence that more and more Russian companies started understanding the importance of the issues of gender diversity and put more focus on board composition and director selection, nomination and election.

Less than half of Russian companies include at least one female (40%) in the composition of the board of directors. This is, again, an extremely low reading on the background of such European countries as Norway (100%), France (100%), Finland (100%), Belgium (98%), the UK (98%), the US (98.3%), Italy (99%), Sweden (98%), Switzerland (95%), Germany (93%), Spain (83%) and the Netherlands (78%).

Data analysis

Descriptive statistics on Russian board composition are reported in Table 8.1 and Table 8.2. Table 8.1 presents the summary statistics for largest publicly listed Russian companies that represent Moscow Exchange Top List A1 and A2, for which data were available in 2016. Table 8.2 covers the Sverdlovskaya Oblast sample of 22 companies taken from the database of the Territorial Administration of Rosimushchestvo.

Table 8.1 Women on boards of Russian public companies (as of June–December 2016)

Company name	Industry	Board size	Women on boards	Share of women on boards, %	Female NED*	Female ID**	Company website
1 Interregional Distribution Grid Company of Centre	Energy	11	3	27.27	3	–	www.mrsk-1.ru/ www.mrsk-1.ru/en/
2 Unipro	Energy	9	2	22.22	–	–	www.unipro.energy/ www.unipro.energy/en/
3 Interregional Distribution Grid Company of the North-West	Energy	11	2	18.18	–	–	www.mrsksevzap.ru/ www.mrsksevzap.ru/en/home
4 Interregional Distribution Grid Company of Urals	Energy	11	2	18.18	–	–	www.mrsk-ural.ru/ www.mrsk-ural.ru/en/
5 Inter RAO UES	Energy	11	1	9.09	1	1	www.interrao.ru/ www.interrao.ru/en/
6 Enel Russia	Energy	11	1	9.09	–	–	www.enelrussia.ru/ru/investors.html
7 Interregional Distribution Grid Company of Volga	Energy	11	1	9.09	–	–	www.mrsk-volgi.ru/ www.mrsk-volgi.ru/eng/
8 T+ Group	Energy	12	1	8.33	–	–	www.tplusgroup.ru/company/organy-upravlenija/governing-bodies/
9 MOSENERGO	Energy	12	1	8.33	–	–	www.mosenergo.ru/investors/
10 United Company RUSAL	Metallurgy	18	4	22.22	4	1	www.rusal.ru/index.php www.rusal.ru/en/index.php
11 Polymetal International	Metallurgy	9	2	22.22	1	1	www.polymetal.ru/ www.polymetal.ru/?sc_lang=EN
12 Magnitogorsk Iron and Steel Works	Metallurgy	10	2	20.00	1	1	http://mmk.ru/ http://eng.mmk.ru/

(Continued)

Table 8.1 (Continued)

	Company name	Industry	Board size	Women on boards	Share of women on boards, %	Female NED*	Female ID**	Company website
13	MMC NORILSK NICKEL	Metallurgy	13	1	7.69	–	–	www.nornik.ru/ www.nornik.ru/en/main
14	PICK Group	Construction and real estate	9	3	33.33	2	1	www.pik.ru/
15	LSR Group	Construction and real estate	9	1	11.11	–	–	www.lsrgroup.ru/ www.lsrgroup.ru/en/
16	MOSTOTREST	Construction and real estate	11	1	9.09	1	1	http://mostotrest.ru/ http://mostotrest.ru/en/
17	OTKRITIE Bank	Banking	9	2	22.22	–	–	www.otkritiefc.ru/about/supervisory www.open.ru/en
18	Sberbank Group	Banking	14	2	14.29	1	1	www.sberbank.com/ru www.sberbank.com/index
19	Credit Bank of Moscow	Banking	10	1	10.00	–	–	https://mkb.ru/ https://mkb.ru/en/
20	MegaFon	Telecommunications	7	1	14.29	–	–	https://corp.megafon.ru/ https://corp.megafon.com/
21	Mobile TeleSystems	Telecommunications	9	1	11.11	1	1	www.company.mts.ru/comp/ir/control/directors/
22	TransContainer	Transport	11	2	18.18	1	1	www.trcont.ru/ru/ www.trcont.ru/en/
23	Europlan	Transport	9	1	11.11	1	1	https://europlan.ru/
24	ALROSA	Mining	15	3	26.67	3	2	www.alrosa.ru/ http://eng.alrosa.ru/

No	Company	Industry		NED*		ID**		Source
25	POLYUS	Mining	9	2	22.22	1	1	http://polyus.com/ru/company/board_of_directors/ http://polyus.com/en/company/
26	LUKOIL	Oil and gas	10	1	10.00	–	–	www.lukoil.ru/Company/CorporateGovernance/ BoardofDirectors www.lukoil.com/Company/CorporateProfile
27	Nizhnekamskneftekhim	Oil and gas	11	1	9.09	–	–	www.nknh.ru/direction/board_of_directors/ www.nknh.ru/en/direction/board_of_directors/
28	Moscow Exchange	Finance and insurance	12	3	25.00	3	2	https://moex.com/s258 https://moex.com/en/
29	ROSGOSSTRAKH	Finance and insurance	11	2	18.18	–	–	www.rgs.ru/about/management/directors_council/ index.wbp
30	Sollers	Machine building	9	2	22.22	–	–	www.sollers-auto.com/ru/about/directors/
31	RPC United Wagon Company	Machine building	10	1	11.11	–	–	www.uniwagon.com/ru/investors/corporate_ governance/board_of_directors/ www.uniwagon.com/en/investors/corporate_ governance/board_of_directors/
32	Yandex	It	8	2	25.00	2	2	http://ir.yandex.com/directors.cfm

Source: study database

Notes: *NED – non-executive director;
 **ID – independent director

Our study of Russian joint stock companies (Table 8.1) is based on an initial sample of all 65 public companies listed in 2016 in the Moscow Exchange Top List A1 and A2. We eliminate the companies with all-men boards, which reduces the sample size to 32 companies. In other words, approximately half (49.23%) of our initial sample companies have female representation in the boardroom. The sampled companies are active in various industries: energy – 28.13%; metallurgy – 12.5%; construction and real estate and banking – 9.37% each. Six industries (telecommunications, transport, mining, oil and gas, finance and insurance, and machine building) are equally represented – 6.25%. The technology industry is represented by one company (3.13%). We did an internet search to identify companies' gender composition of the boards of directors.

Female representation is measured using five alternatives: the total number of board members (board size); number of female members on the board; proportion of female members on the board; number of female non-executive directors; and number of female independent directors on the board.

Our analysis shows that in 12 out of 32 companies, the proportion of female board members exceeds 20%. The average board in Russia consists of 10.1 directors, a continued reduction from 10.6 and 10.3 in the previous two years (Spencer Stuart, 2017).

In our sample, the board of MegaFon is the smallest with seven members, while the largest, RUSAL, has 18. Though the Law on JSC (1995) does not set any requirements for the number of independent directors on the board, the prevailing majority (90% in 2014) of Russian public companies reported that they set limits on the number of board members in their in-house documents (e.g. charters, articles of association, terms of reference). The following requirements for the number of independent directors on the board are provided by the Moscow Exchange listing rules: at least three independent directors for list A1 and A2, and at least one director for lower lists (Spencer Stuart, 2017). Among the European countries studied in the 2016 Russia Board Index, the average number of directors is 10.5. The majority of companies continue to have between nine and 11 directors as compared with the average board sizes across Europe, ranged from 8.2 to 14.1. The smallest boards were in Finland and the largest were in Germany, where boards include employee representatives.

In our sample, nine out of 32 companies work in the energy industry. The share of women on corporate boards of these companies varies from the lowest 8.33% in T+ Group and MOSENEGRO (one female member out of 12 total) to the highest 27.27% in Interregional Distribution Grid Company of Centre (three female members out of 11 total). This company has the corporate governance rating 7+ 'Developed corporate governance practice' on the scale of the Russian Institute of Directors (RID) National Corporate Governance Rating (NCGR).[3]

Four metallurgical companies in the sample are the business world leaders in the market of precious metals, aluminum, nickel, and ferrous and nonferrous metals. These companies are building a model of excellence, adhering to the CG standards and principles, and introducing social reporting. Since 2011, the shares of Polymetal International have been quoted at the London Stock Exchange and the company is included in the FTSE100 index. Due to these facts, Polymetal International has to comply with not only the Russian CG Code but also the CG Code of the UK that promotes gender diversity.

As stated on the company website, RUSAL adheres to the principles of equality and diversity in the board composition. The company believes that a pool of various experiences and opinions, regardless of gender, age and ethnicity, is an important factor for making balanced corporate decisions. In the reporting year, the RUSAL corporate board included four women. Board diversity is one of the essential board member selection criteria set by RUSAL CG Committee and the Nomination Committee, along with independence, age, professional competence, and willingness to devote sufficient time and efforts to serving as a board member.

In Magnitogorsk Iron and Steel Works, one-fifth of the board members are women. As Russia is still a relationship-based society, firms tend to engage female directors who are family members. That is exactly the case: one director is the daughter of the chairman. There is a thread that board nominations driven mainly by personal relationships (see also Polyus) may restrict the pool of potential candidates, and there is greater likelihood of nominating less qualified women (Siegel et al., 2011). Nevertheless, since 2012, female directors of Magnitogorsk Iron and Steel Works have been nominated for the National award 'Director of the Year' and '50 Best Independent Directors' several times. The company's corporate secretary, Valentina Khavantseva, has been in the rating of '25 Best Corporate Governance Directors – Corporate Secretaries' more than once.

Among the three companies that are in the construction and real estate business, PICK Group has the highest percentage of female directors: 30%. PICK Group is one of the leading development and construction companies. Its management is committed to adhering to the best international CG practice, which helps gain investors' trust. The company shares are traded on the Moscow Exchange and the London Stock Exchange. In order to improve the efficacy of the corporate board, the company strives to attain the optimal balance between executive, non-executive and independent directors. Four out of nine board members are independent directors, including one woman – Zumrud Rustamova, who is also a member of the corporate boards of Magnitogorsk Iron and Steel Works and RPC United Wagon Company.

Among three banks in our sample, OTKRITIE Bank is the largest private bank in Russia and the fourth in terms of assets among all Russian banking groups. Two board members out of nine are women.

ALROSA is the leader of the diamond industry, a Russian mining company with state participation. The company is improving its CG system and ensures its compliance with the world's best standards. The NCGR is 7++ 'Developed corporate governance practice'. ALROSA has approximately 27% female representation on its board. Two women are independent directors. In two from 32 companies, women constitute a quarter of the board members: Yandex and the Moscow Exchange.

Women in companies with state participation

The current estimates show that approximately 70% of all companies in the Russian economy are companies with state participation. What place do women occupy in CG of this type of companies?

According to Rosimushchestvo data, collected from over 650 joint stock companies with state participation, at the end of 2016, corporate boards and audit committees were composed of more than 5,700 members, 37% of which were women. There were approximately 3,700 board members, with 2,800 men and 900 women. The percentage of female board members stood at 24.3%. Totally, 2,000 members were elected in audit committees but in this case, the percentage of female members exceeded male ones: 60% (1,200 women) versus 40% (800 men).

The largest number of female board and audit committee members was recorded in joint stock companies, controlled by the Ministry of Agriculture and the Ministry of Industry and Trade of the Russian Federation. This might be explained by the fact that these two ministries supervise the largest number of joint stock companies.

Table 8.2 covers the Sverdlovskaya Oblast sample of 22 companies taken from the database of the Territorial Administration of Rosimushchestvo. Sverdlovskaya Oblast is one of the top ten leading Russian regions. It is ranked eighth in terms of gross regional product; fourth with regard to wholesale trade turnover; seventh in terms of shipped industrial output; and tenth by investments in fixed capital.

Women are present in the boards of 17 out of 22 companies. Three companies have 60% female board members; two – 40% female board members; one company – around 30%; 11 companies – 20% female board members. Thus, the average percentage of females on the board is 30%. Female independent directors are present in five companies. Their academic qualification is quite high: two out of five women hold a doctoral degree.

Women's representation in audit committees is more significant. All-female audit committees exist in four companies. In 13 firms their representation stands at around 67%; in three companies the proportion of female audit committee members accounts for approximately 33%. Thus, in 20 firms with audit committees the average percentage of female members is 68%. The number of corporate secretaries in the sampled companies is extremely low – only in three companies the position of a corporate secretary is held by a woman.

As in the case with the all-Russia company analysis, on the regional (oblast) level the gender factor is not the focus of special consideration as compared to the essential requirements for the professional criteria set for both male and female board members.

Research suggests that the impact of women's board participation on performance is conditional on a minimum critical mass (Konrad et al., 2008), which makes women comfortable to voice their views. Konrad et al. (2008) suggest three women as the number beyond which gender ceases to be a barrier to acceptance and communication. Only five out of 32 (around 16%) of Russian companies and three out of 22 (about 14%) of local firms we studied have passed this threshold.

Table 8.2 Women on boards of companies with state participation in Sverdlovskaya Oblast (as of July 2016)

	Company name	State-own interest, %	Board size	Women on board	Share of women on board, %	Presence of female ID*	Share of women in audit committee, %	Presence of female CS**
1	Kamyishlov Seed Breeding Station	100	5	2	40.0	–	100.00	–
2	Ayat Peat Mining Company	100	5	3	60.0	–	66.67	–
3	Irbit Seed Breeding Station	100	5	1	20.0	–	66.67	–
4	Research Institute of Asbestos Production	100	5	0	0	–	33.34	–
5	Northern Geological Survey Expedition	100	5	3	60.0	–	66.67	–
6	Central Research Institute of Prevention of Pneumoconiosis and Safety Measures	100	5	2	40.0	–	100.00	–
7	Uralstroysvyaz	100	5	1	20.0	–	66.67	–
8	Sverdlovsk Fuel Company	100	5	0	0	–	66.67	–
9	Beloyarskoye Fuel Cycle Company	100	5	3	60.0	–	66.67	–
10	Research Institute of Mining and Processing Machinery Manufacturing	100	5	1	20.0	–	66.67	+
11	Sverdlovsky Breeding Poultry Enterprise	100	5	0	0	–	–	–
12	Ural Institute of Standardized Design	100	5	0	0	.	66.67	–
13	Sverdlovskaya Film Studio	100	5	1	20.0	+	66.67	+
14	Sverdlovskagropromstandart	100	5	1	20.0	–	66.67	–

(Continued)

Table 8.2 (Continued)

	Company name	State-own interest, %	Board size	Women on board	Share of women on board, %	Presence of female ID*	Share of women in audit committee, %	Presence of female CS**
15	PROGESS	100	5	1	20.0	+	66.67	–
16	URALSKIY RABOCHIY, Printing and Publishing Company	100	5	0	0	–	100.00	–
17	URALETS, Instructional and Experimental Farm	100	5	1	20.0	+ (Chairperson)	100.00	+
18	Ural Management of Amusement Devices	100	5	1	20.0	–	66.67	–
19	NORD, Cold Store Complex	49.0	5	1	20.0	–	33.34	–
20	Uralgiproruda Institute	34.11	5	1	20.0	+	–	–
21	Ural Institute of Metals	25.5	7	2	28.58	+	33.34	–
22	TECHNOSVYAZ'	24.0	5	1	20.0	–	66.67	–

Source: study database

Notes: *ID – independent director;
**CS – corporate secretary

Conclusion

Russian research related to board gender diversity and financial performance of firms in imperfect markets offers two conceptually different approaches: instrumental and regulatory (Ankudinov, 2013). An instrumental approach considers a variety of measures for attaining gender diversity through the lens of the main objective of a business – maximizing stock value for its owners. The regulatory approach to the challenge of board diversity in CG, by definition, does not attribute the achievement of the objectives to economic efficiency; it puts forward the moral obligation to the discriminated part of society – that is, women. In this regard, the regulatory approach perfectly fits the stakeholder model of CG. However, empirical studies of Russian board gender diversity will be faced with certain difficulties caused by the characteristics of the emerging markets, such as limited access to data due to lack of information transparency in non-public companies, or/and a high proportion of women in corporate governance representing the family of the business owners.

The experience of one of the authors of this publication (Tkachenko) as a professional independent director in boardrooms of several Russian companies with state participation allows us to share some personal observations about the impact of diverse boards on board efficacy and firm performance. We believe that there is no significant difference between male and female attributes of boardroom roles as long as a board member is professional, knowledgeable, proactive; exhibits leadership and collaborative skills; and applies high ethical standards.

Overall, gender diversity in boardrooms can be viewed through the prism of the stakeholder model of CG, bearing in mind that women can be treated as holders of original ideas, due to socio-psychological characteristics of women leaders (Bataeva, 2014). Female directors are not inclined to traditional approaches to management and more often consider the variable way of the company development. Female board members are more educated than men and presumably have greater knowledge and expertise (Horton et al., 2012), which translates to a greater perspective on social responsibility (Byron and Post, 2016).[4]

The company can also benefit from a better use of the pool of individual talents (Terjesen et al., 2009) who have expertise in corporate law and governance, corporate finance, strategic management and risk management. Women show more thorough and more careful approaches to information-gathering and financial data analysis. Building a pool of female talent is the key to promoting more women on boards. Companies can attract and retain qualified, talented women by developing a gender diversity strategy suited to its unique environment and needs. In this sense, the participation of women on boards will ensure that women bring new business models implementing in that way the idea of diversity of opinions.

At the same time, the presence of female members in the board can affect decision-making due to a variety of perspectives and non-traditional approaches to problems (Adams et al., 2015). In general, gender diversity in boardrooms can be viewed through the prism of the stakeholder model of CG bearing in mind that female directors are more likely to be stakeholder oriented and concerned about ethical principles and socially responsible behaviour (Adams and Ferreira, 2009).

When the board of directors performs as a team, it presents different views, including those differentiated by gender. In that way, stakeholders' divergent interests will be represented and promoted more adequately.

And some more facts in conclusion. In 2016, 14 women (ten corporate directors and four corporate secretaries) were included in the Russian TOP-50 Best Corporate Governance Directors list (Топ-1000 российских менеджеров, 2016). The 2016 Russian Institute of Directors Rating of the top 250 executives of Russian companies reported 33 women (13.2%). The 2016 National Award 'Director of the Year' initiated by the Association of Independent Directors was given to three women out of the 50 best independent directors. Eight women were nominated among 'The 25 Best Corporate Governance Directors – Corporate Secretaries'. In the nomination 'The Professional Director of the State Company' (held with the participation of Rosimushchestvo) the award went to Tatiana Olifirova, the chairperson of OAO Crystall, Smolensk. Is this not the evidence that Russian women do accelerate their representation in executive roles and do it successfully?

Notes

1 The Federal Agency for State Property Management (Rosimushchestvo)is a subdivision of the Russian Ministry of Economic Development that manages Russia's federal state property and specifically focuses on ranking the level of corporate governance in companies with state participation.
2 The 'Committee of 20's' is a nonprofit organization of the most successful Russian businesswomen, who hold top positions in leading companies, have achieved their success in a comparatively short period by starting their companies from scratch and growing them into recognized industry leaders.
3 The National Corporate Governance Rating (NCGR) is a barometer of a company's current situation in terms of corporate governance practices. It combines four indicators: shareholders' rights, efficacy of corporate boards, information disclosure, and corporate social responsibility and sustainability.
4 For a complete literature review, see Campbell, K. and Bohdanowicz, L. (2015).

References

Adams, R.B., de Haan, J., Terjesen, S., van Ees, H. 2015. Board diversity: Moving the field forward, *Corporate Governance*, 23(2), 77–82.

Adams, R.B., Ferreira, D. 2009. Women in the boardroom and their impact on governance and performance, *Journal of Financial Economics*, 94, 291–309.

Alekseeva, S. 2017. "Опора России" представила исследование женской деловой активности ["Opora Russiyi" presents the research on female business activity], http://firrma.ru/data/analytics/14492/, accessed 6 March, 2017.

Ankudinov, A. 2013. Концептуальные подходы к интеграции принципов гендерного разнообразия в корпоративный менеджмент [Conceptual approaches to integrating principles of gender diversity in corporate management], Экономический Вестник Республики Татарстан, 1, 78–81.

Bataeva, V. 2014. Социально-психологические особенности женщин-руководителей [Social-psychological characteristics of women leaders], Economic psychology in the modern world. Internet conference, http://epsy.fa.ru/forum/5-1-1, accessed 6 March, 2017.

Byron, K., Post, C. 2016. Women on boards of directors and corporate social performance: A meta-analysis, *Corporate Governance*, 24(4), 428–442.

Campbell, K., Bohdanowicz, L. 2015. Corporate governance and the growing role of women in the boardroom in Aluchna, M., Aras, G. (eds.), *Transforming Governance: New Values, New Systems in New Business Environment*, Farnham: Gower, 121–142.

Catalyst 2016 2015. *Catalyst Census: Women and Men Board Directors*. New York: Catalyst.

Cherkaev, D. n.d. Роль женщин в корпоративной ответственности и управлении [The role of women in corporate responsibility and corporate governance]. Межд. Фонд социально-экономических и политологических исследований (Горбачев-фонд) The International Foundation for Social-Economic and Political Issues (The Gorbachev Foundation), www.gorby.ru/activity/conference/show_585/view_27307/, accessed 6 March, 2017.

Davies Report 2015. Improving the gender balance in British boards. London.

Deloitte Global Center for Corporate Governance. 2015. *Women in the boardroom: A global perspective*, 4th edition. https://www2.deloitte.com/global/en/pages/risk/topics/dttl-global-center-for-corporate-governance.html

European Commission 2012. Women in decision-making in the EU. European Union, Brussels.

European Commission 2014. Improving the gender balance in company boardrooms. European Union, Brussels.

Federal Law No. 208-FZ of 26 December 1995 "On Joint Stock Companies".

Freeman, R. 1984. *Strategic Management: A Stakeholder Approach*, Boston: Pitman.

Freeman, R.E., Velamuri, S.R. 2008. A new approach to CSR: Company stakeholder responsibility, https://papers.ssrn.com/sol3/Papers.cfm?abstract_id=1186223, accessed 30 July, 2017.

Hope, K. 2015. FTSE 100 firms appoint more women to their boards. BBC News. March 25, www.bbc.com/news/business-3203856, accessed 25 March, 2017.

Horton, J., Millo, Y., Serafeim, G. 2012. Resources or power? Implications of social networks on compensation and firm performance, *Journal of Business Finance & Accounting*, 39, 399–426.

International Labour Organization n.d. Women on boards: Building the female talent pipeline, Geneva.

Konrad, A.M., Kramer, V.W., Erkut, S. 2008. Critical mass: The impact of three or more women on corporate boards, *Organizational Dynamics*, 37(2), 145–164.

Mastercard Index of Women Entrepreneurs (MIWE). 2017, https://newsroom.mastercard.com/wp-content/uploads/2017/03/Report-Mastercard-Index-of-Women-Entrepreneurs-2017-Mar-3.pdf, accessed 20 March, 2017.

MSCI ECG Research. 2014. Governance Issue Report. 2014 Survey of women on boards. https://30percentclub.org/wp-content/uploads/2014/11/2014-Survey-of-Women-on-Boards-1.pdf, accessed 20 March, 2017.

OECD 2004. OECD Principles of corporate governance, www.oecd.org/corporate/ca/corporategovernanceprinciples/31557724.pdf, accessed 20 March, 2017.

PWC 2013. Russian Boards: Selection, Nomination and Election, www.pwc.ru/en/boardsurvey/assets/e-nomination_survey_eng.pdf, accessed 20 March, 2017.

Qian, M. 2016. Women's leadership and corporate performance. ADB Economics Working Paper Series No. 472, Asian Development Bank.

Schwab, K., Sala-i-Martín, X. The Global Competitiveness Report 2016–2017, www3.weforum.org/docs/GCR2016–2017/05FullReport/TheGlobalCompetitivenessReport2016–2017_FINAL.pdf, accessed 6 March, 2017.

Siegel, J., Pyun, L., Cheon, B.Y. 2011. Multinational firms, labor market discrimination, and the capture of competitive advantage by exploiting the social divide, Harvard Business School Working Paper, 11–011, February 10.

Spencer Stuart 2017. 2016 Russia Board Index, www.spencerstuart.com/research-and-insight/2016-russia-board-index,accessed 6 March, 2017.

Terjesen, S., Lloyd, A. The 2015 Female Entrepreneurship Index. Analyzing the conditions that foster high-potential female entrepreneurship in 77 countries. GEDI the Global Entrepreneurship and Development Institute, https://thegedi.org/research/womens-entrepreneurship-index/, accessed 6 March, 2017.

Terjesen, S., Sealy, R., Singh, V. 2009. Women directors on corporate boards: A review and research agenda, *Corporate Governance*, 17(3), 320–337.

Женщины в современной экономике: вызовы и решения n.d. Women in modern economy: Challenges and solutions, www.womenofrussia.org/new.aspx?id=255, accessed 6 March, 2017.

Топ-1000 российских менеджеров [Top-1000 Russian managers] 2016. Коммерсант.ru, 182, October 10, www.kommersant.ru/apps/102663, accessed 6–10 October, 2016.

9 Female representation on Swedish corporate boards

Gunnar Rimmel, Petra Inwinkl,
Anna Lindstrand and Ida Ohlsson

Introduction

That women hold few corporate board seats is a discussion that has been central during the last two decades (Wang and Clift, 2009; Adams and Ferreira, 2009; Arfken et al., 2004; Ryan and Haslam, 2006). Female board representatives represent a scarce but needed resource because it is believed that female directors can handle crises and riskier tasks better than male directors (Nekhili and Gatfaoui, 2013). Since the collapse of Lehman Brothers in 2008, it has been argued that everything might have turned out differently if there had been a higher number of female representatives on bank boards (Branson, 2012; Tremblay et al., 2016). The assumption that a higher number of women on boards would have reduced unnecessary risk-taking and greed (Tremblay et al., 2016) led Levi et al. (2010: 166) to utter the incisive quote, "What if Lehman Brothers had been Lehman Sisters?"

This situation is likely to change because boards around the world are under increasing pressure to choose female directors (Adams and Ferreira, 2009). International organisations such as the World Economic Forum (2016a) stress the importance of gender diversity in the boardroom by publishing a yearly Global Gender Gap Index measuring economic, political, educational and health gaps between men and women since 2006 (World Economic Forum, 2016b). Nordic countries have been identified as 'women-friendly' countries, based on the large share of women who participate in politics, education and the labour market in general (Siim, 2013). For example, in 2016, Iceland, Finland and Norway were ranked as having the smallest gender gap in the world followed by Sweden (World Economic Forum, 2016c). However, the representation of women in Sweden on corporate boards in listed companies has not followed these trends in equality development (Freidenvall and Hallonsten, 2013). In most Swedish companies, boards are still dominated by males (Langvasbråten, 2008; Freidenvall and Hallonsten, 2013).

Some countries address the issue of gender equality with legislation imposing quotas for female representation on corporate boards. The first prominent legislation for such gender diversity was passed in Norway, where since January 2003 all listed companies must abide by a 40% gender quota for female directors or face dissolution (Huse et al., 2009). Spain has followed Norway's lead by enacting a law requiring companies to increase the share of female directors to 40% by 2015 (Adams and Ferreira, 2009). France adopted the idea of quotas as well by enacting a minimum 40% quota for female board members in large listed and unlisted companies from 2016 on (Nekhili and Gatfaoui, 2013).

The debate to introduce a gender quota began in Sweden in 2006 (Freidenvall and Hallonsten, 2013). At that time, the Swedish Department of Justice (*Justitiedepartementet*) proposed at least a 40% quota for female directors of corporate boards. When the proposal was brought up in Parliament, however, the ruling government voted against it. It was argued that it seemed to be enough that Swedish listed companies had to strive for gender balance on their boards, following the Swedish Corporate Governance Board (2016).

An important argument in the gender gap discussion is economic. Gender discrimination may harm a company's performance when capable and competent candidates are not appointed to board positions due to gender (Brammer et al., 2007). Potential investors might hesitate to invest money in a company that does not promote equal opportunities for men and women (Singh and Vinnicombe, 2004).

The economic evidence provided by the literature is mixed, however. Some studies show that having female representatives on corporate boards may lead to higher quality of earnings, i.e. more sustainable and reasonable profit levels (Srinidhi et al., 2011). Others provide a less positive view on female representatives on boards (Arena et al., 2015; Adams and Ferreira, 2009). Adams and Ferreira (2009) argue that having women on boards will hinder effectiveness in firms that are already well managed, because women will increase the monitoring of the firms and the boards activities, and how the firm is managed. This can be counterproductive for well-managed firms since it will take more time than necessary (Adams and Ferreira, 2009). There is also an argument that having minorities on boards can result in power conflicts whereas women are often a minority on boards. Looking from this perspective, the influence from the females on boards becomes weakened and results in smaller contributions to the firm (Westphal and Milton, 2000). Gender-diverse boards have no specific impact on the efficiency in the corporate board and thus gender diversity does not improve performance (Hillman et al., 2000).

Even though criticisms against board diversity exist, the vast majority of literature provides vital arguments favouring having female board representatives (Arena et al., 2015; Nielsen and Huse, 2010; Campbell and Mínguez-Vera, 2008). From this considerable literature, we summarise three benefits of a female presence on boards.

First, women directors compared to men are claimed to be more patient and open-minded (Arfken et al., 2004) and tend to have fewer attendance problems (Adams and Ferreira, 2009). These are characteristics that can enhance communication and help mediate information to investors and other stakeholders. As a consequence, such boards have a better monitoring of the company and its activities, and accordingly, stakeholders sense a higher accountability for these firms (Adams and Ferreira, 2009). This can be a way to reduce the chance for agency conflicts between shareholders and the boards (Farrell and Hersch, 2005; Arfken et al.,

2004). Second, boards with female representatives are more quick to adopt new recommended practices of corporate governance compared to corporate boards with only male representatives (Terjesen et al., 2009). Third, women contribute to more open discussions and questioning in boardrooms, which may bring new perspectives and ideas to the firm (Singh and Vinnicombe, 2004). Diversity can thus help boards to avoid 'groupthink' when more various opinions are represented (Branson, 2012; Arfken et al., 2004).

The remainder of the chapter is organised as follows. The next section presents previous literature and theoretical perspectives. The third section illustrates the specific structure of the model used in the study. The fourth section shows the empirical findings regarding female representation on Swedish corporate boards. In the following sections, the results are interpreted in the light of the current debate about female representatives on corporate boards and thus constitute a contribution to the ongoing debate on corporate reporting practices. This chapter concludes with a summary of the study's findings and suggestions for further research.

Previous literature and theoretical perspectives of women on corporate boards

The scholarly debate identifies several arguments explaining why women are underrepresented on boards. A metaphor frequently used in the discussion to explain the underrepresentation of women on boards or their absence in the highest positions within companies is the 'glass ceiling'. In short, the notion refers to the assumption of invisible barriers to reach specific company positions (Arfken et al., 2004). Despite the fact that many women operate in middle management within companies, the number of women who break through the glass ceiling and reach higher positions is small (Singh et al., 2001).

The glass ceiling occurs at different levels in different companies, and it is argued that if a woman feels that her career is held back by an invisible ceiling, she is likely to move to another company. In turn, this can result in a loss of competence and knowledge for companies (Singh and Vinnicombe, 2004). On the other hand, there is some criticism against the concept of the glass ceiling. For example, Yousry (2006) states that some people view the glass ceiling as an excuse for not successfully climbing higher on the corporate ladder. Those who claim that the barrier of the glass ceiling exists focus too much on how to break it, in situations when it would be of greater importance to focus on value creation for the company. Focusing on the wrong things can thus weaken the company and its performance.

Ryan and Haslam (2006) describe an invisible 'glass cliff'. This aims to explain the phenomenon that women are more likely to be appointed to higher positions and leadership roles in organisations that are not managed well. A result of this can be that if the company fails, the blame of bad management and failure would fall on these women. This contributes to the positioning of women as 'bad managers' and gives them a poor reputation, which becomes an additional barrier. Furthermore, Krishnan and Parsons (2008) argue that top positions are appointed based on competence and skills, not gender.

Gender stereotypes, that is to say the perception about how women and men act in different roles and situations in management, leadership and communication styles, offer a second explanation of why woman are seen to be underrepresented on boards (Singh and Vinnicombe, 2004).

A third factor is the ownership structure of companies, which is claimed to affect board diversity, appointment of women on boards and the boards' effectiveness (Ben Amar et al., 2013). The incentives and efforts to appoint women to boards differ across different ownership structures, for example, family and non-family firms (Ben Amar et al., 2013; Brunzell and Peltomäki, 2015; Nekhili and Gatfaoui, 2013). A higher proportion of the board members are likely to be women in family owned firms than in non-family owned firms (Dang et al., 2014).

One example of this is that families in family firms typically have controlling power in the company through board representation, and in this way the family can control decision-making and thereby the appointment of new members to the board (Maury and Pajuste, 2005). Muttakin et al. (2015) find that in family firms, a large proportion of the board of directors is made up of family members or other relatives and that family owned firms in general have more female representatives on their boards.

According to Campbell and Mínguez-Vera (2008), family owned firms strive for continuity, and therefore they are more likely to appoint family members to higher positions, no matter their gender. Furthermore, Nekhili and Gatfaoui (2013) found that the ownership structure could also affect the appointment of female representatives. Their research shows that family ownership and higher educational level among female representatives on boards are negatively correlated to each other, i.e. that family firms do not appoint females with higher levels of education to the same extent as non-family firms. Claessens et al. (2000) argue that females in family firm boards might be unqualified for the directorship, but appointed because they are family members. In the light of this it seems like both ownership structure (Ben Amar et al., 2013) and educational level (Hambrick and Mason, 1984) can affect the appointment of females to corporate boards.

A fourth contributing factor when it comes to appointing women to corporate boards is their workforce, expertise, knowledge and skills. The directors of corporate boards all bring unique capacities to the board, referred to as human capital (Becker, 1962). A company's resources include human capital in terms of the workforce, and their expertise, knowledge and skills. To appoint the most appropriate board of directors is thus one way to increase the value of a company's resources (Singh et al., 2008). The human capital theory is based upon the idea that every person in the company adds value to it, through his or her experience, education and abilities (Geiger and Marlin, 2012). Carter et al. (2010) state that board diversity contributes to a more valuable human capital in the company and in the board, which in turn will enhance both the company's and the board's performance. The educational level of individuals within a company is one contributing factor to its success, since education raises the level of human capital (Hambrick and Mason, 1984). The effects of discrimination, such as gender discrimination, are likely to be compensated by higher educational qualifications (Hillman et al., 2002).

Hence, women are more likely to strive for higher education in order to reach higher positions in companies. It has been argued that women do not put in the same effort as men in getting higher education, and the literature suggests this to be one factor causing a lower amount of promotions and lower pay for women (Terjesen et al., 2009). However, this seems not to be true. Singh et al. (2008), for example, show in their study of several dimensions of human capital that women are more likely than men to have higher education such as MBA degrees (master's degree in business administration). More women are graduating with higher education (Parker, 2008), and Singh and Vinnicombe (2004) argue that higher education among women increases the likelihood of companies appointing more females to corporate boards. The Global Gender Gap Index shows that in Sweden the level of education among men and women does not differ significantly, i.e. participation in education is not lower for women than for men (World Economic Forum, 2016a). Since the gender gap concerning educational level is low in developed countries, the underrepresentation of women on corporate boards cannot be explained by such things as a higher level of education among men than among women (Terjesen and Singh, 2008).

Common for all investments in human capital is that they aim to improve people's abilities, both mental and physical (Becker, 1962). Other types of human capital that often are invested in are, for example, health care and on-the-job training. On-the-job-training will add value to the company since employees, trained for their specific tasks, will be more productive than employees who are not specialised. This theory is relevant for the study since diversity on boards will lead to a broader variety in human capital, which has been proven to favour companies in different ways (Terjesen et al., 2009). Further the theory can be used to explain the exclusion of women in boardrooms that previously existed and still exist (Singh et al., 2008).

Data and methodology

The initial sample consisted of 87 large-cap companies listed on the NASDAQ OMX Stockholm with a market capitalisation equivalent to 1 billion Euros or more for the period 2011–2015. The hand-collected variables of board size, number of female representatives, level of education and ownership structure were retrieved from each company's annual report and corporate governance report. A total of 15 companies had to be excluded either due to a lack of factor (variable) information or because they were not listed on the stock market for the entire period of investigation. This led to a final sample consisting of annual data from 72 companies and 360 firm-year observations.

For the 360 firm-year observations we counted manually the number of female directors for each company. In doing so we searched for nonfinancial information about the female directors that were disclosed in company reports. The descriptive statistics shows a steady increase in female directors during 2011–2015 (see Table 9.1). The average number of female directors ranged from 2.01 in 2011 to 2.61 in 2015. The total increase was 0.6 female directors over this period. In 2015, all companies evidenced female representatives.

For measuring the level of education and ownership structure, a binary coding system was used. A female with a master's degree or PhD degree was coded 1. If the female had a bachelor's degree or lower, her education was coded as 0. Ownership structure was coded as 1 when a firm was a family firm where the

Table 9.1 Average number of women on boards and percentage of women on boards

Years	Average number of women on board	Percentage of women on board
2011	2.01	25.51
2012	2.04	25.84
2013	2.18	27.66
2014	2.40	30.42
2015	2.61	33.18

Note: total number of firm-year observations = 360 = 100%

Table 9.2 Percentage of women on the boards over each sample year

Years	Percentage of firms with no women on board	Percentage of firms with one woman on board	Percentage of firms with two women on board	Percentage of firms with three women on board	Percentage of firms with four women on board	Total (%)
2011	5.56	22.22	43.06	23.60	5.56	= 100
2012	4.17	20.83	45.83	25.00	4.17	= 100
2013	4.17	18.05	41.67	27.78	8.33	= 100
2014	2.78	12.50	37.50	36.11	11.11	= 100
2015	0.00	8.30	36.11	41.67	13.89	= 100

Note: total number of firm-year observations = 360 = 100%

family held at least 5% of the equity. A family firm is defined as when a family as a shareholder holds more than 5% of the equity and can thus impact the governance in the company (Nekhili and Gatfaoui, 2013). If a family owns less than 5%, or alternatively no family ownership exists at all, the firm is coded as 0.

Table 9.2 displays that the range of number of female board members was between zero and four in all studied companies. There was no company that has more than four women on its board. A clear improvement in representation, or more correctly underrepresentation, can also be seen in the column 'Percentage of firms with no women on board', as the percentage of firms with no female representatives reached 0.00% in 2015, compared to 5.56% without female representatives in 2011. Furthermore, the percentage of firms that had only one woman on their board decreased from 22.22% to 8.33% over the five-year period. The percentage of firms with three women on their board showed the largest positive development, with an increase from 23.61% to 41.67% from the year 2011 to 2015. The percentage of firms with the highest number of female representatives, four women on their board, increased from 5.56% in 2011 to 13.89% in 2015. The decrease in percentage of firms with zero and one woman on the board and the increase of firms with three and four women on the board indicate a positive development of female representation during this five-year period.

In the analysis, tests were performed on the relationship of the variables a) "ownership structure" (whether the firms are family firms or not); b) the "number of female representatives"; c) the "level of education"; and d) "board size".

To examine the association between the dependent variables (factors c) and b)) and independent variables (factors a) and d)) first a Chi-square test is performed. Next, a Poisson regression analysis for the variables d) board size, b) the number of female representatives, a) ownership structure and b) the number of female representatives is executed. Count data are best handled by using the Poisson regression model (Greene, 2009). For the binary variables (c) educational level and a) ownership structure, we use a logistic regression analysis, since the Poisson regression cannot be used for binary variables (Ge and Whitmore, 2010).

All variables are tested at a significance level of 1%. Those which do not show a relationship at a 1% level are tested for significance at a 5% level. A significance of 1% means that there is 99% probability that there is a significant relationship and a 1% margin that the results would have occurred by chance due to an error in sampling. A significance level of 5% in turn means that the margin of error is 5% and the results are correct with a likelihood of 95%. The lower the significance level, the lower margin of error and the more likely that the results are correct (Bryman, 2016).

Empirical results

Development of female representatives on boards and board size

If board size affects the number of female directors on the board, then we expect to have more female directors the larger the board size is. Thus, we began by analysing the different numbers of female directors in relation to the board size with a minimum of five directors and maximum of 13 directors. Most companies have seven or eight directors sitting on the company board.

The Chi-square test we used displays in Table 9.3 a significant relationship between board size and number of female representatives at a 1% level. Further

Table 9.3 Number of female representatives and board size

	Board size – total number of directors in the boards (ranging from 5 to 13)									
	5	*6*	*7*	*8*	*9*	*10*	*11*	*12*	*13*	*χ2*
Number of female representatives										
0	3	7	1	0	2	0	0	0	0	124.651** (p=0.000)
1	3	18	25	7	5	0	0	0	0	
2	7	17	47	40	26	6	2	2	0	
3	4	3	15	38	27	8	7	6	3	
4	0	0	8	10	6	0	4	2	1	
Total	17/360	45/360	96/360	95/360	66/360	14/360	13/360	10/360	4/360	=360/360

Notes: **significant at a 1% level

360 = total number of firm-year observations

the table presents the 360 firm-year observations in relation to board size (five to 13 members) and the number of female directors (zero to four female board members) therein. The results show that boards with the maximum board size of 13 members have three or four female directors throughout the observational period. In boards with five and six members the maximum number of females on a board is three, compared to boards between ten and 13 board members where the number of women therein reaches four. None of these boards between ten and 13 board members have one woman. The results suggest a positive relationship between board size and the number of females appointed to a board. The observation performed for Swedish companies is in line with earlier research, and shows that the larger the size of the board, the higher the number of female representatives on boards (Gregoric et al., 2017; Brammer et al., 2007; Sealy et al., 2007).

Ownership structure and appointment of women

Because board size is one internal factor that affects the likelihood of appointing females to boardrooms, we take ownership structure as an outside dominating factor for female appointment. This means that we consider in our sample female directors, as they are appointed due to ties to family firms and non-family firms. Table 9.4 shows at a 1% level a significant result of the Chi-square test for the relationship between the number of female directors and the ownership structure. Out of the 360 firm-year observations 70 firm years (19.44%) show appointments in family firms and 290 (80.56%) in non-family firms.

The largest proportion from our total 360 firm-year observations is non-family firms with two female directors (31.94%), while the smallest proportion is family firms with no female directors (0.00%) meaning that no family firm had zero female directors during this five-year period. All family firms have at least one female director, in opposition to non-family firms. This indicates

Table 9.4 Number of female representatives in family firms and non-family firms

Number of female representatives	Non-family firms	Family firms	χ^2
0	13 (3.61%)	0 (0.00%)	19.506** (p = 0.001)
1	54 (15.00%)	4 (1.11%)	
2	115 (31.94%)	32 (8.89%)	
3	90 (25.00%)	21 (5.83%)	
4	18 (5.00%)	13 (3.61%)	
Total	290 (80.56%)	70 (19.44%)	= 360 (100.00%)

Note: ** significant at a 1% level

Table 9.5 Poisson regression analysis and Chi-square correlation test

Educational level	Non-family firm	Family firm	Total number of companies	χ2
0	62 (22.30%)	30 (42.86%)	92	12,149** (p = 0.000)
1	216 (77.70%)	40 (57.14%)	256	
Total	278 (100.00%)	70 (100.00%)	348	

Notes: statistics of the educational level are only provided for firm-year observations where there is at least one woman present on the board (348 firm-year observations = 100.00%)

** significant at a 1% level
0 = bachelor's degree or lower education
1 = higher education than bachelor's degree

that family firms are more likely to appoint female representatives than non-family firms.

By using regression analysis we show that there is a relationship between the ownership structure and the number of female directors in the boards of our sample, which is in line with the findings from Dang et al. (2014) and Campbell and Mínguez-Vera (2008). They argue that family firms are more likely than non-family firms to appoint female directors – a pattern which applies in the case in Sweden as well.

Table 9.5 shows the results from the Chi-square correlation tests and the Poisson regression analyses. One star (*) and two stars (**) means that the test is significant at a 5% and a 1% level, respectively. The correlation test between the variables "ownership structure" and "number of female directors" shows significance at a 1% level, while the regression analysis showed a significance at a 5% level (0.023 < 0.05). For the variables "board size" and "number of female directors", both the correlation test (Table 9.5) and the regression analysis show significance at a 1% level. The regression analysis further strengthens the results of the correlation analysis that there is a relationship between the variables and also the strength of the relationship.

The significantly higher proportion of female representatives in family firms than in non-family firms could be explained family owned firms being more likely to appoint family members to their boards, regardless of their gender (Campbell and Mínguez-Vera, 2008). This results in female family members obtaining a greater chance to be appointed to these specific boards, than if they were not family members. One reason for the high likelihood of appointing family members could be that family firms often strive for continuity, as an incentive to keep the firm as a family firm (Campbell and Mínguez-Vera, 2008). On the other hand, non-family firms are less likely to appoint women to their board. Instead, their appointments are rather based on other qualities, partly on gender (men are more likely than women to be appointed), but also on characteristics and skills.

Educational level and ownership structure

If the family firms represent a specific type of ownership structure that promotes the appointment of female directors, then we would expect female directors on family firms to have a lower educational level than female directors of non-family firms. We expect that female directors of non-family firms are principled in the human capital theory; that is to say that only skills, abilities and qualifications for the job are the underlying criteria for the appointment as a board member.

The relationship between ownership structure and educational level is displayed in Table 9.6. The Chi-square correlation test shows a significant relationship at a 1% level. All non-family firms (77.70%) have women with a higher education on their boards compared to the corresponding proportion of female representatives in family firms, where only 57.14% have higher education. We can use this result to confirm the assumption that non-family firms are more likely to appoint female directors with a higher education than family firms.

We provide evidence consistent with this hypothesis in Table 9.7 which shows the results from the correlation test and the logistic regression analysis of the variables "ownership structure" and "educational level". Both the correlation test and the binary logistic regression analysis show a significance at 1% level

Table 9.6 Number of female representatives and educational level within family firms and non-family firms

Dependent variables versus independent variables	Educational level	Chi-square correlation
	Bivariate logistic regression	
Family ownership	0.001**	12.149** (p = 0.001)

Note: **significant at a 1% level

Table 9.7 Bivariate logistic regression analysis and Chi-square correlation test

Dependent variables versus independent variables	Number of female directors Poisson regression	Chi-square correlation
Family ownership	0.023*	19.506** (p = 0.001)
Board size	0.000**	124.651** (p = 0.000)

Notes: **significant at a 1% level
*significant at a 5% level

Dependent variables versus independent variables	Educational level	Chi-square correlation
	Bivariate logistic regression	
Family ownership	0.001**	12.149** (p = 0.001)

Note: **significant at a 1% level

(P = 0.001). In consequence, the most appropriate person is appointed for the top positions, which gives equal chances for both genders. By this, it can be argued that the theoretical standpoint of the human capital theory becomes more and more common among Swedish companies, which is also supported by the findings of Freidenvall and Hallonsten (2013).

The negative relationship between higher education and family ownership is confirmed by previous research. One possible explanation why family firms are more likely to appoint family members or other relatives regardless of their educational level is that they tend to value the continuity of the firm within the family (Nekhili and Gatfaoui, 2013; Campbell and Mínguez-Vera, 2008). On the other hand, firms that are not family owned are more likely to appoint women who have higher educational qualifications. Such an argument might confound the interpretation of the results that the performance quality of non-family firms' boards is higher than in family firms, simply because the overall educational level among women is higher. Instead more diversity on corporate boards increases the value of companies' human capital and since family firms are more likely to have a higher gender diversity on their boards, their human capital tends to be highly valued (Terjesen et al., 2009). Whereas, on the other hand, higher education does also necessarily contribute to an increase in human capital (Becker, 1962; Geiger and Marlin, 2012). A strong family relationship might instead bring a better ability to cooperate, which in turn can favour both the firm and the board. Furthermore, even if family firms in general have higher board gender diversity, the appointment of family members, instead of other appropriate candidates, could possibly make other aspects of board diversity suffer, for example ethnicity or nationality (Siim, 2013).

Conclusions

Female representation on corporate boards is a central theme of institutional and governance reform efforts worldwide. However, Swedish studies on board characteristics for female appointments are rare and consequences resulting of changing the gender diversity of the board are little known.

In this study, we provide some evidence that the presence of female directors in Swedish large-cap listed companies increased during 2011–2015, even though the country has no binding legislation on gender quotas. We also found that the female representation on boards was positively related to measures of board size and ownership structure when companies were family firms. Female directors appeared to be appointed in family firms more often as in non-family firms regardless of their level of education. Female directors in non-family firms get more frequently appointed due to their skills, abilities and knowledge as described in human capital theory. In non-family firms, women are more likely to be appointed on corporate boards if they have higher education than a bachelor's degree. In the light of this we tested the relationship between ownership structure and level of education among female directors.

Although a positive relation between ownership structure and level of education existed, the increase in firm performance through gender diversity – as often cited in the popular press – might not show robustness on an educational level. The true relation between gender diversity and firm performance appears to be more complex. More generally, our results show that for female directors, the glass ceiling is stronger in non-family firms than in family firms. But this evidence does not provide support for quota-based policy initiatives. In line with the Swedish policy, no evidence suggests that such policies would improve firm performance on average.

References

Adams, R.B., Ferreira, D. 2009. Women in the boardroom and their impact on governance and performance, *Journal of Financial Economics*, 94(2), 291–309.

Arena, C., Cirillo, A., Mussolino, D., Pulcinelli, I., Saggese, S., Sarto, F. 2015. Women on board: Evidence from a masculine industry, *Corporate Governance*, 15(3), 339–356.

Arfken, D.E., Bellar, S.L., Helms, M.M. 2004. The ultimate glass ceiling revisited: The presence of women on corporate boards, *Journal of Business Ethics*, 50, 177–186.

Becker, G.S. 1962. Investment in human capital: A theoretical analysis, *Journal of Political Economy*, 70(5), Part 2: Investment in Human Beings, 9–49.

Ben Amar, W., Francoeur, C., Hafsi, T., Labelle, R. 2012. What makes better boards? A closer look at diversity and ownership, *British Journal of Management*, 24(1), 85–10.

Brammer, S., Millington, A., Pavelin, S. 2007. Gender and ethnic diversity among UK corporate boards, *Corporate Governance: An International Review*, 15, 393–403.

Branson, D. 2012. Initiatives to place women on corporate boards of directors: A global snapshot, *Journal of Corporation Law*, 37(4), 793–814.

Brunzell, T., Peltomäki, J. 2015. Ownership as a determinant of chairperson activity: A study of Nordic listed companies, *Qualitative Research in Financial Markets*, 7(4), 412–428.

Bryman, A. 2016. *Social Research Methods*, 5th ed., Oxford, UK: Oxford University Press.

Campbell, K., Mínguez-Vera, A. 2008. Gender diversity in the boardroom and firm financial performance, *Journal of Business Ethics*, 83(3), 435–451.

Carter, D.A., D'Souza, F., Simkins, B.J., Simpson, W.G. 2010. The gender and ethnic diversity of US boards and board committees and firm financial performance, *Corporate Governance: An International Review*, 18(5), 396–414.

Claessens, S., Djankov, S., Lang, L.H.P. 2000. The separation of ownership and control in East Asian corporations, *Journal of Financial Economics*, 58(1), 81–112.

Dang, R., Bender, A.-F., Scotto, M.-J. 2014. Women on French corporate board of directors: How do they differ from their male counterparts?, *Journal of Applied Business Research*, 30(2), 489–507.

Farrell, K.A., Hersch, P.L. 2005. Additions to corporate boards: The effect of gender, *Journal of Corporate Governance*, 11, 85–106.

Freidenvall, L., Hallonsten, H. 2013. Why not corporate gender quotas in Sweden? *Representation*, 49(4), 467–485.

Ge, W., Whitmore, G.A. 2010. Binary response and logistic regression in recent accounting research publications: A methodological note, *Review of Quantitative Finance and Accounting*, 34(1), 81–93.

Geiger, S.W., Marlin, D. 2012. The relationship between organizational/board characteristics and the extent of female representation on corporate boards, *Journal of Managerial Issues*, 24(2), 157–172, 122.

Greene, W. 2009. Models for count data with endogenous participation, *Empirical Economics*, 36(1), 133–173.

Gregoric, A., Oxelheim, L., Randøy, T., Thomsen, S. 2017. Resistance to change in the corporate elite: Female directors' appointments onto Nordic boards, *Journal of Business Ethics*, 141(2), 267–287.

Hambrick, D.C., Mason, P.A. 1984. Upper echelons: The organization as a reflection of its top managers, Academy of Management, *The Academy of Management Review*, 9(2), 193–206.

Hillman, A.J., Cannella, A.A., Harris, I.C. 2002. Women and racial minorities in the boardroom: How do directors differ?, *Journal of Management*, 28(6), 747–763.

Huse, M., Nielsen, S.T., Hagen, I.M. 2009. Women and employee-elected board members, and their contributions to board control tasks, *Journal of Business Ethics*, 89(4), 581–597.

Krishnan, G.V., Parsons, L.M. 2008. Getting to the bottom line: An exploration of gender and earnings quality, *Journal of Business Ethics*, 78(1–2), 65–76.

Langvasbråten, T. 2008. A Scandinavian model? Gender equality discourses on multiculturalism, *Social Politics*, 15(1), 32–52.

Levi, M., Li, K., Zhang, F. 2010. Deal or no deal: Hormones and the mergers and acquisitions game, *Management Science*, 56(9), 1462–1483.

Maury, B., Pajuste, A. 2005. Multiple large shareholders and firm value, *Journal of Banking and Finance*, 29(7), 1813–1834.

Muttakin, M.B., Khan, A., Subramaniam, N. 2015. Firm characteristics, board diversity and corporate social responsibility, *Pacific Accounting Review*, 27(3), 353–372.

Nekhili, M., Gatfaoui, H. 2013. Are demographic attributes and firm characteristics drivers of gender diversity? Investigating women's positions on French boards of directors, *Journal of Business Ethics*, 118(2), 227–249.

Nielsen, S., Huse, M. 2010. Women directors' contribution to board decision-making and strategic involvement: The role of equality perception, *European Management Review*, 7, 16–29.

Parker, L.D. 2008. Strategic management and accounting processes: Acknowledging gender, *Accounting, Auditing & Accountability Journal*, 21(4), 611–631.

Ryan, M., Haslam, A. 2006. What lies beyond the glass ceiling?, *Human Resource Management International Digest*, 14(3), 3–5.

Siim, B. 2013. Gender, diversity and migration – challenges to Nordic welfare, gender politics and research, equality, *Diversity and Inclusion: An International Journal*, 32(6), 615–628.

Singh, V., Terjesen, S., Vinnicombe, S. 2008. Newly appointed directors in the boardroom: How do women and men differ?, *European Management Journal*, 26(1), 48–58.

Singh, V., Vinnicombe, S. 2004. Why so few women directors in top UK boardrooms? Evidence and theoretical explanations, *Corporate Governance: An International Review*, 12, 479–488.

Singh, V., Vinnicombe, S., Johnson, P. 2001. Women directors on top UK boards, *Corporate Governance: An International Review*, 9, 206–216.

Srinidhi, B., Gul, F.A., Tsui, J.S.L. 2011. Female directors and earnings quality, *Contemporary Accounting Research*, 28(5), 1610–1644.

The Swedish Corporate Governance Board. 2016. The Swedish Corporate Governance Code, www.corporategovernanceboard.se, accessed 13 February, 2017.

Terjesen, S., Sealy, R., Singh, V. 2009. Women directors on corporate boards: A review and research agenda, *Corporate Governance: An International Review*, 17, 320–333.

Terjesen, S., Singh, V. 2008. Female presence on corporate boards: A multi-country study of environmental context, *Journal of Business Ethics*, 83(1), 55–63.

Tremblay, M.-S., Gendron, Y., Malsch, B. 2016. Gender on board: Deconstructing the "legitimate" female director, *Accounting, Auditing & Accountability Journal*, 29(1), 65–190.

Wang, Y., Clift, B. 2009. Is there a "business case" for board diversity?, *Pacific Accounting Review*, 21(2), 88–103.

Westphal, J.D., Milton, L.P. 2000. How experience and network ties affect the influence of demographic minorities on corporate boards, *Administrative Science Quarterly*, 45(2), 366–398.

World Economic Forum 2016a. The Global Gender Gap Report 2016, https://reports.weforum.org/global-gender-gap-report-2016/the-global-gender-gap-report-2016/, accessed 9 February, 2017.

World Economic Forum 2016b. Measuring the Global Gender Gap, https://reports.weforum.org/global-gender-gap-report-2016/measuring-the-global-gender-gap/, accessed 13 February, 2017.

World Economic Forum 2016c. Top Ten, https://reports.weforum.org/global-gender-gap-report-2016/top-ten/, accessed 9 February, 2017.

Yousry, M. 2006. The glass ceiling – isn't glass, *Business Renaissance Quarterly*, 1(1), 93–111.

10 Females on corporate boards

French perspectives: towards more diversity?

Nabyla Daidj

Introduction

The 1990s have been characterized by profound economic changes in France, the increasing role of financial markets and globalization, a wider uptake and use of ICT by businesses across all sectors of the economy. The challenges came with the rising Europeanization (involving the integration in a single European market) leading French firms to expand operations on a broader geographical base. Deregulation in sectors such as telecommunications led to higher competitive pressures on existing groups (incumbents). The share of large state enterprises of the economy started to decline considerably.

The French corporate governance system has significantly changed over the years aiming at a more widely dispersed ownership and greater transparency. In the 1990s, the government's privatization policy led to improving corporate governance of large firms allowing them to acquire more and more resources through market financing rather than through bank borrowing. Foreign funds have begun to play an increasingly important role in the French economy and to impact corporate governance of big companies through the transformation of ownership structures (towards a more dispersed ownership).

Several corporate governance principles have been applied successfully and have strengthened the rights and responsibilities of shareholders, the duties and responsibilities of the board of directors, the development of independent directors and external auditing, disclosure and transparency practices. The introduction of monitoring and control mechanisms has had also a significant impact on corporate governance rules. The presence of foreign ownership in CAC 40 listed firms has increased as well as the percentage of independent directors in CAC 40 firms.

In June 2013, AFEP and MEDEF published a new version of the code of corporate governance. This revision is part of a codification process begun in 1995 and regularly updated since then, particularly in 2007, 2008 and 2010. The 2010 version made in particular recommendations regarding the representation of women on boards of directors. This chapter aims at analyzing the evolution since the end of the 1990s of the representation of women in the economic sphere and in decision-making positions (mainly CAC 40 listed firms) in France.

The chapter proceeds as follows: the next section reviews the main features of the French capitalist system relying mainly on large public corporations and family companies and on closed links between economic and political elites. It documents the evolution of public and private large companies showing the leading role of men at the top of the CAC 40 companies. The following section analyzes the most recent corporate governance rules focusing on the representation of men and women on boards. The last section concludes.

The evolution of large groups in France

The evolution of the French capitalist system

Three decades of prosperity (1960–1980) have been followed by economic uncertainty. The 1990s were characterized by profound economic changes in France, the increasing role of financial markets and globalization, a wider uptake and use of ICT by businesses across all sectors of the economy. As Piketty (2014) points out,

> [W]hat is distinctive about the French trajectory is that public ownership, having thrived from 1950 to 1980, dropped to very low levels after 1980, even as private wealth – both financial and real estate – rose to levels even higher than Britain's: nearly six years of national income in 2010, or 20 times the value of public wealth. Following a period of state capitalism after 1950, France became the promised land of the new private-ownership capitalism of the twenty-first century.
>
> (p. 138)

In the 1990s, the challenges came with the rising Europeanization (involving the integration in a single European market) leading French firms to expand operations on a broader geographical base. Deregulation in sectors such as telecommunications led to higher competitive pressures on existing groups (incumbents). The share of large state enterprises of the economy started to decline considerably.

In the 1990s and the 2000s, the conglomerate restructuring has taken place in several sectors and has been facilitated in the context of a growing number of M&A and a sharp rise of foreign investments in French large companies (Daidj, 2016). This has been made possible because of the partial unravelling of the *noyaux durs* (Morin, 2000, 2009). This situation has not been observed for all firms. As Clift (2007: 41),

> in particular, large family-owned firms have in many cases not followed these prevalent trends (Goyer, 2003b). Family dominates ownership and firm structures in approximately 50 of the top 100, including such household names as Michelin, Leclerc, and Peugeot (MacLean, 2002: 211–12; Schmidt, 2003: 540–1).
>
> (2007: 41)

The notion of large companies

Even if large companies are usually and often identified on the basis of national rankings rather than actual size, it is worth briefly restating the definitions of this notion (Exhibit 10.1). According to France's National Institute of Statistics and

Economic Studies (*Institut National de la Statistique et des Études Économiques*: INSEE), a Directorate General of the Ministry of the Economy, Industry and the Digital Sector and of the Ministry of Finance and Public Accounts, a large enterprise is a company employing over 5,000 people. A company with fewer than 5,000 employees but an annual turnover greater than 1.5 billion Euros and a balance sheet total of more than 2 billion Euros is also considered to be a large enterprise. A group is a set of companies interlinked through shareholdings and controlled by a single company. In the case of diversified conglomerate, each 'autonomous' segment (or strategic business unit) is considered an enterprise (INSEE, 2015).

Exhibit 10.1 New definition of the enterprise and initial approach

Article 1 of **Decree no. 2008–1354**, promulgated to implement the Economic Modernization Act, defines the enterprise in the same terms as European Economic Community (EEC) Council Regulation no. 696/93 of March 15, 1993: "the smallest combination of legal units that is an organizational unit producing goods or services, which benefits from a certain degree of autonomy in decision-making, especially for the allocation of its current resources". Accordingly, a group may have one subsidiary dedicated to the manufacture of goods and another to their sale. These two legal units, which are subsidiaries of the same group, must be combined in order to constitute an enterprise in the economic sense of the term.

This is an **approximation**, as certain diversified conglomerates (such as Bouygues, LVMH, and General Electric) comprise relatively autonomous segments engaged in different businesses. By logic, such segments should be viewed as separate enterprises operating in different sectors. Identifying enterprises under the criteria of the Decree within large, complex groups is a vast undertaking known as group **profiling**. It is currently under way in France and the other European countries. It will alter the number of large enterprises (whose order of magnitude may rise from 200 to 300) and, marginally, the number of intermediate-sized enterprises (by about 100, out of nearly 5,000), as well as certain distributions by sector. However, there will be practically no impact on the main findings of this study.

The **principal activities** of groups are defined by an algorithm from those of the affiliates and subsidiaries. The principal activity is the one that occupies the largest share of the workforce, not counting the head office and support functions.

Source: Adapted from INSEE, www.insee.fr/en/statistiques/1281374 and www. insee.fr/en/insee-statistique-publique/connaitre/rae/rae14-en-withprofiling.pdf, accessed 12 March, 2017.

If the large firm in France was associated with an increase in state ownership in the 1960s, the privatization waves in the late 1980s and in the 1990s didn't lead to the disappearance of large-scale enterprises. Big corporations still dominate the French economy as shown in Exhibit 10.2.

Exhibit 10.2 The current role of large companies in the French economy

With over 100 members, AFEP represents large French and foreign companies operating in France. Worldwide, this accounts for 6 million employees and a turnover of around 1,700 billion Euros. These companies are typical of strong multinational groups; their necessary presence on markets abroad brings growth and jobs to France. They contribute to the image of France beyond our borders.

INSEE counts 217 large French companies out of a total of 2.7 million companies (which include 4,600 intermediate-size companies and 130,000 small and medium-size companies).

As defined in the French law of modernization of the economy, large companies are those with staff of over 5,000 employees or with a turnover exceeding 1,500 million Euros. In 2009, these companies accounted for:

31% of total employment (that is, 3.5 million employees)
Half of turnover achieved through exports
30% of gross operating profit
A third of added value generated in France (or 17% of GDP)
Nearly two-thirds of internal spending on research and development (R&D)

As far as pay is concerned, data from the French Ministry of Work show a level of pay for large companies' employees exceeding the average by nearly 15% (28,710 Euros a year against 25,100 Euros a year).

Source: AFEP (the French Association of Large Companies), www.afep.com/en/content/large-companies/the-role-of-large-companies-in-the-french-economy, accessed 22 May, 2017.

Complex interactions between business, public administrations and political leaders

Since the 1960s, the ties between political leaders and businessmen have been very close. Network-based monitoring devices such as interlocking directorships, corporate cross-shareholdings and personal ties among managerial and financial elites are widespread and dominate the French capitalist system.

Exchanges between political elites, public administrations and business were a powerful driver for the post-war economy and underpinned French *dirigisme*.

Another distinctive feature is that the fact that the *Grandes Écoles* train the core of the French elite (education based on tough selection criteria).

> French capitalism was "organized", in the sense of being characterized by a multiplicity of networks – linking companies together, linking companies and the state, and connecting the larger and more active firms with internationally oriented investment banks that "answered industrial firms' requests for advice, expertise and investments". These networks were strengthened by personal, family and friendship links that held together the economic, political and financial elites.
>
> (Djelic and Amdam, 2007: 489)

The French establishment network referred to as 'the 200 top executives' by Bauer and Bertin-Mourot (1987).

The dense networks of crossed ownerships and interlocking directorships that characterized French capitalism have been achieved also through personal links between heads of companies and government members. Networking was decisive in managers' success (Cassis, 1997, 2008). The situation remains the same today as shown in Table 10.1. We have identified in the table the main CAC 40 (France's main stock market index) companies for which business leaders have developed strong links with the government administration (the remaining list can be found in Appendix 1). The CAC 40 Index represents the 40 largest equities listed in France.

These economic, political and financial networks have been strengthened thanks also to the cross involvement and reciprocal representation in the boards of directors of listed companies. High levels of cross-shareholdings have characterized the French system.

The second comment refers to the absence of women at top executive managing positions as chairman and/or CEO of one of the CAC 40 companies (Table 10.1 and Appendix 1). Yet, the representation of women is more and more emphasized as a key success factor (Appendix 2). Several consultant studies have shown linkages between women's presence and performance. For example, McKinsey's study, 'Women Matter', has argued since the end of the 2000s that firms that included women in management performed better:

> [Our] research has consistently shown a correlation between the proportion of women on executive committees and corporate performance. While correlation does not prove causality, we have also found that a diversity of leadership styles can contribute to more effective decision-making, and that the leadership behaviors women typically display can have a positive impact on many dimensions of an organization's performance and health
>
> (2016: 4)

The next section will present the main evolutions of the rules about the balanced representation of men and women.

Table 10.1 Links between the heads of CAC 40 companies and the French political elite (2015)

Company/sector	Chairman and/or CEO education	Links between business and political elites
Airbus Group (formerly EADS) (Aerospace, Defense)	Tom Enders Doctorate in political science (University of Bonn and University of California) Denis Ranque X-Mines	Tom Enders spent two years (1989–1991) in the planning staff of the German defense ministry. Assistant at the German Federal Parliament. Denis Ranque held various management positions in the French Ministry of Industry in the 1970s and 1980s.
Alcatel-Lucent (Telecommunications)	Michel Combes X (1981) – Télécom ParisTech (1986)	1991–1995: occupied posts within the Ministry of Telecommunications and the Cabinet of Minister.
Alstom (Transport and energy)	Patrick Kron X (1973) – Mines Paris (1976)	Started his career at the French Ministry of Industry (1979–1984) and at the *Direction régionale de l'Industrie, de la Recherche et de l'Environnement* (DRIRE) Pays-de-la-Loire.
Axa (Insurance)	Henri de Castries ENA (1980), HEC Paris (1976)	Started as auditor of the Minister of Finances (1980–1984) and as member of the French Treasury (1984–1989) he participated in the privatization policy initiated by Jacques Chirac's government (1986).
BNP Paribas (Bank)	Jean Lemierre Institut Politique de Paris, ENA (1976) Jean-Laurent Bonnafé X (1981) – Mines ParisTech	Various functions in the tax administration. Director of Cabinet (Ministry of Finances). 1987–1992: various positions in the French administration.
Capgemini (Consulting services)	Paul Hermelin X (1972), ENA (1978)	1991–1993: started his career in the French government in various ministries: Economy, Finance, Research and Technology. Chief of staff in the Ministry of Industry and Foreign Trade.
Crédit Agricole (Bank)	Jean-Marie Sander Jean-Paul Chifflet Institut des hautes finances de Paris	Politician (local level).
EDF (Energy)	Jean-Bernard Lévy (Président) X (1973) – Telecom ParisTech	1986: worked in the Ministry of Post and Telecommunications under the secretary of state. 1982–1986: part of the Directorate General of Telecommunications within *PTT France*.
Engie (formerly GDF Suez) (Energy)	Gérard Mestrallet X (1968), ENA (1978), ENAC, IEP Toulouse	1982–1984: in charge of industrial affairs under the Minister of Economics and Finance.

Company/sector	Chairman and/or CEO education	Links between business and political elites
Orange (formerly France Telecom)	Stéphane Richard HEC (1983), ENA (1987)	1987–1991: assigned to "Inspection Générale des Finances". 1991–1992: appointed technical adviser to the Minister of Industry and Foreign Trade, and was in charge of the electronics and computer industries. 2007–2009: Chief of Staff to the Minister for the Economy, Industry, and Employment.
Pernod-Ricard (Wines and spirits)	Pierre Pringuet X (1969), Mines ParisTech	Held numerous functions in the public service and various positions on ministers' staffs.
Saint-Gobain (Building materials)	Pierre-André de Chalendar ENA (1983), ESSEC (1979)	1983–1987: General Inspection of Finance (IGF). 1988–1989: deputy director in the General Directorate for Energy and raw materials of the Ministry of Industry and Energy.
Société Générale (Bank)	Lorenzo Bini Smaghi Master's degree in economics (1980), University of Southern California; PhD, University of Chicago (1988) Frédéric Oudéa X (1981), ENA (1987)	1987–1995: civil service (several functions in the Audit Department of the Ministry of Finance, the Ministry of Economy and Finance, the Budget Ministry, and the Cabinet of the Ministry of Treasury and Communication). Also worked as technical adviser in Ministry of Budget and Communication in 1993.
Solvay (Chemicals)	Jean-Pierre Clamadieu Mines ParisTech (1983)	1991–1993: worked for the French Ministry of Industry and as technical adviser to the Minister of Labor.
Total (Petroleum)	Patrick Pouyanné X (1983), Mines ParisTech (1989) Thierry Desmarest X (1964), Mines ParisTech (1967)	1995–1997: several functions in the Ministry of Information Technology and then of Space. 1993–1995: technical adviser of the French first minister at the time. 1992–1993: Ministry of Industry. 1975–1980: technical adviser (Ministry of Industry).
Valeo (Automotive industry)	Jacques Aschenbroich	1987–1988: member of the Prime Minister Cabinet. 1981–1987: different positions in the French public service.

Source: elaborated by the author

The evolution of corporate governance rules

The French corporate governance system

The French corporate governance system has significantly changed over the years aiming at a more widely dispersed ownership and greater transparency. In the 1990s, the government's privatization policy led to improve corporate governance of large firms allowing them to acquire more and more resources through market financing rather than through bank borrowing. Foreign funds have begun to play an increasingly important role in the French economy and to impact corporate governance of big companies through the transformation of ownership structures (towards a more dispersed ownership). As Morin states:

> Directly inspired by the American shareholder value model, the largest French groups are going through a managerial revolution, whose consequences are only now beginning to become apparent, most noticeably in the new way in which the French stock exchange operates.
>
> (2000: 3)

Regulatory bodies were developed to regulate the French financial market: the *Commission des Opérations de Bourse* (COB) based on the model of the US Securities and Exchange Commission (SEC) in 1967, the *Conseil des Marchés Financiers* (CMF) and the *Conseil de Discipline de la Gestion Financière* (CDGF). The *Autorité des Marchés Financiers* (AMF) was created by the Financial Security Act of 1 August 2003, which merged the COB, the CMF and the CDGF. Since its creation, the AMF has continued its monitoring of the French securities market by improving securities regulation. The law for financial security (*Loi de sécurité financière*, 2003) was ratified one year after the US Sarbanes-Oxley Act following various scandals such as WorldCom and Enron (Chabrak and Daidj, 2007).

The law for financial security passed in order to increase transparency in the French market.

At the European level, several directives have been taken since the end of the 1980s and then adopted in the French law promoting the shareholder model. At the same time, several groups of experts, think tanks, professional associations concerned with these issues offered detailed recommendations. Thus a number of reports have been written on corporate governance reform such as Viénot I (*Conseil National du Patronat Français* and *Association Français des Entreprises Privées*, July 1995), Hellebuyck Commission (*Association Française de la Gestion Financière – Association des Sociétés et Fonds Français d'Investissement*, 1998), Viénot II (*Association Française des Entreprises Privées and Mouvement des Entreprises de France*, July 1999) and Bouton (*Association Française des Entreprises Privées, Association des Grandes Entreprises Françaises* and *Mouvement des Entreprises de France*, September 2002). This collection of recommendations has been developed by working parties composed of chairmen of French listed corporations, at the request of the *Association Française des Entreprises Privées* (AFEP) and the *Mouvement des Entreprises de France* (MEDEF).

French corporate governance standards combine legislative provisions and the recommendations of the AFEP-MEDEF code. This code is a code of reference with which businesses must comply or explain how their practices differ from it, and why. In the 2000s, the code was written with reference to corporations with a board of directors (the most common form of organization). Corporations with a supervisory board and management board, as well as partnerships limited by shares (*société en commandite par actions*), had to make adjustments as appropriate to implement them (Exhibit 10.3).

Exhibit 10.3 The AFEP-MEDEF code of reference

The Board of Directors: a collegial body

Regardless of its membership or how it is organized, the Board of Directors is and must remain a collegial body representing all shareholders collectively. It is required to act at all times in the interests of the company.

Separation of the offices of chairman and chief executive officer

The diversity of forms of organization of the management and supervisory powers under French law.

Only French law offers an option between a unitary formula (Board of Directors) and a two-tier formula (Supervisory Board and Management Board) for all corporations, including listed corporations.

In addition, a recent statute has provided for corporations with Boards of Directors an option between separation of the offices of chairman and chief executive officer and maintenance of the aggregation of such duties. As recommended by the Viénot report of July 1999, the statute does not favor either formula and allows the Board of Directors to choose between the two forms of exercise of executive management. It is up to each corporation to decide on the basis of its own specific constraints.

French *sociétés anonymes* accordingly can choose from among three forms of organization of the management and supervisory powers.

Independent directors

> "A director is independent when he or she has no relationship of any kind whatsoever with the corporation, its group or the management of either that is such as to colour his or her judgment".

Accordingly, an "independent director" is to be understood not only as a "non-executive director", i.e. one not performing management duties in the corporation or its group, but also one devoid of any particular bonds of interest (significant shareholder, employee, other) with them.

(. . .)

The independent directors should account for half the members of the Board in widely-held corporations and without controlling shareholders. In others, the rule of "a third at least" set by the Viénot report of July 1999 should be observed.

Source: AFEP and MEDEF (2003), brief excerpts, www.ecgi.org/codes/documents/cg_oct03_en.pdf, accessed 17 May, 2015.

Consequently, several corporate governance principles have been applied successfully and have strengthened the rights and responsibilities of shareholders, the duties and responsibilities of the board of directors, the development of independent directors and external auditing, disclosure and transparency practices. The introduction of monitoring and control mechanisms has had also a significant impact on corporate governance rules. The presence of foreign ownership in CAC 40 listed firms has increased as well as the percentage of independent directors in CAC 40 firms.

In June 2013, AFEP and MEDEF published a new version of the code (Exhibit 10.4). This revision is part of a codification process begun in 1995 and regularly updated since then, particularly in 2007, 2008 and 2010. The 2013 updated code represents a new step in regulation combining transparency, responsibility and oversight. Stakeholders were widely consulted for the first time in 2013. Recommended by the AFEP-MEDEF code, 'say-on-pay' has been also applied for the first time in France at the annual meetings of shareholders held in 2014. In addition, the High Committee on Corporate Governance (*Haut Comité de Gouvernement d'Entreprise*) was created in 2013.

Exhibit 10.4 The corporate governance revised code:
towards more transparency and responsibility

The revised code introduces new steps forward in corporate governance:

- Establishment of a high committee on corporate governance. This is made up of seven members, i.e. four experienced individuals who hold or have held positions in international groups and three qualified individuals, i.e. investor, legal expert and compliance officer. This committee is responsible for monitoring compliance with the principles set out in the code. It may have cases referred to it by boards and may also examine cases on its own initiative if a company does not comply with a recommendation without providing an adequate explanation. A company which does not follow a recommendation made by the high committee must mention this in its annual report and explain why it decided not to act on this recommendation. The committee may also propose changes to the corporate governance code;
- Introduction of an advisory vote on executive compensation (AMF, 2014). At the annual ordinary general meeting, the board shall present the components of the compensation due or allocated for the past financial year to each executive director. This presentation shall be followed by an advisory vote by shareholders. If the meeting votes against it, the board, on the advice of the compensation committee, shall discuss the matter at its next meeting and immediately publish a press release on the company's website stating how it intends to act on shareholders' expectations;

Reinforcement of the "comply or explain" principle: the explanation given in the event of non-compliance with a recommendation of the code should be detailed and tailored to the specific situation of the company; it should indicate any alternative measures adopted. The non-compliances and related explanations must be shown under a specific heading or table in the annual report;

Restriction on the number of offices for executive directors to two other offices in listed companies outside of the group, including those abroad, and for directors a restriction on this number to four other offices in listed companies outside of the group, including those abroad;

Transparency of multi-year variable compensation, following the same principles as annual variable remuneration;

Transparency of start-of-contract pay and reinforcement of recommendations concerning severance and non-competition pay;

Reinforcement of recommendations relating to performance conditions applicable to stock options and performance shares, as well as to the requirements to keep shares resulting from the exercise of options or performance shares. Formal commitment required of directors not to use any hedging instrument, in accordance with the recommendation of AMF;

Inclusion of a specific chapter on employee directors which specifies that, like any director, they may be appointed by the board to take part in board committees. Furthermore, they shall receive training appropriate for the performance of their duties;

Limitation on supplementary pensions to 45% of the reference income.

Source: AFEP, www.afep.com/en/content/challenges/corporate-governance-transparency-responsibility-and-oversight, accessed 24 July, 2015.

Steps towards the legal recognition of balanced gender representation on boards

At a more general level, "France has a long-standing tradition of legislating in favor of gender equality in the domain of employment and professional life with the first legislation dating from 1972 and the establishment of no less than 12 laws between 1972 and 2014" (Lépinard and Lieber, 2015: 7).

More specifically, regarding boards, several initiatives (non-mandatory codes and laws) have been carried out in parallel in order to meet quotas for female membership.

The 2010 AFEP-MEDEF updated code has also made recommendations regarding the representation of women on boards of directors (Exhibit 10.5).

Exhibit 10.5 Proportion of women on boards

The AFEP-MEDEF code states that, from April 2010, "each board should consider what would be the desirable balance within its membership and within that of the committees of Board members which it has established, in particular as regards the representation of men and women and the diversity of competencies, and take appropriate action to assure the shareholders and market that its duties will be performed with the necessary independence and objectivity".

Consequently, "in order to reach such balance, the objective is that each board shall reach and maintain a percentage of at least 20% of women within a period of three years and at least 40% of women within a period of six years [from April 2010] or from the date of the listing of the company's shares on a regulated market, whichever is later" (§ 6.3).

Source: AFEP, www.afep.com/uploads/medias/documents/Rapport_annuel_sur_le_code_Afep-Medef_Novembre_2011_EN.pdf, accessed 19 February, 2017.

But as this code has not been applied consistently and rigorously, the issue has required a new law. Several European countries have required quotas to ensure that corporations add female board members. France is one of them:

> Compliance with corporate codes is not mandatory but rather is voluntary for French companies. Based on 2011 figures, it did not appear that such voluntary approaches were producing effective results. According to the fundamental corporate governance principle "comply or explain," the reasons for non-compliance only have to be explained in the companies' annual reports. Hence, as long as the companies explain it, they are not subject to any sanctions. Considering that self-regulation has not been effective, in January 2011 France adopted a new law implementing gender quotas on corporate boards.
>
> (Hastings, 2013: 79)

In July 2008, the French Constitution was modified to enable the introduction of board gender quotas into French law. The Article 1 states that "French law favors equal access for men and women to elective functions and political mandates as well as to social and business functions". Therefore, equality between men and women is now mandatory in both public and private sectors and can be guaranteed through the implementation of quotas. After the revision of the French Constitution, a new law, aimed at establishing quotas for women on corporate boards, was proposed in December 2009. Finally, the French Parliament passed a law, called Coppé-Zimmerman, on 13 January 2011 setting quotas for gender-balanced representation on boards. The law dictates that 40% of board members of CAC 40 companies (and of companies with more than 500 employees, with a turnover exceeding 50 million Euros over the previous three years) must be women by 2017 (the currently prevailing level is 35%). If these thresholds are not reached, the sanction for non-compliance is annulment of board members' appointments, and board members' benefits can be suspended.

In 2012, at a more general level, a new law was implemented to complete the 2011 law requiring a 40% gender quota to be reached by 2018 for nominations to executive functions in the public service. This quota applies to administrative and supervisory boards of public institutions, high councils, juries and selection committees in public service procedures.

According to OECD (2016),

> [A] higher percentage of WOB (women on board) can be seen in countries where legal requirements have been passed or are being considered. In 2003, Norway adopted quota legislation for corporate boards and following the introduction of sanctions has 36% WOB17 in 2015. Since then, some countries have followed suit. For example, the share of WOB in France grew from approximately 10,7% in 2009 to 33% in 2015, following a quota in 201.
>
> (p. 21)

In comparison with other OECD countries, the French situation is still poor but a little better (Figure 10.1). But it's the old idea that you can't see the forest for the trees, as analyzed in the next section (Fagan et al., 2012; Smith, 2010; Smith et al., 2012; St-Onge and Magnan, 2013).

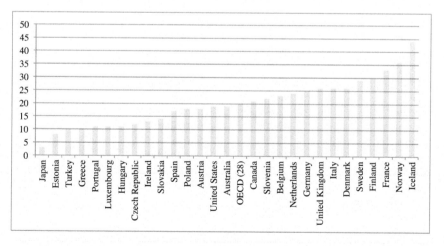

Figure 10.1 Share of female board members (2015 or latest)

Source: EC (2016) Database on women and men in decision making; Catalyst (2015) Catalyst Census: Women Board Directors quoted in OECD (2016: 21)

The glass ceiling is still very real in many French companies' boards

Efforts are still needed as shown in Table 10.2. The real equality between women and men is not yet achieved in practice in boards in France in spite of new rules and practices. CAC 40 corporations are racing to comply with the law requiring 40% of women on French boards. But only 21 of them respect this percentage.

The scarcity of qualified women in France is also one of the reasons frequently stated for this situation. Table 10.3 presents the most emblematic women representatives on the boards. They have various backgrounds, graduated from the *Grandes Écoles* and/or universities (see section 1), as mentioned by Magnier and Rosenblum (2014):

> Male directors are most often graduates of the French *Grandes Écoles*. Female directors also do not have the same experience at the top executive levels as male directors. One may therefore infer a correlation between the feminization

Table 10.2 Percentage of women board members at CAC 40 companies in France (2016)

The adoption of good practices		*The laggards . . .*	
Kering	63.60	Schneider Electric	38.50
Publicis	54.50	Vinci	35.70
Engie	52.40	Essilor International	35.70
BNP Paribas	50.00	LVMH	35.30
Société générale	50.00	Saint-Gobain	35.30
Danone	50.00	Veolia Environnement	35.30
Bouygues	46.70	Renault	35.30
L'Oréal	46.70	Capgemini	33.30
Sanofi	46.10	Solvay	33.30
Air Liquide	45.40	Valeo	33.80
Michelin	44.40	Pernod-Ricard	28.60
Axa	43.80	Airbus	26.70
Vivendi	42.80	Crédit agricole	23.80
Peugeot	42.80	Carrefour	23.50
Sodexo	42.80	Safran	23.50
Technip	41.70	ArcelorMittal	23.10
AccorHôtels	41.70	Nokia	20.00
Legrand	40.00	Lafarge-Holcim	7.10
Unibail-Rodamco	40.00		
Orange	40.00		
Klépierre	40.00		

Source: Datawrapper–Le Figaro (2016).

www.lefigaro.fr/economie/le-scan-eco/decryptage/2016/02/10/29002-20160210ARTFIG00223-conseils-d-administration-seules-cinq-societes-du-cac-40-respectent-la-parite.php of boards of directors and some diversification of skills and points of view on how to run a business. In practical terms, the participation of women on boards of directors should offer corporations a larger pool of skills and expertise than a pool composed exclusively of males.

(p. 257)

These arguments have been corroborated by other findings. Rosenblum and Roithmayr (2015) have conducted an in-depth analysis by interviewing 24 members of the CAC 40 firms between October of 2011 and February of 2012. They have posed a range of questions designed to assess the effect of the quota and of

Table 10.3 French women on CAC 40 companies' boards in France (2016)

Name	Background/current position
Clara Gaymard	Institut Politique de Paris, ENA (1986)
	Former head of General Electric in France (2006–2016)
	Co-founder of Raise, a capital investment company
	Has joined LVHM, Bouygues, Danone and Veolia boards
	VP or member of board of several non-profit foundations as College de France, Fondation Valentin Haüy and IMS Entreprendre pour la Cité
Laurence Boone	London School of Economics and University of Paris Nanterre
	Bank of AmericaMerrill Lynch (2011–2014)
	Adviser of the former French President François Hollande (2014–2016)
	Since 2016, Chief Economist AXA Group
	Member of Kering board (2010–2014 and from 2016)
Natacha Valla	PhD (European University Institute)
	Currently deputy director of CEPII, a French economic think tank
	Member of LVMH board
Delphine Arnault (the daughter of Bernard Arnault, chairman and chief executive officer (CEO) of LVMH)	EDHEC Business School, London School of Economics
	Since 2003, member of the Management Board of the group LVMH
	Executive vice president of Louis Vuitton
Marie-Laure Sauty de Chalon	IEP Paris and University of Paris 2
	Currently the CEO of the auFeminin.com group
	Member of LVMH board
Bernadette Chirac	IEP Paris
	Former First Lady of France (Jacques Chirac's wife)
	Member of LVMH board

the increased presence of women on corporate governance. Their conclusions are particularly interesting. First, they have found that in the view of corporate board members themselves, the quota has not substantively affected corporate governance decisions. In addition,

> [T]he quota has in fact had a substantive impact, but not because of the sex of newly added board members. Rather, [our] interview results suggest that in the view of board members, newly added female members have had a substantive impact on corporate governance because they are outsiders. For strategic reasons . . . , to comply with the quota, French boards have appointed women members who are more likely to be foreign, from non-elite professional and educational networks, less experienced and from specialties not traditionally represented on boards, like environment or labor. Participants suggest that these traits, which are associated with women's outsider and newcomer status and not their sex, are potentially responsible for any difference in substantive board decision-making after the quota.
>
> (p.891–892)

Conclusion

Several international studies (EWOB, 2016; OECD, 2016) record the widest gaps between men and women when it comes to access to resources and economic opportunities, power and decision-making. The low level of representation of women is particularly weak in the highest level and managerial positions and on boards.

In France, in spite of an important legislative framework,

> the implementation of gender equality policies in France is often heterogeneous and varies over time depending on the political will of the respective governments and social partners. Legislation that applies voluntary measures and self-regulation from social actors, rather than imposing sanctions, has rarely met its goals.
>
> (Lépinard and Lieber, 2015: 7)

The percentage of women representation on French boards is still far short of the objective set by the law. 'Breaking the glass ceiling' must not only remain a flourishing modern slogan.

References

AFEP & MEDEF 2003. Corporate Governance of Listed Corporations, Principles for corporate governance based on consolidation of the 1995, 1999 and 2002 AFEP and MEDEF's reports, Paris: AFEP and MEDEF.

AMF 2014. Report on corporate governance and executive compensation, Press release, September 24, www.amf-france.org/en_US/Actualites/Communiques-de-presse/AMF/annee_2014.html?docId=workspace://SpacesStore/c9c2db6c-b4a1-44bb-ac66baff1f7eec3a, accessed 17 July, 2015.

Bauer, M., Bertin-Mourot, B. 1987. *Les 200: Comment Devient-on Grand Patron?* Paris: Seuil.

Cassis, Y. 1997. *Big Business: The European Experiences in the Twentieth Century*, Oxford: Oxford University Press.

Cassis, Y. 2008. Big business in Jones, G., Zeitlin, J. (eds.), *The Oxford Handbook of Business History*, Oxford: Oxford University Press, 171–193.

Chabrak, N., Daidj, N. 2007. Enron: Widespread Myopia, *Critical Perspectives on Accounting*, 18(5), 539–557.

Clift, B. 2007. French corporate governance in the new global economy: Mechanisms of change and hybridisation within models of capitalism, *Political Studies*, 55(3), 546–567.

Daidj, N. 2016. *Strategy, Structure and Corporate Governance: Expressing Inter-Firms Networks*, Aldershot, Hampshire, England: Taylor & Francis Group.

Djelic, M.-L., Amdam, R.P. 2007. Americanization in comparative perspective: The managerial revolution in France and Norway, 1940–1990, *Business History*, 49(4), 483–505.

European Women on Boards (EWoB) 2016. Progress and challenges for women on company boards, http://european.ewob-network.eu/ewob-publishes-landmark-report-on-the-progress-of-women-on-the-boards-of-major-european-companies, accessed 26 March, 2016.

Fagan, C., Menéndez, M.G., Ansón, S.G. 2012. *Women on Corporate Boards and in Top Management: European Trends and Policy*, Basingstoke, UK: Palgrave MacMillan.

Hastings, P. 2013. Breaking the glass ceiling: Women in the boardroom. Paul Hastings LLP, www.paulhastings.com/genderparity/pdf/Gender_Parity_Report.pdf, accessed 29 January, 2017.

INSEE 2015. Directory of companies in which the State has a controlling interest (RECME), www.insee.fr/en/themes/tableau.asp?reg_id=0&ref_id=nattef9302, accessed 18 August, 2015.

Lépinard, E., Lieber, M. 2015. The policy on gender equality in France, document requested by the Committee on Women's Rights and Gender Equality, European Parliament, www.europarl.europa.eu/RegData/etudes/IDAN/2015/510024/IPOL_IDA(2015)510024_EN.pdf, accessed 19 January, 2017.

Magnier, V., Rosenblum, D. 2014. Quotas and the transatlantic divergence of corporate governance, *Northwestern Journal of International Law & Business*, 34(2), 249–298.

McKinsey & Co. 2016. Women Matter 2016. Reinventing the workplace to unlock the potential of gender diversity, www.mckinsey.com/global-themes/women-matter, accessed 14 March, 2017.

Morin, F. 2000. The transformation of the French model of shareholding and management, *Economy and Society*, 29(1), 36–53.

Morin, F. 2009. Transformation in the French model of shareholding and management in Clarke, T., Chanlat, J.-F. (eds.), *European Corporate Governance: Readings and Perspectives*, New York, NY: Routledge.

OECD 2016. Background Report. Conference on improving women's access to leadership. 8 March 2016. Paris, www.oecd.org/daf/ca/OECD-Women-Leadership-2016-Report.pdf, accessed 11 February, 2017.

Piketty, T. 2014. *Capital in the Twenty-First Century*, Cambridge, MA and London, England: The Belknap Press of Harvard University Press.

Rosenblum, D., Roithmayr, D. 2015. More than a woman: Insights into corporate governance after the French sex quota, *Industrial Law Revue*, 48(3), 889–930.

Schmidt, V. 2003. French capitalism transformed, yet still a third variety of capitalism, *Economy and Society*, 32(4), 526–554.

Smith, M. 2010. Analysis note: The gender pay gap in the EU – what policy responses? EGGE – European Network of Experts on Employment and Gender Equality issues – Fondazione Giacomo Brodolini.

Smith, M., Srinivasan, P., Zhuk, K. 2012. Women in top management in France: A time of change in Fagan, C., Menèndez, M.G., Ansón, S.G. (eds.), *Women on Corporate Boards and in Top Management: European Trends and Policy*, Basingstoke, UK: Palgrave Mac-Millan, 150–168.

St-Onge, S., Magnan, M. 2013. Les femmes au sein des conseils d'administration: bilan des connaissances et voies de recherche futures [Women on corporate boards: Taking stock and future research], *Finance Contrôle Stratégie*, 16(1), 49–68.

Appendix 1

CEO and chairman with no official functions in the French public service source: elaborated by the author

Company/sector	Chairman and/or CEO Education
Accor (Hotels)	Sébastien Bazin
	1985: master's degree in management (finance) from the University Paris I – Sorbonne
Air Liquide (Industrial gas)	Benoît Potier
	Centrale Paris (1979), INSEAD
ArcelorMittal (Steel)	Lakshmi Mittal
	Bachelor's degree in commerce (University of Calcutta (1970))
Bouygues (Construction)	Martin Bouygues
	Baccalaureate (the French secondary school exit exam)
Carrefour (Wholesale)	Georges Plassat
	Ecole hôtelière de Lausanne
Danone (Food)	Franck Riboud
	Ecole polytechnique de Lausanne (Switzerland)
	Emmanuel Faber
	HEC (1986)
Essilor International	Hubert Sagnières
(Optical equipment)	MBA INSEAD (1985), Centrale Lille (1980)
Gemalto (New	Olivier Piou
technology)	Centrale Lyon
Kering (formerly PPR)	François-Henri Pinault
Retail	HEC (1985)
Lafarge SA (Cement)	Bruno Lafont
	ENA (1982), HEC (1977)
Legrand (Electrical equipment)	Gilles Schnepp
	HEC (1981)

(*Continued*)

(Continued)

L'Oréal (Cosmetics and beauty)	Jean-Paul Agon
	HEC 1978
LVMH (Luxury)	Bernard Arnault
	X- (1969)
Michelin (Rubber)	Jean-Dominique Senard
	HEC (1976)
Publicis Group	Maurice Lévy
(Advertising)	Degree in computer science (New Jersey City University)
Renault (Automotive)	Carlos Ghosn
	X (1974), ParisTech (1978)
Safran (Aerospace)	Jean-Paul Herteman
	X (1970), Sup'Aéro (1975), chief arms engineer
Sanofi (Pharmaceuticals)	Olivier Brandicourt
	Physician
	Serge Weinberg,
	ENA (1976), IEP Paris
Schneider Electric	Jean-Pascal Tricoire
(Electrical equipment)	ESEO Angers, MBA CESMA Lyon (1986)
Technip (Oil engineering)	Thierry Pilenko
	ENSG Nancy (1981), ENSPM (1982)
Unibail-Rodamco	Christophe Cuvillier
(Property)	HEC (1984)
Veolia Environnement	Antoine Frérot
(Environmental	X (1977), PhD in civil engineering (École Nationale des Ponts et
services)	Chaussées)
Vinci (Construction)	Xavier Huillard
	X (1973), École Nationale des Ponts et Chaussées (1978)
Vivendi	Vincent Bolloré
	Doctorate in law
	Arnaud de Puyfontaine
	Graduate of the ESCP Europe Business School (1988), the Multimedia Institute (1992) and Harvard Business School (2000)

Appendix 2

Extracts from Mr Emmanuel Macron speech at women's forum for the economy and society (December 2, 2016)

Claire Doole: Mr Macron, are quotas the silver bullet? Or would you like to see more quotas, if you were to be president? Is it something that you think could be legislated and actually enforced?

Emmanuel Macron: I don't believe it's the silver bullet, but I think it allows behaviors to change. And you mentioned this law, passed a few years ago, called Coppé-Zimmerman for the presence of women on executive boards. It allows in our country to go from 10% to 36%. So, I mean, it provides some effects. I think now, our key issue is not to have women on boards, but, I mean, as top executive members. It's something difficult, because you have to reorganize the company, you have to promote women progressively, at different levels. But I do think that we will probably need some quotas for top executive members, and I do agree with this idea. But I do agree with what you mentioned, the fact that it is not a silver bullet. For me, the best way to succeed in this way, is to say "you need innovation and inclusivity". For me the two legs of modernity today are innovation and inclusivity. When you are in a country, or in a company, where you don't innovate, it can go very well on a day-to-day basis, but you are already dead . . . because of the fact that a competitor will suddenly arrive, innovate, disrupt your market and will kill your business. When you don't have inclusivity, in terms of gender policy, minority policy, in your neighbourhood, you are dead as well, on the mid to long-run. Because you cannot succeed by excluding part of your society, by not providing, precisely, a due role to everybody. So, I do believe today, that our companies, and our policy-makers, will integrate into their model, I have to say, into their own decisions, these two legs.

Source: https://en-marche.fr/article/emmanuel-macron-women-forum-for-the-economy-and-society-discours

11 The 2017 New Zealand Stock Exchange directors' network analysis and the effect of 'soft' reporting regimes on board diversity

Rosanne Hawarden

Introduction

The 2017 New Zealand Census of Women on Boards (WOB), originally released through the website Counting for Change, www.countingforchange.nz, is the initiative of two researchers, Professor Judy McGregor, now head of School of Social Sciences and Public Policy at AUT, and formerly Equal Employment Opportunity (EEO) commissioner, Human Rights Commission, and Dr Rosanne Hawarden, director, businesswoman and currently president of Governance New Zealand Inc. In her role as EEO commissioner, McGregor and her staff produced five censuses of women's participation from 2004 to 2012. Each one built on the previous one in breadth and depth, winning international acclaim. During this period Hawarden completed a doctorate in business and administration at Massey University on women directors' networks, the first network study to locate women in the networks of publicly listed companies. Meeting at the 2016 Women in Governance Awards, an annual event to celebrate the achievements of women directors organized by Governance New Zealand Inc, a conversation took place concerning the likelihood that the WOB census would not continue. To ensure that the gender gap on New Zealand's boards continued to receive the attention of directors of both sexes, officials and other regulatory bodies concerned with gender equity in the boardroom, it was important that this research be maintained. Both researchers resolved to continue this important tradition by jointly under-taking a 2017 census of women directors on the boards of companies listed on the New Zealand Stock Exchange. The results of this research were announced at the Women on Boards Conference in Auckland on 18 May 2017 with the launch of the website to facilitate dissemination of accurate and timely information on the progress of board diversity in New Zealand. The name of the website was chosen to reflect the axiom that what is measured is valued and gets changed or, as Waring (1999) so eloquently expressed it, women's contribution will Count for Nothing.

The 2017 WOB Census focused on the New Zealand Stock Exchange which introduced a diversity reporting regime in 2013. This research is the first research that attempts to assess the effectiveness of this regime in the four years it has been in place. It is regarded as a 'soft' initiative as there are limited sanctions for non-compliance. The raw data were supplied on request by the NZX as at the end of January 2017. The research outputs were two papers that analyzed the same data, motivated by the new methodology of crowd science. The paper by McGregor examined the Top 100 companies by market capitalization following the gold standard for international comparisons. Her segment of the research followed the methodology of the earlier five censuses and, as a longitudinal comparison, compares like with like.

This chapter reports on the segment of the research conducted by the author and uses the same data supplied by the NZX but takes a different view, using the data of the 122 companies required to report to the NZX on their gender diversity in 2016. Many of the companies are included in both datasets, but the differences give a richer insight into board diversity and how it is changing. The author took the opportunity to trial a research methodology, 'crowd research', which has not previously been used in WOB research. Using this methodology volunteer researchers were asked to give three hours of their time to check the NZX raw data and to investigate the diversity policies of companies listed on the main board of the NZX. Their learnings during this process are of particular interest as few of these women had investigated NZX companies at this detailed level. Their personal experiences give a qualitative context to what is a quantitative research project. The core of this research was a director network analysis and uses a new network visualization tool, Polinode (Pitts, 2016), which is a major advance in the display of director networks. This research is based on techniques developed in the course of Hawarden's (2010) doctoral research and provides a ten-year comparison with her 2007 dataset of all NZX listed companies.

The research null hypothesis was that the NZX diversity regime had resulted in no or minimal change to the gender gap (Figure 11.1). It was anticipated that the network structure would be unchanged even though the director turnover was expected to be high. The results show that there has been an incremental improvement of 1% per year in the numbers of women directors over the ten-year period. Pressure towards board equity in the New Zealand business community has also led to a rapid rise in the numbers of women who hold multiple board seats, called connector directors in network terminology or 'Golden Skirts' by Huse (2012). There has been a corresponding decline in the number of men with more than one directorship. This is an unintended consequence in the drive to increase New Zealand board gender diversity but is not wholly surprising as this effect was first noted in Norway when a 40% board gender quota was formally introduced in 2008. This was a 'hard' diversity regime with an initial grace period of two years, after which failure to achieve the quota would result in delisting. Now that this effect has been observed in New Zealand with its soft reporting requirement, the increase in female connector directors must lie in causes other than quotas, as previously thought. Glass Network Theory provides an explanation and suggests that this is a predictable effect in the class of networks known as scale free, to which director networks belong. Does this increase in Golden Skirts have implications for ongoing board equity efforts? Should its effects be mitigated, and if yes, how would this be achieved?

The NZX gender gap – how wide is it?

From 2013 the New Zealand Stock Exchange required companies listed on the main board to include a tally of directors and senior officers' gender diversity in their annual reports and to report these numbers to the New Zealand Stock Exchange under their diversity regulations, which may be found at www.nzx.com/regulation/diversity_statistics. Under Listing Rule 10.4.5(j), issuers listed on the NZX Main Board (excluding overseas companies) must include in their Annual Report quantitative data on the gender breakdown of the directors and officers at the financial year end, including comparative figures for the prior financial year end. The listing rule implies that this requirement extends to all companies, but in practice a significant number including some of the largest companies are excluded. Of the 196 listed companies, 74 or 38% are excluded and are not required to report on their board gender (NZX supplied data at 24 January, 2017). With over a third of companies excluded, this dilutes considerably any beneficial impact for this reporting regime.

Figure 11.1, a graphical representation of the NZX Gender Gap is derived from official NZX summary statistics for the year ending December 2016 as retrieved from https://nzx.com/files/static/cms-documents//000000010-251223.pdf. First, this NZX data refers to directorships and not the numbers of individual men and women. Second, it is not a snapshot at a point in time, but reflects quarterly figures as companies submitted diversity statistics at their year end. Third, the detailed statistics provided by the NZX for this research included three companies that were doubled up. These companies appear to have submitted their data twice (possibly reflecting changes to their boards) and the NZX data are therefore inflated.

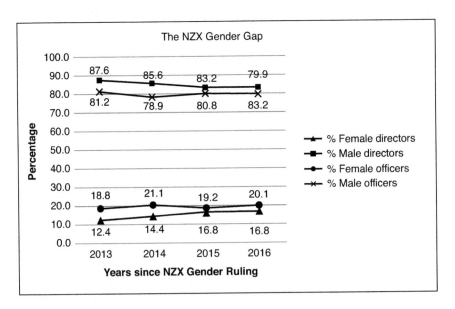

Figure 11.1 NZX Gender Gap (2013 to 2016)

This data includes directors and senior managers/senior executive staff, and so provides valuable insight into the pipeline for future directors. The analyses later in this report are based on the 122 companies in the data, not 125. The NZX's diversity reporting regime reflects a small improvement in the numbers of women directors from 12.4% in 2013 to 16.8% in 2015, where it is now static. The gender gap in NZX companies at top executive and governance levels remains heavily biased against women and favors men in these roles.

Director networks – where are women in gendered networks?

Women directors are not sidelined in director networks but are present throughout the network components and are more likely to be found in the largest component (Hawarden and Marsland, 2011). Unlike the glass ceiling concept which is viewed as a solid barrier to aspiring women directors, Glass Networks (that is, gendered director networks) may be thought of as transparent and semi-permeable. This allows a small but constant proportion of women into boardrooms. All director networks where there is no affirmative action have a few women directors, approximately 5–10%. Single seat women directors are linked into director networks through male colleagues, while the few women who have multiple directorships actively participate in the creation of the network components. Directors who sit on multiple boards create the links or edges between the nodes (directors or companies) in a network. When a network graph is visualized it can be seen that it is not completely connected but consists of a number of components. Starting with a random director and following links, there will be several subsets of directors whom cannot be reached. For statistical reasons, network analysis usually considers the largest component of the graph where it is possible to reach every node by following a connecting path. The technical analysis of the largest component is not included in this research. Only statistics that apply to the whole network are included. The network visualization tool, Polinode, used here shows all the components and includes directors and companies. This inclusive graph is interesting in its own right and can reveal details that a statistical analysis cannot. The detailed analysis extracting components and splitting out companies will be reported elsewhere.

Director networks belong to a class of networks called 'scale-free' networks. Examples of social and natural scale-free networks are the internet and computer networks, airline and shipping networks, power grids, neural networks, river systems, movie star and academic citation networks. Director networks like other complex networks are similar in structure irrespective of the location, size or scale of the network, and for this reason are called self-similar or scale-free (Newman et al., 2006). A small network will resemble a larger network. Scale-free networks have a specific structure, aspects of which can be mathematically expressed as a power law. This is more familiar if described as 'success attracts success', or the Pareto Principle or the 80/20 rule. A few nodes in the network attract the most links, while the remaining nodes have very few links to other nodes. The actors or nodes change but the underlying network is self-organizing and continues to shape itself organically into a quantifiable form. Once a stable state is reached, both natural and social networks are robust and change-resistant. This is a valuable attribute in power grids or the internet, but a problematical one when affirmative action interventions attempt to increase the number of women directors. If a stable director networks changes very little over time and is not subject to external pressure, gender ratios may similarly stay constant, shedding or adding directors in the same proportion as economies expand or contract.

Three main principles underlie the formation of scale-free networks and can also be observed in director networks. First, *preferential attachment* or increasing attractiveness due to popularity leads to a few nodes having the majority of the links. Examples in the internet are Google and Facebook. In director networks the recruitment of directors through 'shoulder tapping' or personal invitations to known colleagues and acquaintances has this same effect. Second, through *homophily* or a preference for the similar, certain nodes group together forming clusters or communities. It can be statistically demonstrated that directors prefer to sit on boards among peers with similar numbers of board appointments. Third, *salience* or a preference for characteristics that are notable and relevant also leads to the appointment of celebrity or trophy directors who may have little governance experience or be family members.

Where there is pressure for affirmative action, Glass Network Theory suggests that boards will preferentially respond by appointing experienced female directors who already have a substantive board appointment. As these will be in larger companies with bigger boards which form the largest network component, more women connector directors will be found in the largest component. As director networks are dynamic entities, the movement of directors through the network must also be taken into account. High levels of turnover in director networks appears to be the norm. Davis, Yoo and Baker (2003) found this to be 95% over 17 years in the US Fortune 1000 network. Hawarden and Marsland (2011) found 49% of directors had been replaced in the NZX network from 2004 to 2007. Female directors showed a higher average turnover rate of 59% compared to 48% for male directors. Despite high turnover, individual connector directors must gain other board appointments at an equal rate or single seat directors gain a second seat, to give director networks stability.

Having located women directors in the network, Hawarden and Marsland (2011) also examined the percentage of connector directors in a network. This was found to be different to the total percentage by gender and to change over time and in response to external pressure such as quotas. Why certain directors are able to secure the small number of multiple seats available is a question to which diversity researchers have devoted much time and effort. In particular they have looked at the characteristics of successful women directors trying to find common reasons for their success. Glass Network Theory suggests that overlooked differences may exist between them and single seat directors. Connector directors of both genders may share these characteristics, which may relate to competence, leadership ability and other enabling factors, but these are still to be established.

Affirmative action interventions, such as the Norwegian board quota legislation, took place without a program to monitor the effects of social change. Much of the subsequent research in Norway has centered on evaluating and understanding the unintended consequences of the quota regime. Known as 'Golden Skirts', a group of female connector directors emerged in Norway with what were regarded as 'excessive' board appointments (Huse and Seierstad, 2013; Seierstad and Opsahl, 2011). The intention of the quota legislation was to increase the absolute numbers of women directors, or single seat directors, not reduce gender diversity with a limited number of women appointed to most of the seats. This phenomenon was understood to be a response to the imposition of quotas. Contrarily Glass Network Theory predicts that where there is pressure to increase the total percentage of women on boards, the numbers of female connector directors will increase first as they are beneficiaries of the network force of preferential attachment. It can be further argued that rising numbers of Golden Skirts will be the first indication that equity measures are successful in changing board composition. This will be associated with a corresponding decline in the numbers of male connector directors. The ratio of directors with multiple seats to single seat directors can be predicted if there is no affirmative action as it too follows a power law (Hawarden, 2010). Changes to this ratio are a measure of the success of gender equity programs.

Where there is pressure to appoint a woman to a board, a known pair of hands represents a reduced risk and an experienced woman is less likely to disrupt established modes of business. This may also be another indicator of the 'Queen Bee syndrome' or 'Aunt Lydia organizations' where women through a glass ceiling work together to shut out equally competent aspiring women directors. Where the proportion of Golden Skirts (or Golden Suits, the male equivalent) increases beyond the predicted ratio the presence of oligarchic organizations should also be considered. This is a troubling idea for those working towards board gender equity but requires examination. The term 'old boys' network' is a well-accepted concept but hard to demonstrate. The use of these terms, including Golden Skirts, in the research literature means that they cannot be ignored and, as the academic rule of priority taking precedence applies, can continue to be used.

Queen Bees, Golden Tokens/Skirts and Shirts

The 'Queen Bee' concept has had some currency in the WOB literature. Queen Bees (and there is no male equivalent) are defined as women directors with two or more seats, who adopt the behavior patterns of male directors, and are perceived as violating the norms of feminine behavior by behaving in an imperious manner. Seeing other women as competitors, Queen Bees do not champion aspiring directors of their own gender (Hawarden, 2010: 43). Two factors reinforce Queen Bee behavior (Kang et al., 2007). First, women are perceived as unlikely to be part of the old boys' network, which allows them to be independent (meeting governance requirements for independent directors) but lacking in influence and therefore unlikely to undermine the status quo. Second, they may have a better understanding of consumer behavior and needs, and the opportunities for a company to meet them. To provide 'the women's point of view' on a board only one woman is required. Kantor's (1977) classic study found that tokenism creates performance pressure to behave in gender-specific ways where the display of feminine characteristics, or those perceived as such, obscures contributions in the boardroom. Token women directors may respond by constructing a façade that minimizes peer concerns or develop a persona that masks deeper thinking and accomplishment. Gender-limiting strategies in the boardroom that promote Queen Bee behavior and tokenism appear to be a norm. Research by Farrell and Hersch (2005) indicates that departing women directors are replaced with women and the likelihood of a firm adding a woman to its board in a given year is negatively affected by the number of women already on the board.

Branson (2007: 52) introduced the concept of the female trophy director on US boards where a woman director occupies four or more seats at publicly held corporations. A trophy director is appointed because of his or her high visibility and whose contribution to the board is limited to the recognition their celebrity status brings. Branson suggested that such a woman should be called a 'Golden Token'. It is from this discussion that Huse (2011) popularized the term 'Golden Skirts' when the impact of the Norwegian gender quota system became observable with a few women appointed to a large number of public company boards. Describing women as 'skirts' is American English slang and may or may not be pejorative depending on the context. The silhouette of a woman in a skirt as opposed to a man in pants is the ubiquitous indicator for segregated toilet facilities. Huse (2011) also introduced the term 'Golden Sacks' to describe male investors who remained on the 40% gender quota boards while independent male directors were replaced by women. Where the governance literature has focused on the effects of one director holding too many board appointments, the results are mixed with both positive and negative consequences (Ferris et al., 2003). Despite concerns with the gendered nature of the term 'Golden Skirts', this research needed a male equivalent and Golden Suits is used here as the least offensive (Tutchell and Edmonds, 2013: 28).

Another term that is gaining currency in digital discussions is a resurgence of interest in a 1985 novel called *The Handmaid's Tale* by the Canadian author Margaret Atwood, following the release of a new television drama series in April 2017. In a recent Radio New Zealand interview with Kim Hill on 22 April 2017, Margaret Atwood highlighted her depiction of the repressive character, Aunt Lydia. She suggested that Aunt Lydias are women or women's organizations who benefit themselves by supporting a totalitarian or colonial regime to repress other women and enforce the regime's gendered dictates. This is an extreme conceptualization of an 'old girl network' which has limited membership controlled by shoulder tapping or is by invitation only. Circumstances that favor one group over another are likely to lead to gender or other imbalances or the dystopic world of gender segregation. These may occur at lower levels in organizations as is now been seen in the Middle East where educated and skilled women are unable to find employment, a phenomenon being described as 'pipeline block'. If these organizations do exist and are influential in determining board appointments that favor certain women over others, then having baseline statistics becomes important in establishing their presence.

Research methodology

1   In January 2017 the NZX provided an Excel spreadsheet as at 24 January 2017, listing companies by market capitalization and directors by company and by gender. The diversity reporting statistics by quarter were also provided. This list was used as the basis to include or exclude companies in the network analysis and, as three companies appeared twice, 122 companies were used.

2   A crowd sourcing or a crowd research methodology was used for the first time in Women on Boards research. Crowd science also involves multiple teams examining the same data, replicating results and confirming findings while applying innovative methodologies to develop and expand initial results (Silberzahn and Uhlmann, 2015). These new approaches are time efficient, low cost and very productive as they very quickly harness the talents of a diverse community where research budgets are minimal. Crowd science is characterized by open participation in a project by a wide base of potential contributors, with data or problem-solving methods supplied by the researchers (Franzoni and Sauermann, 2014). Critical challenges in crowd science projects are attracting contributors and coordinating the contributions of a large number of participants. The motivation and educational benefits of crowd science are recognized as enhancing an individual's engagement with science and progressing science generally by building in cumulative steps on the work of earlier and other researchers.

Members of the Women on Boards division of Governance New Zealand Inc. were approached by email and asked to volunteer three hours of their time to research companies listed on the New Zealand Stock Exchange. A Gmail email address was set up to collect responses. The email included the NZX Gender Gap graph (Figure 11.1) and a link to the NZX diversity statistics page. In addition, the anticipated benefits were described for a participating researcher as:

- An active contribution to increasing board diversity;
- A detailed look at five to ten NZX companies' annual reports and websites as board member gender was verified and diversity statements explored;
- Improved understanding of corporate governance and information that would assist personal share market investing; and
- Experience with a new research technique.

The email contained a statement clarifying ethical issues. Volunteers were assured that the data used was publicly available or supplied by the New Zealand Stock Exchange on request. All contributors would be acknowledged in any published research and given an opportunity to comment on the draft report. The skills required were a basic knowledge of Excel spreadsheets, an ability to download files from the NZX website and an ability to use word search to find specific information. Researchers were provided with five to ten companies identified by name and ticker code to research and an answer spreadsheet with a sample template and instructions on how to fill it in. Researchers were asked to download annual reports from 2013 if available and search them using 'gender' and 'women' as the key word. Committee members of the WOB Division were first asked to trial and comment on the email and the usability of the templates. Based on feedback the email text was improved. Volunteers were also asked to report on their learnings in four or five short sentences. Qualitative reports on learnings would indicate the levels of stock market literacy in the contributors who were 99.9% female. The invitation to participate stressed that the research was gender inclusive but only one man volunteered but did not submit results. All data returned was double checked and verified.

Every email was replied to personally with the researcher ensuring that all replies were friendly and answered all questions raised by volunteers. The time and effort taken to do this was not onerous and the relationship building between the researcher and the contributors was an important part of the research methodology. The anticipated benefits stressed this educational component as the extent of WOB members understanding of stock market governance and investment in NZX listed companies is unknown. Also unknown is the number of WOB members and/ or volunteers who personally invest in NZX companies and how their portfolio and investment selection is driven. In 2005 the ANZ Banking Group conducted an extensive survey on the financial practices of consumers in Australia and New Zealand (Lusardi and Mitchell, 2007). Low levels of financial literacy highly correlated with low education and income levels. This survey also confirmed the gender gap, with women concentrated in the lowest 20% of the financial literacy distribution. New Zealand women directors' financial literacy levels are unknown, nor is it known whether there are gender differences in stock market research behavior among New Zealand directors. How women directors think and feel when researching and making stock market investment decision needs further research.

Results

This second research segment of the 2017 Women on Boards Census examined the 2016 gender diversity of 122 NZX listed companies required to report on their board gender composition since 2013. Descriptive statistics are given in Table 11.1 which gives a ten-year comparison to the 2007 NZX data. The NZX's diversity reporting regime has led to a small improvement in female directorships or seats from 12.4% in 2013 to 16.8% in 2015, and was unchanged for 2016 (Figure 11.1). This study found the percentage of women directors out of a total 586 directors in these 'diversity reporting companies' to be 14.8%. When all 718 directorships or seats are considered the NZX official figure of 16.8% is confirmed but is much lower than the percentage of 22.1% for the Top 100 companies as reported by McGregor. However, it is the comparison to the 2007 data that shows the greatest improvement. Over the ten-year period, the percentage of female seats/directorships has improved from a low of 7% to 16.8%. This does indicate that increased activism and consciousness raising in this period has led to an average increase in the numbers of female seats of 1% per year both before and after the 2013 introduction of NZX diversity reporting. As a bigger difference would have been

Table 11.1 Descriptive statistics for the mixed gender 2007 NZX and 2016 diversity reporting director networks

	2007 NZX All companies	2016 NZX diversity reporting companies	Direction of change
No. of companies	185	122	
No. of directors	899	586	
Male directors (%)	832	499	
	92.5%	85.1%	⬆
Female directors (%)	67	87	
	7.5%	14.8%	⬇
Gender ratio	12.4	5.7	⬆
No. of seats	1059	718	
No. of male seats	985	597	
	93%	83.1%	
No. of female seats	74	121	
	7.0%	16.8%	⬆
No. of connector directors (%)	117	87	No change
	14.1%	14.8%	
No. of male connector directors (%)	110	63	
	94.0%	72.4%	⬇
No. of female connector directors (%)	7	24	
	6.0%	27.5%	⬆
No. of connector seats (% to total seats)	277	219	Small
	26.1%	30.5%	change
No. of male connector seats (%)	261	161	
	94.2%	73.5%	⬇
No. of female connector seats (%)	16	58	
	5.8%	26.5%	⬆

expected in the percentage increase from 2013 to 2016, the reporting regime is not having a marked effect on the gender balance. However the ratio of male to female directors has improved from 12:1 to 6:1. Women directors are increasingly the norm around the board table.

No conclusions are drawn here regarding the effect of detailed gender policies in quickening the pace of greater female representation in boardrooms as these were reported by McGregor. The wide variability in company gender policies made collation and analysis difficult with multiple contributors but the provision of these reports did save considerable time in validating the data. Both researchers and contributors were in agreement that variability and the lack of accountability undermine New Zealand's corporate diversity reporting regime. The learnings of the contributors (Appendix A) show a positive experience with crowd research techniques. The most common phrase used was the perception of 'lip service' being paid to gender diversity in company annual reports and a boilerplate approach to comply with NZX guidelines. Some researchers were shocked to find that at the company level there was so little interest in diversity.

Rise of the Golden Skirts and decline of the Golden Suits

There has been a marked change to the circumstances of the Golden Skirts, the female connector directors or the group of women holding more than one board appointment in the diversity reporting companies. The Golden Skirts have gained at the expense of the Golden Suits and aspiring women directors.

Table 11.1 shows that a total of 86 connector directors or Golden Skirts and Golden Suits link multiple boards together as they hold from two to five board appointments in the 2016 NZX data. Twenty-four Golden Skirts (28% of women directors) hold 58 seats (47% of the female seats), while the 62 Golden Suits (13% of male directors) hold 161 seats (22% of the male seats). Ten years ago, the 2007 survey of all 185 NZX companies reported seven Golden Skirts holding 16 seats (21% of female seats) and 110 Golden Suits holding 261 seats (27% of male seats). Table 11.2 gives

Table 11.2 Seat spreads for the 2007 all NZX listed companies and the 2016 diversity reporting companies by gender

No. of seats/ directorships per director	2007 NZX companies				NZX diversity reporting companies in 2016			
	2007 male directors	2007 female directors	2007 male seats	2007 female seats	2016 male directors	2016 female directors	2016 male seats	2016 female seats
No. of companies	185				122			
6	2	0	12	0	0	0	0	0
5	3	0	15	0	2	1	10	5
4	5	0	20	0	8	0	32	0
3	14	2	42	6	13	7	39	21
2	86	5	172	10	40	16	80	32
1	722	60	722	60	436	63	436	63
	832	67	983	76	499	87	597	121
Total directors	899		1059		586		718	

the numbers of directors at each level from one to five seats in the NZX data for 2007 and 2016. Figure 11.2 shows how male and female seat distributions converge in the 2016 data compared to the 2007 data, showing the growth in the numbers of women with multiple seats at each level and the reduction in the number of men.

A small group of women directors hold nearly half of all the female seats. This is the first evidence that the NZX's diversity regulations may be contributing to the creation of the same unintended consequences as in Norway where the implementation of gender quotas saw a dramatic rise in the

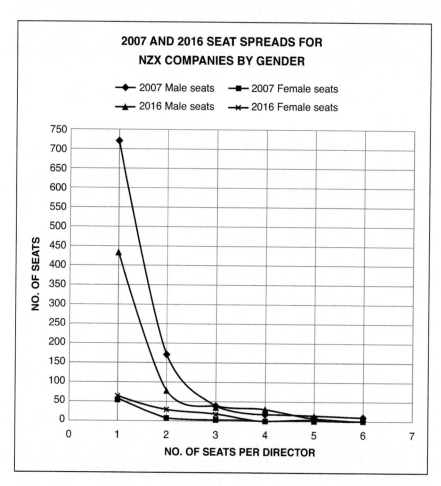

Figure 11.2 Seat spreads by number of seats per director by gender in the 2007 all NZX companies and the 2016 gender reporting companies, showing the decrease in 2016 male directors (triangle) and increase in 2016 female directors (cross) with more than one directorship

numbers of 'Golden Skirts'. Norwegian board diversity was reduced as a limited number of women held a high number of seats. This is now the case in New Zealand and is also reflected in the seat spreads in Table 11.2. In 2007 Golden Skirts did not hold more than three seats each while in 2016 they held up to five seats. In 2007 Golden Suits held up to six seats each while this has reduced to five. As the NZX has imposed a 'soft' diversity reporting regime, this rise of the Golden Skirts cannot be as previously thought, solely a consequence of quota imposition. These results support Glass Network Theory that affirmative action pressure on a director network will result in an increase in the numbers of Golden Skirts, and a decrease in the Golden Suits with the total percentage of connector directors remaining constant at 14–15% in the director network. The total percentage of male to female directors responds slowly i.e. 1% per year to pressures for change unless these are imposed through quotas.

Network analysis

The percentage of total connector directors has remained stable over the ten-year period at 14–14.8% but the gender balance has changed. From a low of 6%, female connector directors now comprise 27.5% and male connector directors have declined from 94% to 72.4%. Of the 67 women in the 2007 NZX dataset, only 13 remained in the 2016 NZX dataset. They are Alison Paterson, Carmel Fisher, Elizabeth Coutts, Jane Freeman, Jenny Shipley, Joan Withers, Joanna Perry, Linda Sanders, Rosanne Meo, Sarah Ottrey, Sharon Hunter, Susan Paterson and Susan Sheldon. While their individual board appointments may have changed, these women continued to be appointed to NZX boards over the ten-year period. Of these women, eight were connector directors and contributed to the stability of the 2016 director network.

Figure 11.3, an online and interactive view of the NZX director network, shows that the unconnected components are largely male (darker circles) and around the rim of the image with the female directors (triangle shapes) in the largest connected component. The numbers of multiple seats are reflected in the size of the nodes and the individual directors can be identified. The largest nodes are the connector directors with the most seats. The small grey nodes are the companies. In the interactive online version of the network, floating a mouse over the node will reveal the identity of the node. Figure 11.4 is a view where boards are grouped into communities based on common links and then separated by seat level where it is easy to see the gender of directors at each level. The largest connected community is on the left. It can be seen that the women directors tend to cluster in certain communities which can be colored separately in the Polinode software. Polinode also can calculate a range of network metrics which are not reported on here but can be accessed online or through the website, www.countingforchange.nz.

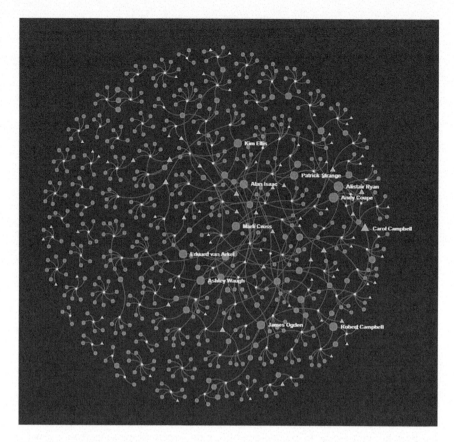

Figure 11.3 2016 NZX network of male and female directors in 122 gender diversity reporting companies (male – circle and female – triangle), size indicates number of seats

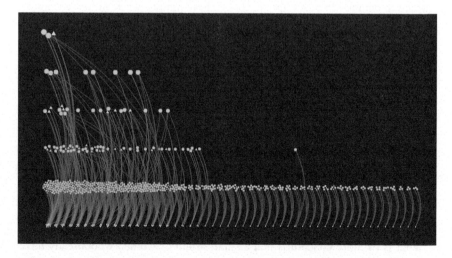

Figure 11.4 2016 NZX network of male and female directors in 122 gender diversity reporting companies by seat spread (male – circle and female – triangle), size indicates number of seats from one to five per director

Learnings analysis

There were 44 responses to the request for volunteers, and from their email signatures many were senior officers and directors. Five dropped out early followed by another six largely due to pressure of work. The names of the respondents indicated a multicultural response and included one man. Seventeen volunteers returned data and gave their learnings (Appendix A). These learnings are all positive about the research and the contributors perceived it to be of high value. It was apparent that exploring the company data on the NZX website was a new experience for some contributors. A number of senior women made constructive comments on NZX governance and comparisons with international practice. In general the tone reflected disappointment in the lack of value placed on diversity in company reporting. Where companies have good programs and policies, respondents commented that these do stand out. As a constructive methodology to increase WOB member engagement and provide an opportunity to contribute to a research project perceived as of high importance, crowd research was an effective tool. Its value also lies in increasing meaningful networking opportunities between researchers and volunteers and an opportunity to publicize research to a wider community engaged in promoting more women onto boards.

Conclusion

In the ten years since the 2007 NZX network analysis (Hawarden, 2010), there has been an increase in the percentage of female directorships/seats from a low of 7% to 16.8%. The average annual increase of 1% in female seats indicates slow change. The governance community of New Zealand is responding to pressure to appoint more women directors but at this rate the target of 40% may only be reached in another 20 years, that is 2037. These figures, while mildly encouraging, do mask the underlying trends that are revealed if the numbers of individual women directors are considered. The major change is in the percentage of women connector directors from 6% to 27.5% of female directors with this small group of women who previously held 5.8% of the female seats now holding 27%. Male directors holding multiple seats have declined. These changes are in line with Glass Network Theory predictions, being the group of directors most likely to change if affirmative action pressures are applied to change board gender. This research reaches the conclusion that these changes will also occur in the absence of legislated quotas such as those imposed in Norway and Europe. Soft or community pressures for change can be effective but will take place at a slower rate. Quotas are an effective way to implement rapid change and maintain it permanently. These gender balance changes resulting from unlegislated pressure may not be permanent if the pressure to change is reduced. Network dynamics suggest that gender balances would drift back to the Pareto ratio of 90/10.

What is of more concern is that a small group of women who already have extensive governance experience and are 'through the glass ceiling' are benefitting from this pressure for more diverse boards. This does have negative implications in that the pool of experienced women directors is limited and aspiring directors continue to be caught in the Catch-22 of directing, unable to get the governance experience to qualify them for the boards of the NZX. There is a suggestion that this may not be a permanent phenomenon as follow-up research into Norwegian quota companies is starting to indicate. There do appear to be spillover effects as companies not affected by quota legislation appoint women to their boards. There is no shortage of qualified women and as they are getting more experience are becoming more visible (Huse, 2012). While the phenomenon of the Golden Skirts with large numbers of board appointments appears to be abating in Norway, there are no regular censuses such as in New Zealand to track this reliably. New Zealand appears to be a world leader in terms of monitoring changes to the gender balance on public boards and to understanding how director network structure impacts the gender balance, particularly of directors with multiple board appointments.

The conclusions drawn here reinforce the requirement for ongoing Census of Women's Participation as research of this nature exerts community pressure on boards to change their gender composition. Where the imposition of quotas seems unlikely, activism on the part of concerned governance and women directors' organizations also needs to be continued. To ensure that the pool of board-ready female directors continues to grow, initiatives that encourage the exposure of aspiring women directors to governance training and real-life learning through observing boards at work are to be encouraged. Connector directors and those through the glass ceiling of NZX boards should be encouraged to mentor and promote other women to boards recruiting new directors. Education of chairs and the members of selection committees as to best practice in terms of open and transparent selection procedures would ensure meritorious selection. Greater emphasis should be placed on developing consensus as to what constitutes best practice for director recruitment and selection. The same level of attention needs to be paid to the appointment of directors as is to the hiring of senior executives. This is the most important role of the chair who needs the foundation of a well thought out gender diversity policy on which to base these decisions.

Acknowledgements

The support of Governance New Zealand Inc in facilitating this research is acknowledged, in particular the contribution of Linda Noble and Joy Tracey. Funding by AUT, Auckland supported the research led by Professor Judy McGregor. Andrew Pitts is acknowledged for his assistance with the Polinode network analysis. Forty-four volunteers came forward and data contributions came from Alison Wood, Annis O'Brien, Carron Blom, Fi Dalgety, Ginnie Denny, Irene Durham, Ithu Ageel, Jennifer George, Josie Fitzgerald, Joy Tracey, Karen Remetis, Megan Sargent, Phillipa Smith, Rebekah Swan, Sandy Jackson, Sophie Davies and Sue Neale.

References

Australia and New Zealand Banking Group 2005. ANZ Survey of Adult Financial Literacy in Australia, November as cited in Lusardi, A., Mitchell, O. 2007. Financial literacy and retirement preparedness: Evidence and implications for financial education programs, CFS Working Paper, No. 2007/15, http://nbn-resolving.de/urn:nbn:de:hebis:30-38250

Branson, D. 2007. *No Seat at the Table: How Corporate Governance and Law Keep Women Out of the Boardroom*, New York: New York University Press.

Davis, G.F., M. Yoo and W.E. Baker (2003), 'The small-world of the American corporate elite, 1982–2001', *Strategic Organization*, 1(3), 301–326.

Farrell, K., Hersch, P. 2005. Additions to corporate boards: The effects of gender, *Journal of Corporate Finance*, 11, 85–106.

Ferris, S.P., Jagannathan, M., Pritchard, A.C. 2003. Too busy to mind the business? Monitoring by directors with multiple board appointments, *The Journal of Finance*, 58(3), 1087–1111.

Franzoni, C., Sauermann, H. 2014. Crowd science: The organization of scientific research in open collaborative projects, *Research Policy*, 43(1), 1–20.

Hawarden, R.J. 2010. Glass networks: The network structure of women directors on corporate boards: A thesis presented in partial fulfilment of the requirements for the degree of Doctor of Business and Administration at Massey University, Palmerston North, New Zealand, http://mro.massey.ac.nz/handle/10179/2047, accessed 30 August, 2017.

Hawarden, R.J., Marsland, S. 2011. Locating women board members in gendered director networks, *Gender in Management: An International Journal*, 26(8), 532–549.

Huse, M. 2011. The golden skirts: Changes in board composition following gender quotas on corporate boards, in Australian and New Zealand Academy Meeting, Wellington, NZ, December, www.anzam.org/wp-content/uploads/pdf-manager/473_ANZAM2011-148. PDF, accessed 30 August, 2017.

Huse, M. 2012. The "golden skirts": Lessons from Norway about women on corporate boards of directors, in Takagi, J., Gröschl, S. (eds.), *Diversity Quotas, Diverse Perspectives: The Case of Gender*, Gower Publishing Ltd., (1), 11–23.

Huse, M., Seierstad, C. 2013. Getting women on to corporate boards: Consequences of the Norwegian gender balance law, *The European Financial Review*, 12, 37–39.

Kang, H., Cheng, M., Gray, S. 2007. Corporate governance and board composition: Diversity and independence of Australian boards, *Corporate Governance: An International Review*, 15(2), 194–207.

Kantor, R.M. 1977. *Men and Women of the Corporation*, New York: Basic Books.

Newman, M., Barabási, A.-L., Watts, D. 2006. *The Structure and Dynamics of Networks*, Princeton: Princeton University Press.

Pitts, A. 2016. Polinode: A web application for the collection and analysis of network data, Advances in Social Networks Analysis and Mining (ASONAM), 2016 IEEE/ACM International Conference, 1422–1425, doi:10.1109/ASONAM.2016.7752435

Seierstad, C., Opsahl, T. 2011. For the few not the many? The effects of affirmative action on presence, prominence, and social capital of women directors in Norway, *Scandinavian Journal of Management*, 27(1), 44–54.

Silberzahn, R., Uhlmann, E. 2015. Crowdsourced research: Many hands make tight work, *Nature News*, October, 526, 189–191.

Tutchell, E., Edmonds, J. 2013. *Made in Norway: How Norwegians Have Used Quotas to Increase the Number of Women on Company Boards*, London: Labour Finance and Industry Group and the Fabian Women's Network.

Waring, M. 1999. *Counting for Nothing: What Men Value and What Women Are Worth*, Toronto: University of Toronto Press.

Appendix A

Learnings from WOB crowd research

These reflections are not ordered and have been anonymized, removing comments on specific companies with minor editing to improve readability.

1 Contributor A

1 The international banking company had no reference to diversity in the NZ annual report while the Australian New Zealand Corporate Governance Framework was very positive with detailed references. This seems more like tokenism rather than being embedded across the organization, and across borders. This bank had one woman on the NZ board out of the seven directors, and this is someone who has many board appointments. It seems there are go-to women across the country.

2 A personal response to doing this is that being on a board is for a certain type of woman and the rest of us are those who contribute in the NGO sector for no financial recognition. I found it a little depressing as I have a lot to contribute and looking through this makes me think that I will never have the opportunity.

3 The property investment company had no women and no diversity statement or reporting. Ironically, the only diversity mention related to the importance of diversity in their property portfolio.

4 The minerals company had two out of five directors as women. Interesting that the founding director was part of IOD mentoring for diversity program. Yet, the other woman on the board was someone she previously worked with on a board. Also the annual report had minimal reference to diversity only, identifying the numbers and nothing in corporate governance framework. Wonder if numbers on the board are personality driven rather than organizationally driven.

5 The news media company had well-developed policies under the corporate governance statement since 2013. Wondering what makes this organization different as it also has two women directors out of the five current directors. There seems a commitment to gender diversity.

2   Contributor B

The lack of women on Boards, and that as short as three years ago, diversity and the role of women within companies, held little value. Out of the five companies I researched there was only one that valued women and diversity in the workplace. As the mother of two daughters, I found this very sad. I felt some of the companies Diversity Policies were nothing more than lip service – doing what had to be done to meet NZX requirements. Again, sad.

3   Contributor C

I found it disappointing that very few women are on the boards I researched. Lip service is being paid to women being appointed. A company can write the word 'diversity' as many times as it likes but that doesn't equate to action. Personally it was good for me as I've never achieved a board appointment in NZ so now do not participate in putting my CV forward. The research gave me better knowledge of NZX and how companies are reporting.

4   Contributor D

The commitment by listed companies to diversity is very disappointing – I was truly surprised that only one of five companies I researched has a diversity policy. It would seem that despite NZX requiring companies, since 2013, to include a diversity statement, this is not being complied with in many cases. It appears NZX are not taking any steps to check, much less ensure, that their diversity requirement is being complied with. It was pleasing to see that there are some women on some of the boards of companies I researched. However the proportion of women does not reflect the composition of our population. I would describe gender diversity, and diversity in general, as merely 'being paid lip service' by influencers in NZ.

5   Contributor E

Very interesting project – I learned heaps!!

6   Contributor F

That there are NZX requirements regarding (limited) gender diversity; how minimal those requirements are; and (on a sample of five companies) how little effort those companies put into improving diversity.

7   Contributor G

I was not previously aware of the requirement to report on diversity – this was interesting. The companies that chose to have a diversity policy and how they defined diversity was interesting and informative and highlighted that diversity definition was up to individual companies. The glaring lack of consistency in the representation of women on boards.

8   Contributor H

Crowd research is a great option. Some companies actively encourage diversity while other sectors don't appear to encourage it at all. I should peruse more Annual Reports and they are readily available. Reinforces my thinking of ensuring your values align with an organization before you try and work with it. It was easy to assist.

9 Contributor I

It was interesting to learn more about the NZX requirements for listed entities and what information is available on the main board website – I hadn't really looked at this in any detail before. Even amongst the five entities I looked at there was a big variation in the content and presentation of information on corporate governance. Compliance with the NZX disclosure requirements does not of itself appear to increase diversity – in most of the reports the diversity information was buried near the back and there was no clear link between having a diversity policy and the quantitative disclosures. One company was a clear stand out having clearly articulated objectives and measurements around diversity.

10 Contributor J

My learning from participating in this research was to get up to speed on the current approach to corporate reporting/governance in NZ and to understand a bit more about the differences in approach versus the UK.

11 Contributor K

1   A common thread are that those who did minimal compliance did not place value on diversity. While I expected male-dominated companies e.g. construction to pay lip service only, some appeared to be totally committed to diversity. Not many companies have actually moved the needle and improved their female/male ratio. A very interesting project!

12 Contributor L

I noted a number of annual reports were 'cut and paste' for each year. In particular companies focused on funding and/or little interest in diversity. As soon as I saw a specific woman was the chair I knew there would be a focus on diversity in the annual reports and I was correct. I noticed gender-based titles – chairman even for woman in the role. I would prefer chairperson as a title. It became evident from reviewing the Annual Reports that board members stay in their roles for a number of years. For some businesses reviewed there was only lip service to diversity and I am not sure how NZX can enforce diversity beyond a statement.

13 Contributor M

Exposure to a new research method, and its logistics (something to squirrel away for future reference and use perhaps). Exposure to the diversity reporting requirements of the NZX and their guidance. Insight into organizational/board reporting in general and the varied, but often poor or cursory coverage of matters such as diversity, inclusion, environment etc.

14 Contributor N

Disappointing to learn that so little regard is paid to diversity. The boards I serve on have a comprehensive diversity policy and enact it in everyday activities throughout the company – diversity in the wide sense not just gender. Most companies have directors who are white male middle aged. I believe it is time for quotas – such as in Norway.

15 Contributor P

The NZX guidelines are pretty lame. You don't have to have a diversity policy, but if you do develop one then you give yourself a lot of reporting requirements. It's the corporately responsible thing to do but it's hardly being effectively promoted by the controlling body. If you have no policy then it's only a matter of reporting a table of actual numbers of board and executive by gender. I can see why we have not really progressed in addressing the gender imbalance. There is NO teeth to any of this.

12 Women on boards

Perspectives from BRIC and Turkey

Güler Aras and Ozlem Kutlu Furtuna

Introduction

In September 2015, 193 world leaders agreed to 17 Global Goals for Sustainable Development which means an end to extreme poverty, inequality and climate change by 2030 if they are completed (UN SDG, 2015). One of these global goals which seeks to change the course of the 21st century is the fifth one, namely gender equality. Gender diversity has become a crucial topic for human development, labor markets and hence GDP growth. In that respect, women labor workforce and women's empowerment in top management has been more crucial in emerging countries. In that study gender diversity has been tackled on BRIC countries and Turkey due to the fact that the association of the Turkey and BRIC countries has grown into a formidable one that collectively account for 21% of the global GDP (WB Statistics, 2016). The growth potential of the BRIC countries has been widely acknowledged and Goldman Sachs economists predicted that the BRIC economies (Brazil, Russia, India and China) would outperform that of the G7 countries (the richest countries) before the middle of the century (Glosny, 2010).

It is evident that the various qualities, talents and perspectives of the male and female board members will provide the firm with a multitude of benefits. In that context, the effect of gender diversity on firm performance, which means that women board members are included in the board of directors, has been a subject of investigation specifically in recent years and many researches have been done about it. Singh and Zammit (2000) state that women directors lead to better performance with their women-specific communication and listening abilities and generally have a graduate degree in business administration. Again, with these women-specific qualities there may be increases in the problem-solving problems in firms.

Brennan and McCafferty (1997) argue that women may have a better understanding of consumer behavior, the needs of customers and opportunities for companies in meeting those needs. Furthermore, Dominguez et al. (2012) highlight that with the same working environment and academic background, women are more successful than men, which emphasizes that the board of directors should be balanced or have more female members. Lückerath-Rovers (2013) reveals a consistent and significant positive relationship between the percentage of women on board and firms' return on equity ratio. They state higher representation of women on board yields to better firm performance.

One of the comprehensive studies related to BRIC and Turkey in that topic belongs to Aras (2015). She investigates the effect of corporate governance mechanisms in terms of women's representation on boards on financial structure in BRICK (Brazil, Russia, India, China and South Korea) between the years 2005 and 2013. She reveals that having women directors on the board not only decreases firm performance but also has no effect on financial leverage for both the common and civil law countries. Moreover, the percentage of women on boards has a negative effect on firms' return on assets. This indicates that the firms that have more women directors on the board are not more efficient in increasing the firm's profitability. She states that women directors on the board are appointed solely to fulfil the BRICK governance recommendations, and they may lack knowledge about the company and therefore add little or no value to the firm in BRICK firms. Moreover, Fauzi and Locke (2012) also indicate that having women on boards decreases the return on assets for New Zealand's listed firms. Most of these, however, are members of the owning families. The question thus remains, what impacts the proportion of women on the quality of decisions and the operational performance of the firm?

Ocak (2013) examine the effects of females on boards in terms of female chairpersons, percentage of independent female members on boards of directors and percentage of females in top management on financial performance in Turkey. He founds a positive and significant effect of the percentage of females in top management only on return on assets between the years 2008 and 2012. In another study related to the Turkish case, Karayel and Doğan (2014) investigate the association between gender diversity on boards and firm performance for listed firms on the Borsa Istanbul (BIST) 100 Index between the years 2009 and 2012. They reveal that gender diversity has a positive effect on return on assets while no effect on return on equity and Tobin's Q.

Aras and Kutlu Furtuna (2015) investigate the effect of female directors on agency cost levels in Turkish listed firms between the years 2005 and 2013. The percentage of female directors is found to increase the agency costs in terms of operating expense and excessive perquisite consumption. This indicates that boards having a higher number of women directors are less efficient in reducing agency costs, perhaps because the low women's representation rate on the boards. Although the percentage of women directors has slightly increased in recent years, a new regulation on the board composition requiring firms to appoint at least one female director on the board of directors will elevate the women ratio in the near future and might lead them to better concentrate on the agency problems. Okoth (2016) evaluates the impact of corporate governance on firm performance using board index between the years 2009 and 2013 with 52 listed firms on BIST. He has found a significant relationship with the performance of the firm. The underlying reason has been stated as the proportion of women on the quality of decisions and the operational performance of the firm.

Schmid and Urban (2015) investigate the reactions of the stock markets upon the exit of a female director due to death or illness to determine the impact of female directors on firm value with 53 countries and over 35,000 firms. They reveal that the stock markets react more negatively to the exogenous departure of female directors (as opposed to male directors), especially when the departing female director is replaced by a male director. A recent and most cited study of Post and Bryon (2015) investigate the effect of women on boards on the financial performance of firms by statistically combining 140 studies for a meta-analysis. Findings reveal that women's representation on boards is positively related to accounting returns and that this relationship is more positive in countries with stronger shareholder protection. Moreover, meta-analysis results exhibit that women on boards and market performance is near zero; however, this relationship is positive in countries with greater gender parity and negative in countries with low gender parity because of gender differences may affect investor's perceptions.

McKinsey & Co. (2010) analysis which consists of 411 firms from six European countries, BRIC countries and the US, underline whether the firm which has the highest number of women in top management has the best corporate financial performance. They exhibit that the financial performance of firms has been compared to the performance of companies having no women in top management and the firms with the highest number of women in top management had the best performance. Another research conducted by MSCI (Modern Index Strategy Indices) (2015) reveals that firms in the MSCI World Index with strong female leadership generated a return on equity of 10.1% per year versus 7.4% for those without. A current McKinsey & Co. (2016) report states that diverse teams have a positive effect on corporate performance through incorporating different opinions, expectations and style. Women may also add valuable insights to customer behavior.

Board diversity has become a major issue within corporate governance, where a number of papers seek to explore the effect of diversity on firm value, performance and risk-taking behavior. As can be seen, there are sometimes positive, sometimes negative, and sometimes no relations with the country where the women board members are affected by the firm performance, according to the time and selected criteria.

The remainder of this chapter is organized as follows. The section on the women labor force in BRIC and Turkey gives statistical perspectives about gender diversity. The following section emphasizes the percentage of women on boards comparatively among the related countries and gives insights for industries in which there are women directors and highly concentrated firms in emerging markets. The last section concludes the chapter.

Women labor force in BRIC and Turkey

Increasing women's participation in the labor force implies significant growth potential for the global economy. Women may have a better understanding of consumer behavior, the needs of customers and opportunities for firms in meeting those needs. International Labour Organization (ILO) states the labor force participation rate "is the proportion of the population ages 15 and older that is economically active: all people who supply labour for the production of goods and services during a specified period".

Figure 12.1 indicates the women labor force participation rate among some part of the Organization for Economic Cooperation and Development (OECD) members and BRIC countries. It has to be noted that the related rate of China (63.3%) and Russia

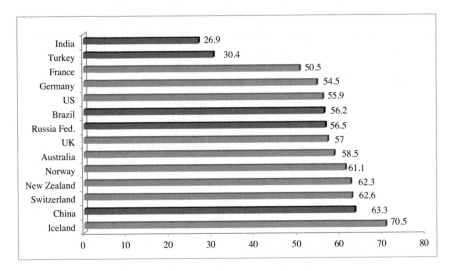

Figure 12.1 Women labor force participation rate (% of female population ages 15+, 2016)

Source: World Bank Database, http://databank.worldbank.org/data/reports.aspx?source=2&series=SL.
TLF.CACT.FE.ZS&country=

(56.5%) compare favorably with that of the US (55.9%) and the UK (57%) while that of China's exceeds that of both the US, UK and other BRIC countries in 2016.

India has the lowest female rate of the BRIC nations. The participation rate among other BRIC nations is almost twice as high as that of India. This is due to factors restricting women from working outside the home. Moreover, India is the only country where the participation rate has declined noticeably over the past ten years among BRIC countries. India's female labor force participation rate declined from 37% in 2005 to 26.9% in 2016.

Turkey has the lowest female labor participation rate after India in 2016. The employment rate of Turkey is a record low with 50.6% of the total workable force due to the traditional low women's participation in the workforce, as we have witnessed in all Islamic countries. In Turkey only 30.4% of the potential female labor force is employed whereas the EU average is 61.7%. Turkish government has set several goals to increase the female labor force. Turkey labor force statistics evidence that the female labor ratio has increased from 22.7% to 30.4% between 2006 and 2016. A 10% increase in ten years' time, although far from the EU standards, is quite remarkable.

Pioneer work of Akerlof's and Kranton's *identity economics* prioritizes identities and norms in the economic activity which states gender is one aspect of identity and a source of social difference. For instance, in emerging countries each of the two categories 'man' and 'woman' is associated with different socially prescribed behavior: typically, men are supposed to pursue a career and women are expected to stay at home (Akerlof and Kranton, 2000) Over the last ten years, Turkey has anticipated a growing momentum in female labor participation as the current government policy provided a fertile climate for the women who wish to express their religious and traditional identities.

Although Turkey has the lowest female labor participation rate among OECD countries with a 30.4% representation rate, it has to be noted that women represent 41% of total employees in leading firms in Turkey. When financial services have been considered, this percentage increases to 56%. The main underlying reason is the urbanization and decline in agricultural employment. Turkish women migrate from a high participation rural environment because of urbanization.

Pillay (2014) investigates how women workers in the five BRIC countries fare with regard to key labor market indicators. She reveals that although the labor market outcomes for women workers are varied across the BRIC countries, there are some similarities. The majority of BRIC countries conform to the gender segregation of employment as depicted by a marked presence of women workers in services, a negligible proportion in industry and the majority of countries having just above 40% of women employed in the non-agricultural sector.

Women on boards in BRIC countries and Turkey

Women directors can add additional skills and perspectives that are different from those of male directors as well. However, in some countries women directors on the board can be appointed solely to fulfill the country governance recommendations, and they may lack knowledge about the firm and therefore may add little or no value to the firm.

Table 12.1 reveals that the number of women holding seats of the largest publicly listed firms is still lower than that of men in the related years.

Table 12.1 Women share of seats on boards of the largest publicly listed firms (as percentage)

	2010	2013	2016
Iceland	16	48	44
Norway	39	42	41
France	12	30	37
Sweden	26	26	36
Finland	26	30	30
Netherlands	15	25	28
UK	13	21	27
Denmark	18	23	27
Germany	13	21	27
US	12.3	12.2	16.4
OECD-Average	12.2	16.8	20
Turkey	10	8	12
India	4.5	6.5	11.4
China	8	8.4	9.4
Brazil	4.7	5.1	6

Source: OECD Statistics Database; http://stats.oecd.org/index.aspx?queryid=54753

Several countries have adopted quotas or passed legislation mandating more women's representation on corporate boards. In Nordic firms, women are best represented in the top management as a result of gender quotas. The greatest gender diversity has been registered in the firms of the Iceland (44%) which is the first country among OECD countries. In Norway, the proportion of women on board was 41% and in Sweden this percentage was 36% in 2016. Norway first introduced gender quotas in some public sector entities in the 1980s and extended them in 2003 under legislation requiring at least 40% of women on boards of public limited companies (known as ASA), inter-municipal businesses and state-owned enterprises. France, Germany, Norway and Iceland have implemented legally binding gender quota requirements for corporate boards. The reason of the high percentage of women directors on the board within those countries is the new amendments emphasizing the representation of both genders on the board.

Denmark, Finland and the Netherlands required target setting around 30–40% based on a comply-or-explain approach. The US and UK have required mandatory disclosure of board diversity policies that were endorsed and supported by business-led campaigns. The UK has made great progress under a voluntary, business framework with a 14% increase from 2010 and 2016.

For BRIC countries, the percentages of women on boards is remarkably low. For India, a law that was realized in 2015 states that firms are supposed to have at least one woman on their board. However, compliance has been uneven, with a number of firms appointing firm insiders and even the wives of CEOs to the board in order to comply. Among these nations, India has the leading the trend – the share of women's seats on boards has grown there by 6.9% from 2010 to 2016. The Indian Revised Companies Act which was issued in 2013 made it mandatory for all listed firms and other large public limited firms to appoint at least one woman on the board (Deloitte, 2016).

There are no gender quotas in Russia. There have been no initiatives and provisions about gender diversity. According to McKinsey& Co. (2016), Russia has been found to have fewer women in executive committees than Europe or the US, but more than BRIC countries in general. In that report it has been explained by the principles of gender parity applied during Soviet times. For Brazil, initiatives on gender quota which were first proposed in 2015 by the Brazilian government have been drafted and discussed. Women held only 6% of board seats in Brazil in 2016, a mere 1.3% increase in 2010. For China, there are recently no quotas for women on boards. While the percentage of women on boards was 8% in 2010, a mere 1.4% increase resulted in 9.4% in 2016. Hence, lower representation of women directors indicates that the involvement of women on the board is still rare in firms operating in BRIC.

Aras (2015) exhibits the proportion of women directors in BRICK firms between the years 2005 and 2013. The mean values of women's participation on board in Brazil, Russia, and India vary between 5% and 6%, as has been stated. In China, women represent 8% of the board, which might be evidence that the country is modelling not only Western production methods but also Western management styles, which have a higher contribution from women. For South Korea, women's participation on boards has been found to be only 1% which represents the traditional conservative approach of far-Eastern countries.

Turkey has the largest percentage of women on boards among firms operating in Brazil, India and China. There are no quotas for women on boards in Turkey, except the provisions and initiatives of Capital Markets Board of Turkey (CMBT). CMBT has made several regulations about the board composition for women directors on the board. According to the Amendments of the CMB Communique Serial: IV, No. 57 amending the Communique Serial: IV, listed companies may appoint at least one female to the board of directors as of 2009. Four years later, in 2013, CMBT revised its recommendation by asking the firms to set and disclose a voluntary target level of women on boards, which should not be less than 25%, by a target date they specified. An analysis of mandatory corporate governance compliance reports of companies with all male boards or with less than 25% women revealed that the vast majority of the companies ignored the ruling. For accomplishing the target 25% gender diversity level, for every listed firm, women must fill 574 additional board seats. Given the current average of 1.28 seats per woman on boards, this would mean that 448 new female directors are required to reach the minimum target (Sabancı University Women on Board Joint Project Report, 2015). However, firms continued to ignore the CMBT's recommendation and the obligation to provide an explanation for non-compliance. A related report states that two factors may change this picture and encourage firms to consider women candidates more in 2016. The first factor is the social pressure on companies resulting from various campaigns demanding or facilitating election of a gender-diverse board. The second factor is potentially the CMBT's new project that aims to improve the listed firms' compliance with the corporate governance principles. Moreover, there are 50 firms listed in the Corporate Governance Index in 2015. The percentage of female directors in the companies that are included in that index (10.76%) is lower than the percentage of the female directors in firms that are not included in the Corporate Governance Index (13.23%).

In March 2017, the 30% Club was launched in BIST. This launch means that Turkey's listed firms are seeking a higher percentage of women on boards. Thirty CEOs and board chairs had become members of this club as of March 2017.

Although the percentage of women on boards was 8% in 2010, a mere 4% increase resulted in 12% in 2016. Additionally, 44.5% of BIST companies have not yet appointed female directors on boards. The 190 largest firms in the Turkish economy still do not have any women on their boards. Although there has been a small increase in the percentage of females on boards in recent years, male directors on boards in Turkey are still dominant. Notwithstanding, the 23x2023 project, which aims to increase the percentage of women on boards to 23% by 2023 by encouraging companies to nominate women to fill the independent director quota, is a response to the call for corporations to comply with the voluntary provision of the CMBT's corporate governance principles related to boards' gender diversity. This represents a 100% increase from today, and more

SaaS

Table 12.2 Women directors in different industries in Turkish listed firms

	Total number of directorships	Female directorships	
	#	#	%
Education, health, sports and other social services	35	0	–
Electricity, gas and water	0	4	10
Energy	12	0	–
Administrative and support services	17	2	12
Manufacturing industry	1,289	150	13
Construction and public works	49	3	8
Mining	34	5	15
Financial institutions	1,002	133	14
Professional, scientific and technical activities	3	1	33
Agriculture, wood products and fishing	16	7	44
Technology and defense	102	13	13
Wholesale and retail trade, hotels and restaurants	43	32	13
Transportation, telecommunication and storage	74	4	5

Source: Sabanci University Corporate Governance Forum of Turkey, 3rd Annual Report, Women on Board, Independent Women Directors Project, 2015.

than 600 new board seats for women (Sabancı University Women on Board Joint Project Report, 2015).

Table 12.2 indicates an overview of women directors serving on BIST company boards in different sectors. There are no women directors in energy and social services sectors. Finance and manufacturing sectors that include the vast majority of firms reveal no significant difference with respect to the percentage of women directors: 14% and 13%, respectively (Sabancı University Women on Board Joint Project Report, 2015). According to that comprehensive report, in parallel to the increase in the ratio of women on boards, the ratio of women among independent directors has also increased to 9.9%. This represents an increase of 6.5% since 2015 compared to a 5.7% increase in 2014 and a 7.4% increase in 2013. Agriculture, wood products and fishing industries have seen the highest female percentage rate but it makes little sense to draw conclusions for industries in which less than a dozen listed companies are operating (e.g. professional, scientific and technical activities).

McKinsey & Co.'s (2010) comprehensive report analysis which consists of 411 firms from six European countries (the UK, France, Germany, Spain, Sweden and Norway), BRIC countries and the US states that the number of women in the top management also varies depending on the industry. For instance, women are relatively well represented both in executive committees (16%) and in corporate boards (12%) in the segment of retail trade and consumer goods, while in such sectors as transportation, logistics, real estate and construction their proportion is noticeably lower: 6–9% in executive committees and 8–9% in corporate boards.

Conclusion

Despite the various global, regional and country-level interventions, the progress in improving the gender diversity of boards has been a hot debate to discuss in recent years. Equal representation of women and men at every level of economic, political and social life is vital for inclusive growth and sustainable development, because gender equality has a multiplier effect across all development areas. Related studies highlight that women bring more creativity and innovation, better problem-solving and improved decision-making at the top stemming from greater cognitive diversity. Women directors can add additional skills and perspectives that are different from those of male directors as well. However, in some emerging markets women directors on the board can be appointed solely to fulfill the country's governance recommendations, and they may lack knowledge about the firm and therefore may add little or no value to the firm. Increasing women's participation in the labor force implies significant growth potential both for the global and Turkish economy. This chapter explores how women workers in Turkey and BRIC countries fare with regard to key labor market indicators so as to gain an insight into the gender segregation of employment sectorally, industrially and firm-wise.

Having women participate in corporate decision-making is good for business and good for Turkey's economy, as well as ensures competitiveness in the global arena. Although the number of women who make up the workforce has increased in recent years, women on boards has not been at satisfactory levels. Lower representation of women directors indicates that the involvement of women on the board is still rare in BRIC firms. Affordable childcare and a more flexible labor market regulation have been needed. Furthermore, women directors can add additional skills and perspectives that are different from those of male directors. It has to be noted that good corporate governance enables firms to improve performance, increase firm value, manage risks and attract investors with requiring diversified skills of boards, which is closely related to gender diversity.

Executives of several firms have realized that gender diversity in business management is crucial for achieving high corporate firm performance. However, ensuring gender diversity in the top management very rarely becomes a strategic priority of a company. Meanwhile, unless comprehensive measures aimed at increasing the proportion of women in the top management are taken, the situation will not improve. Academic studies reveal that the countries which have strongest shareholder protection level have more women on board. Shareholder protection motivates boards to use the differing knowledge, experience and values that each member represents. Consequently, this study not only contributes in revealing female representation on boards but aims to contribute to the literature on cross-national comparisons of females on boards.

References

Akerlof, G.A., Kranton, R. 2000. Economics and identity, *Quarterly Journal of Economics*, 115, 715–753.

Aras, G. 2015. The effect of corporate governance practices on financial structure in emerging markets: Evidence from BRIC countries and lessons for Turkey, *Emerging Markets Finance and Trade*, 51(2), 5–24.

Aras, G., Kutlu Furtuna, O. 2015. Does governance efficiency affect equity agency costs? Evidence from Borsa Istanbul, *Emerging Markets Finance and Trade*, 51(2), 84–100.

Brennan, N., McCafferty, J. 1997. Corporate governance practices in Irish companies, *Irish Business and Administrative Research (IBAR)*, 18, 116–135.

CMB Amendments Communique Serial: IV, No. 57 amending the Communique Serial: IV, No. 56 on Corporate Governance Principles dated by the Official Gazette December 11, 2012, no. 28201.

Deloitte 2016. *Women in the boardroom: A global perspective, Deloitte Global Center for Corporate Governance Publishing*, 5th ed., London, England.

Dominguez, L., Sanchez, L., Maria, I., Alvarez, I. 2012. Explanatory factors of the relationship between gender diversity and corporate performance, *European Journal of Law & Economics*, 33(3), 603–620.

Fauzi, F., Locke, S. 2012. Board structure, ownership structure and firm performance: A study of New Zealand listed-firms, *Asian Academy of Management Journal of Accounting and Finance*, 8(2), 43–67.

Glosny, M.A. 2010. China and the BRICS: A real (but limited) partnership in a unipolar world, *Polity*, 42.

ILO, www.ilo.org/global/statistics-and-databases/research-and-databases/kilm/lang-en/index.htm, accessed 17 April, 2017.

Karayel, M., Doğan, M. 2014. Yönetim Kurulunda Cinsiyet Çeşitliliği ve Finansal Performans İlişkisi: BİST 100 Şirketlerinde Bir Araştırma, Suleyman Demirel University, *The Journal of Faculty of Economics and Administrative Sciences*, 19(2), 75–88.

Lückerath-Rovers, M. 2013. Women on boards and firm performance, *Journal of Management and Governance*, 17(2), 491–509.

McKinsey & Co. 2010. Women Matter. Gender diversity, a corporate performance driver. Paris: McKinsey and Company, www.mckinsey.com/locations/swiss/news_publications/pdf/women_matter_english.pdf, accessed 13 April, 2017.

McKinsey & Co. 2016. Women Matter Turkey 2016. Turkey's Potential for the Future: Women in Business, TUSIAD (Turkish Industry and Business Association) Publishing, Istanbul, Turkey.

MSCI ESG Research Paper, Women on board global trends in gender diversity on corporate boards, prepared by Linda-Eling Lee Ric Marshall Damion Rallis Matt Moscardi.

Ocak, M. 2013. Yönetim Kurulu ve Üst Yönetimde Yer Alan Kadınların Finansal Performansa Etkisi: Türkiye'ye İlişkin Bulgular, *Muhasebe ve Finansman Dergisi*, 107–126.

OECD Statistics Database, http://stats.oecd.org/index.aspx?queryid=54753, accessed 13 April, 2017.

Okoth, B. 2016. Evaluating the Impact of Corporate Governance on Firm Performance using Board Index, Unpublished Master's Degree Dissertation, Anadolu University, Eskisehir.

Pillay, P. 2014. Gender influences in the labour market: The case of BRICS, *Mediterranean Journal of Social Sciences MCSER Publishing*, 5(10).

Post, C., Bryon, K. 2015. Women on boards and firm financial performance: A meta-analysis, *Academy of Management Journal*, 58(5), 1546–1571.

Sabancı University Corporate Governance Forum of Turkey, 3rd Annual Report, Women on Board, Independent Women Directors Project, 2015.

Schmid, T., Urban, D. 2015. Women on corporate boards: Good or Bad? AFA 2016 San Francisco Meetings Paper. Available at SSRN, http://dx.doi.org/10.2139/ssrn.2344786, accessed 13 April, 2017.

Singh, A., Zammit, A. 2000. International capital flows: Identifying the gender dimension, *Journal of World Development*, 28(7), 1249–1268.

UN, www.un.org/sustainabledevelopment/gender-equality/, accessed 13 April, 2017.

World Bank, http://data.worldbank.org/indicator/NY.GDP.PCAP.KD.ZG, accessed 20 April, 2017.

World Bank Database, http://databank.worldbank.org/data/reports.aspx?source=2&series=SL.TLF.CACT.FE.ZS&country, accessed 10 April, 2017.

Part V
Conclusion

Conclusion

Women on boards: what will be the next step?

Güler Aras and Maria Aluchna

Corporate boards are essential bodies for governance and management and their efficiency determines the company's performance. The board is a crucial element of the corporate governance structure and its efficiency and performance determines the success of monitoring and the operation of the company. The board is viewed as the liaison between providers of capital (shareholders) and managers who use this capital to create value. The board role is to represent, formulate and fulfil the interests and expectations of shareholders as the owners of the companies. From the perspective of influence, power, responsibilities and prestige, as well as organizational hierarchy, corporate boards are the top corporate gremials. The discussion on women's participation in business inevitably needs to refer to their presence on corporate boards. It is also a reliable indicator of gender equality advancement and policy adopted by countries and companies.

In spite of the various global, regional and country-level interventions, the progress in improving the gender diversity of the boards has been a hot debate in recent years. Equal representation of women and men at every level of economic, political and social life is vital for inclusive growth and sustainable development, because gender equality has a multiplier effect across all development areas. One of the global goals for sustainable development, 'gender equality' has become a crucial topic for human development, labour markets and hence GDP growth. Governments from all regions of the world have made the achievement of gender equality and the empowerment of women a high priority of the Sustainable Development Goals (SDGs).

On the academic side, board diversity has also become a major issue within corporate governance, where a number of researches indicated the effect of diversity on firm value, performance and risk-taking behaviour. Changing gender dynamics on corporate boards introduce a wider range of perspectives, attributes and skills in board discussions, which improve board performance. Despite a large body of literature examining the relationship between women on boards and firm financial performance, the evidence is mixed. Findings suggest that board diversity is neither wholly detrimental nor wholly beneficial to firm financial performance. This relationship can be more positive in countries with stronger shareholder protections. Additionally, board representation may be positively related to boards' two primary responsibilities in terms of monitoring and strategy involvement (Post and Bryon, 2015).

Moreover, women's participation on corporate boards increases firms' ESG disclosure and favourably influences the ESG-firm's performance relationship (Arayssi et al., 2016; Bear et al., 2010). For supporting social spending, investment and reporting, governments could provide more incentives such as reduced taxation of income. This would recognize the firm's engagement in efficient sustainability projects as a legitimate and fairly rewarding investment outlet.

While gender diversity has a crucial effect on achieving high corporate firm performance, the efficiency of women's presence on boards within the organizations is also dependent on the firms' structural efficiency. International instances indicate that the ecosystem in which institutions are located, related regulations, principles and standards shape the status of women on corporate boards. Discriminatory practices in the recruitment of directors should attract scrutiny by regulators. Related studies (Sila et al., 2016) find evidence of gender bias; their results at first glance support mandatory gender quotas. However, regulations such as gender quotas could cause a deviation from optimality and adversely impact on firm value. Therefore, regulations around increased diversity disclosure and demands for more diversity by outside stakeholders offer a more cautious route towards encouraging firms to bring more gender diversity to their boardrooms. Therefore, for improving gender diversity on corporate boards, different strategies are adopted in different countries, namely legislative intervention (mandatory quotas), a liberal approach, and a collaborative, business-led approach.

References

Aras, G. 2015. The effect of corporate governance practices on financial structure in emerging markets: Evidence from BRICK countries and lessons for Turkey, *Emerging Markets Finance and Trade*, 51(2), 5–24.

Aras, G., Kutlu Furtuna, O. 2015. Does governance efficiency affect equity agency costs? Evidence from Borsa Istanbul, *Emerging Markets Finance and Trade*, 51(2), 84–100.

Arayssi, M., Dah, M., Jizi, M. 2016. Women on boards, sustainability reporting and firm performance, *Sustainability Accounting, Management and Policy Journal*, 7(3), 376–401.

Bear, S., Rahman, N., Post, C. 2010. The impact of board diversity and gender composition on corporate social responsibility and firm reputation, *Journal of Business Ethics*, 97(2), 207–221.

Post, C., Bryon, K. 2015. Women on boards and firm financial performance: A meta-analysis, *Academy of Management Journal*, 58(5), 1546–1571.

Sila, V., Gonzalez, A., Hagendorff, J. 2016. Women on board: Does boardroom gender diversity affect firm risk?, *Journal of Corporate Finance*, 36, 26–53.

Index

Note: Page numbers in **bold** indicate tables and those in *italic* indicate figures